Please remember that this is a library book,
and that it belongs only temporarily to each
person who uses it. Be considerate. Do
not write in this, or any, library book.

Learning to Teach
in an Age of Accountability

Learning to Teach
in an Age of Accountability

Arthur T. Costigan
and
Margaret Smith Crocco

with

Karen Kepler Zumwalt

2004

LAWRENCE ERLBAUM ASSOCIATES, PUBLISHERS
Mahwah, New Jersey   London

Lawrence Erlbaum Associates, Inc., Publishers
10 Industrial Avenue
Mahwah, New Jersey 07430

Cover design by Kathryn Houghtaling Lacey

Library of Congress Cataloging-in-Publication Data

Costigan, Arthur T.
    Learning to teach in an age of accountability / Arthur T. Costigan, Margaret Smith Crocco with Karen Kepler Zumwalt.
        p. cm.
    Includes bibliographical references and index.
    ISBN 0-8058-4707-3 (cloth : alk. paper)
    ISBN 0-8058-4708-1 (pbk. : alk. paper)

    1. Educational accountability—New York (State)—New York—Case studies. 2. First year teachers—New York (State)—New York—Case studies. 3. Education, Urban—New York (State)—New York—Case studies. I. Crocco, Margaret. II. Zumwalt, Karen Kepler, 1943–   . III. Title.
LB2806.22.C67   2004
371.1—dc22   2004043633
                                                                        CIP

Books published by Lawrence Erlbaum Associates are printed on acid-free paper, and their bindings are chosen for strength and durability.

Printed in the United States of America
10   9   8   7   6   5   4   3   2   1

Contents

Part II: Teaching as an Autobiographical Act

Part III: Encountering Classrooms and Schools

Part V: Confronting the Age of Accountability

Preface

This book documents the "brave new world" of teacher, administrator, school, and student accountability that has swept across the United States over the last 10 years. The particular vantage point taken by this book is the perspective of dozens of new teachers trying to make their way through their first months and years working in schools in the New York City metropolitan area. Novices all, these new teachers encounter schools rife with problems related to overcrowded and underresourced classrooms, immigrant students who speak little English, acute literacy challenges, burnt-out administrators and teachers, chaotic operations, and, in some cases, violence. Although these schools are clearly marked by their urban setting, experienced teachers and teacher educators all know that such problems are by no means unique to city schools, having found their way to some degree into most suburban and rural schools as well. What makes this portrait different from past accounts of young, White teachers in urban schools are the stories of their encounters with the new culture of accountability and the strategies they develop for coping, and even succeeding, within such demanding settings.

The portrait painted here is not a pretty one, but it is realistic. The book relies on excerpts from lengthy interviews done with scores of new teachers over the last 3 years who were graduating from two large teacher education programs in New York City and beginning work in middle and secondary schools in New York, New Jersey, and Connecticut. The passages from those interviews incorporated into the book vividly document the difficult circumstances in which many teachers, novice and veteran, pursue their teaching careers. We believe that this book makes a singular contribution to the expanding educational literature on new teachers; we also believe it is unique in its extensive portrayal of new teachers' encounters with issues of accountability. The theme of accountability via high-stakes testing pervades each chapter in this book. Readers may find this recurrent theme amounting to a drumbeat of bad news throughout the book. Still, as Karen Zumwalt points out in the final chapter, possibilities for good teaching do exist within classroom climates shaped by unprecedented pressures on new teachers.

It is important to note that the book is not just one more addition to the "gloom and doom" genre of urban education. Instead, what the reader will encounter here are portraits of resilience alongside stories of turmoil; that is, new teachers facing the realities of contemporary schooling squarely and finding ways to succeed despite the challenging circumstances they confront.

We have written this book for all those interested in the contemporary world of teaching, especially teaching in a major metropolitan area in the United States. Primarily, however, our audience will be those preparing to teach. When we address ourselves to "you"—the reader—we mean the prospective and practicing teachers who, we hope, will engage most deeply and personally with the issues presented in this book.

We believe it is crucial for all school teachers and administrators to think through the issues raised in this book and their reactions to these issues. As Part I amply demonstrates, teacher retention looms large as a contributing factor to the so-called "teacher shortage" these days. Our immodest hope is that this book will help preview the real-life circumstances of beginning teachers today so that teacher education students can better prepare themselves to deal with the challenges lying ahead. "Rehearsing" responses to these circumstances may prevent new teachers from becoming discouraged by them and departing the profession after only a few years.

Secondarily, we address this book to other teacher educators. Documenting the challenges of the educational field in which we work is vital. Stories of accountability and its toll in urban and suburban schools are vital considerations for beginning teachers and teacher educators, the public—especially parents of school children—as well as politicians and policymakers. Teacher educators do their work at the crossroads of many competing influences; of late, their own legitimacy and utility have been challenged by many prominent figures in the federal government. Indeed, over the last several years, the influence of the federal government has grown markedly. In a democratic society, debate over education and its providers is to be expected. Nevertheless, accusations against the profession by policymakers and the press are often made absent any real understanding of the work of teacher education. Moreover, some of the profession's critics fail to acknowledge the underresourced conditions in which so much educational work is done, especially the work of meeting new state and federal mandates these days.

OVERVIEW

Learning to Teach in an Age of Accountability is organized into five parts: Part I and Part V engage the "big ideas" concerning teacher research: what we know and where that leads us. In other words, Part I introduces research on teaching. Parts II, III, and IV develop according to what might be called an "expanding horizons" orientation—offering a rich set of new teacher narratives that widen the angle of vision from personal biography, to classrooms, school, and society. These parts of the book include questions and activities that encourage discussion and further research about the issues raised in those chapters. Part V addresses the possibilities for curriculum decision making and making a difference in light of preceding chapters.

Part II situates the new teachers, who are the subjects of this book, in their personal as well as social contexts. Decisions to become a teacher typically get made within the nexus of family and friends. Individual relationships, partners, and perhaps even children all play a role in the decision-making process, both in terms of becoming and remaining a teacher. We found that gender, ethnicity, and class all contribute to shaping reactions of significant others to this career choice. These narratives suggest the difficulties new teachers face in "having a life," especially as they embark on their careers.

Part III broadens the analysis to include classrooms, schools, neighborhoods, and school districts. The cultures associated with each of these domains have an enormous impact on the daily life of new teachers, from classroom management strategies to expectations about what is appropriate or "recommended" at a school in terms of homework and academic achievement. Although many teachers consider teaching a solitary endeavor, facing 175 students a day leaves the teacher with little adult interaction and support. Such a volume of intense intergenerational encounters reinforces the impact of personal, social, and communal histories on shaping classroom life. Success or failure in classrooms, especially in urban schools where teachers tend to be White and students of color, often depends on how well such cultural divides are crossed. As products of different backgrounds, both students and teachers carry different mental scripts into their classrooms, a set of preconceptions about what should or should not occur there. The narratives of classroom life contained in this book will help teacher education students uncover their own set of expectations about classroom and school life.

Part IV examines the historical and political forces that shape contemporary teaching and learning in the United States. It is no accident, for example, that most teachers are female or that most school administrators, even at the primary level, are male. This gendered profile within the educational profession is a product of social, economic, and political forces at work over the last 150 years. Likewise, schooling in the United States has been shaped by the competing agendas of local, state, and increasingly national governments, which have produced different results in different places. Understanding the political and historical contexts of schooling in the United States is critical if prospective teachers are to make informed decisions about the kinds of schools and communities in which they wish to work.

The author of Part V, Karen K. Zumwalt, is a highly knowledgeable teacher educator and former dean at Teachers College, Columbia University. Along with many noted teacher educators, she has recently completed a review of research on teacher education for the American Educational Research Association. Her experience and expertise makes her well situated to comment on the implications of the research contained in this book. This section will help readers understand better how they can find room for their own voices as teachers in the age of accountability.

The first four parts of the book are each divided into three or more chapters. Each chapter is subdivided into sections revolving around a key theme articulated by those interviewed for this book. In Parts II, III, and IV, each chapter follows a similar format: introduction to the theme, excerpts from teacher narratives, and a set of questions and activities designed to encourage further reflection and action. Once again, the themes and narratives presented here were selected because they represent issues widely voiced across scores of interviews with new teachers over the last several years.

Because we believe that teaching is a messy, complex, customized, and humanistic endeavor, we resist the notion that it can be reduced to a "10-step program," or any set of rules. That is not to say that principles of good practice do not exist. However, the conditions in which these principles get enacted play a large role in shaping practice. Professional judgment is necessary in determining when, how, and to what extent these principles should shape classroom practice. Thus, we adopt an inquiry-oriented perspective to the problems presented here. We call on readers to make up their own minds about the problems illustrated by these narratives. We present a set of reflective questions at the end of each thematic section and a set of activities at the end of each chapter. These exercises call on readers to use their own personal stories and investigative skills to deliberate further about these issues. Perhaps some readers will create artistic responses to the teaching issues presented here, like Tracy Barsoti, whose poetry opens Part I. Others might be moved to write ethnographies of classroom life, develop action research projects, or keep diaries of their first year in the classroom. Whatever framework readers use to respond to these issues concerned with becoming and remaining a teacher, making such reflection a habit early in their teaching life and sharing dilemmas with colleagues will help new teachers cope with the demands of becoming a teacher. Moreover, such habits will help them sustain this work over the long haul.

ACKNOWLEDGMENTS

In bringing this book to press, we wish to acknowledge the encouragement and expertise of our editor, Naomi Silverman, and her assistant, Erica Kica, and the reviewers for Lawrence Erlbaum Associates: Barbara B. Levin, University of North Carolina–Greensboro; Kenneth M. Zeichner, University of Wisconsin–Madison; Marilyn Johnston, Ohio State University; and Holly Thornton, University of North Carolina–Greensboro. We also acknowledge the helpful suggestions made by various individuals who read earlier versions of the manuscript, including Shirley Brown, Jennifer Blaxall Buice, Andrea Mandel, and Sarah Melvoin. Special thanks go to Eric Rothschild, who suggested the interview project at Teachers College, and with whom the ongoing research concerning social studies teachers continues to be a real pleasure. Thanks also go to David Gerwin, Queens College, City University of New York, for introducing the authors to each other and inspiring this book project.

Most of all, we thank the many new teachers who participated in this study by sharing their precious time with us, many repeatedly. Their generosity in sharing the news of their work—their struggles as well as their triumphs—is testimony to the fine work that many teachers do today in difficult and demanding circumstances.

Part I

CHOOSING
TO BECOME A TEACHER

INTRODUCTION

How have I come to understand myself as a teacher?
Tracy Barsoti

I have come to understand myself as a teacher, Or have I?
I am a joker and a yeller.
I am kind and often rude.
I stand in front of the room saying, listen, listen, listen in a quiet voice.
I yell at kids for talking, but laugh at what they say.
I am patient (often).
I do not want to make my students cry.
I am crushed by my administration
(and I still don't have the books).
Without a curriculum, I teach what I know
and sometimes what I don't
I listen to their questions,
and try to answer. And I say when I don't know.
I am giving all I have.
I am giving all I have.
I have come so far so fast.
I have come to understand myself a teacher.
That's the most that I can do.

In her poem, Tracy expresses the rush, confusion, exhilaration, challenges, and concerns that accompany becoming a teacher, a process perhaps more complex today than ever. Tracy, a new teacher at a suburban high school, focuses on the chief reason she chose to teach: her desire to work with young people. The opportunity to forge relationships with students is a key attraction of teaching. This field is all about working with people—young and old, students and administrators, colleagues and parents. Navigating the often intense personal landscape of teaching is, unavoidably, a highly personal process. Teachers bring their personalities, personal and familial histories, and certainly their own school histories to bear on the task of teaching every time they step into the classroom. Computers, numbers and recordkeeping, and paperwork also form an important part of their daily rituals, to be sure, but the fundamental project of teaching remains dealing with other people: learning how to motivate others, help them learn, offer useful feedback, and evaluate whether students have succeeded or failed in mastering subject matter. There's simply no way to escape one's autobiography in becoming a teacher and claiming responsibility for motivating others (and self) to succeed academically.

Yet many factors outside the classroom also influence a teacher's relationship with his or her students and thus shape what is possible in classroom practice. The size of a school, its administration, district, community, home cultures of students, educational philosophy, and practices of colleagues all influence the type of teaching in which Tracy can, and will, engage. These factors external to classrooms have a strong impact on the nature of the relationships Tracy develops with her students. These days, state and federal mandates for high-stakes testing and new mechanisms for teacher and student accountability press harder and harder on the decisions Tracy makes about her classroom priorities. Despite the fact that some scholars posit a "slow revolution" toward greater teacher professionalism (Grant & Murray, 1999), others note the explosive potential of coming to terms with the demands of "teaching in the knowledge society" (Hargreaves, 2003); many policymakers seem focused on educational achievement as measured through the most simplistic of testing mechanisms, valuing cheaper and faster over better. Such approaches often reduce teachers' daily routine to providing scripted lessons, leaving little room for teacher autonomy. As a result of the "teacherproofing" of the curriculum, the best teachers, those who have the greatest need for autonomy and creativity in their work, often find the work so "dumbed down" that they leave the profession entirely.

All these factors associated with the brave new world of teaching will be explored in this book. In moving the focus from family to classroom and school contexts, and on to political and historical contexts, we ask you, the reader, to engage imaginatively with these environments. The narratives of the new teachers featured in this book make these contexts real, vivid, and personal—but hardly unique to the teachers we talked to for this book. The individual voices of teachers you will read in this book outline and clarify many issues, problems, and opportunities all new teachers face in the increasingly complex world of teaching.

You, too, bring an autobiographical context to your decision to teach. If you have not done so already, soon you will be negotiating your own way through the complex cultures of classroom and school, questioning perhaps how and why schools look and operate as they do. For anyone who has ever lived in another country or has read about how schooling is conceptualized or managed outside the United States, the singular nature of the American public school structure will be obvious.

Traveling across city and state lines illuminates the degree to which local and state control influences American education. Any two schools in this country can be radically different sorts of places. In the New York City metropolitan area, we find poor schools, in the Bronx and Harlem, for example, and wealthy ones in reasonable proximity to these in Scarsdale (Westchester County, NY), Syosset (Long Island, NY), and Tenafly (Bergen County, NJ). Rich schools can be quite impressive in their physical plant, curriculum offerings, and level of college acceptance for their students; poor schools can be incredibly impoverished in these regards, and are often horribly rundown, depressing, and even dangerous places. The chief feature of the New York City public school system is its size—over 1 million students and 65,000 teachers.

Although the larger historical, political, and economic landscapes play a role in shaping schools, research indicates that teachers' goals and methods are heavily influenced by who the teacher is (Munby, Russell, & Martin, 2001; Richardson & Placier, 2001). In Tracy's case, her sense of teaching as vocation (Hansen, 1994), understanding of self (Britzman, 1986; Grossman, 1990), and beliefs about students and teaching (Calderhead, 1987; Richardson, 1996) already contribute greatly to forming the decisions she makes.

Over time, the weight of these personal influences might change to be sure, with growing professional knowledge shifting the balance. One teacher education textbook posits four stages of teacher development, labeling them "Survival, Consolidation, Renewal, and Maturity." In the beginning stage, Survival, teachers "move from day to day, trying to get through the week and wondering if teaching is the right job for them" (Sadker & Sadker, 2000, p. 493). Not surprisingly, you will encounter many narratives associated with this stage in the coming chapters.

In dealing with issues of survival, you will also read stories that represent standard, even "classical," situations most new teachers encounter. Even though these situations are common, that does not make them any easier for novices to manage. Many new teachers, however, struggle in isolation to overcome these commonplace issues. From dealing with students and administrators to dealing with classroom management every new teacher experiences these issues as if they were totally new. This book attempts to assist preservice and beginning teachers to see and understand, and to work through, these commonplace problems. Still, a pervasive and recurring background issue shaping almost every foreground issue is the new climate of accountability and high-stakes testing. As you will see, even where the main thrust of a chapter or a section is something other than high-stakes testing, the topic intrudes. The repeated intrusion of this topic represents a faithful, not a loaded or manipulated circumstance. Even when we did not ask about high-stakes testing, the teachers we interviewed brought it up. No other topic shapes contemporary practice, or the perception of the possibilities of contemporary classroom practice, more than high-stakes testing does for beginning teachers.

Many new teachers, especially those working in urban areas, do not survive the Survival stage. However, teacher retention is not just a problem of cities, although it is more acute there. The so-called teacher shortage is an enormous national problem. We now know that this problem actually has more to do with retention than recruitment of sufficient numbers of new teachers. With a few exceptions in certain subject areas, enough teachers gain their certification each year to replace those who retire or leave the profession. The problem is that many new teachers choose to leave after their first few years of teaching. This book attempts to present, honestly and forthrightly, the issues that challenge new teachers and sometimes move them out of the profession before they have worked out strategies for coping with these issues. In short, this book is directed at keeping you in the profession, so that you evolve through the growth stages of Consolidation, and Renewal into Maturity as an expert and experienced teacher.

We will look more fully at teacher retention in the next chapter. By reading excerpts from hundreds of interviews done by the authors with novice teachers and those on the verge of entering the profession, you will have an opportunity to confront and rehearse your reactions to many of the problems new teachers, especially those working in urban areas, deal with today. It is our hope that through these "virtual encounters" with the complex and messy world of teaching today, you will find that you are not alone in figuring out ways of coping with these challenges and succeeding in the process of becoming the teacher you want to be.

REFERENCES

Britzman, D. P. (1986). Cultural myths in the making of a teacher: Biography and social structure in teacher education. *Harvard Education Review, 56*, 442–456.
Calderhead, J. (Ed.). (1987). *Exploring teachers' thinking*. London: Cassell.

Grant, G., & Murray, C. E. (1999). *Teaching in America: The slow revolution*. Cambridge, MA: Harvard University Press.

Grossman, P. (1990). *The making of a teacher: Teacher knowledge and teacher education*. New York: Teachers College Press.

Hansen, D. (1994). Teaching and the sense of vocation. *Educational Theory, 44*(3), 259–275.

Hargreaves, A. (2003). *Teaching in the knowledge society: Education in the age of insecurity*. New York: Teachers College Press.

Munby, H., Russell, T., & Martin, A. K. (2001). Teachers' knowledge and how it develops. In V. Richardson (Ed.), *Handbook of research on teaching* (pp. 877–903). Washington, DC: AERA.

Richardson, V. (1996). The role of attitudes and beliefs in learning to teach. In J. Sijula, T. J. Buttery, & E. Guyton (Eds.), *Handbook of research on teacher education* (2nd ed., pp.102–119). New York: Simon & Schuster Macmillan.

Richardson, V., & Placier, P. (2001). Teacher change. In V. Richardson (Ed.), *Handbook of research on teacher education* (2nd ed., pp. 905–947). New York: Simon & Schuster Macmillan.

Sadker, M. P., & Sadker, D. M. (2000). *Teachers, schools, society* (5th ed.). New York: McGraw-Hill.

Chapter 1

Teaching Is Messy Work

This book rests on the assumption that an inquiry-oriented approach to learning to teach provides the best means by which prospective teachers can consider the range of issues they will face in meaningful, effective ways (Tabachnick & Zeichner, 1991). This type of engagement with the work of teaching is essential. Once again, it is important to remember that no mathematical formulas exist for reducing the work of teaching to quantitative relationships among people, processes, and products. Teaching is not only a skill, a set of learned lessons for "delivering a lesson"; who you are, what you think, and how you feel about the people, social conditions, and structure of education matter in an essential way. One cannot deliver a lesson in the way one delivers a pizza—just get it to them and they will eat it. Nor is it simply acquiring the art of developing knowledge in one's students, or assimilating a set of techniques for controlling and managing student behavior (Zellermayer, 2001). Teaching includes elements related to these domains, but reducing the profession to a list of such activities is to misunderstand the nature of the work.

The act of teaching is situated within the context of your life history. This life history will influence how you relate to supervisors, students, colleagues, and parents. How you view students who might be different from you, how you conceptualize teaching and learning, the type of community in which the school is located, and the backgrounds of your students all interact in shaping what is possible for you as a teacher. Teaching is a "situated" autobiographical act (Resnick, 1987). This "situatedness" means that you bring a wealth of life experiences, many of them from the classroom, to your work in schools. Fundamentally, teaching is a humanistic activity—one interwoven with all aspects of the human condition: moral, physical,

7

emotional, and intellectual. As you teach, you work within a web of relationships that are very much influenced by who you are and where you have come from.

We know a great deal more today than we once did about many aspects of teaching: learning theory, brain development, multicultural education, linguistic and literacy issues, and effective leaders and effective schools. Still, putting this knowledge to work in the myriad settings of school and classroom with the resources available is not a simple process. Schools are set in historical and social contexts that limit the options for change, or at least circumscribe the teacher's ability to put theory into action. In short, the complex, messy, intellectual work that teaching demands is a daily reality. This reality is only intensified when a teacher has 150 students a day or more in his or her classroom, as is commonly the case in New York City's secondary schools.

In Tracy's case, we see that she embarked on a personal transformation when she chose to become a teacher, one involving a long-term effort at adjusting to a dynamic profession (Cook-Sather, 2001). As a result of this process, Tracy must accommodate herself to the changing demands of her profession and to her students' personalities and needs. The knowledge base of subject content and teaching skills essential to success 30 or 40 years ago in schools is not the same one that drives the profession today.

Many reasons explain this fundamental change. First of all the United States has become more diverse linguistically, culturally, ethnically, socially, and economically over the last 40 years. The American economy has moved to a postindustrial, service-oriented, and information-based economy. Schools have been slow in changing to meet the demands of this economy. The digital revolution has not made the inroads in most urban schools that it has in those of Silicon Valley. In many urban schools, the resources available to teachers and students—blackboards, chalk, and desks lined in rows—are very much the same ones that were available to teachers around World War I. Yet teachers are expected to prepare students who are ready for the Information Age economy with resources that are antiquated. As Tracy's future unfolds in the classroom, social and technological changes could very well reshape the work of education. Still, it will probably be up to Tracy to help her students and herself figure out how to deal with the demands of the Information Age despite the limited resources made available to them.

In meeting all these challenges, the most adaptive educational environments are ones in which teachers function as communities of inquiry. As such, teachers engage in regular investigation of their own practice, assumptions, and goals. Student learning remains the chief goal, of course, but teachers become accustomed to asking regularly: Learning what? How? Why? As the 21st century unfolds, with its high premium on knowledge, skills, and global understanding, the professional work of teaching will demand even greater preparation than in the past, and this preparation will be ongoing throughout teachers' careers. Teachers must become adept learners themselves, as well as investigators of teaching practice, diagnosticians of student learning problems, and friendly critics of school cultures that promote or inhibit teaching, learning, and their own professional growth.

Although Tracy might not be aware of it, her first years in teaching will, if she sticks it out, move her toward the stage of teacher growth called Consolidation. As she survives the Survival stage, she shifts focus from staying afloat to concentrating on her students' learning (Sadker & Sadker, 2000). She becomes less preoccupied with classroom management, and more attuned to different facets of teacher understanding—domains commonly called content knowledge, pedagogical content knowledge (Shulman, 1986), practical knowledge (Carter, 1990), and professional knowledge (Tom & Valli, 1990). As she recognizes what she knows and does not know, she might seek opportunities to enhance her knowledge. If she is motivated to succeed, her ambition and reflective capacity will ultimately help her become an experienced and expert teacher (Richardson & Placier, 2001; Rust & Orland, 2001). However, Tracy will always be a unique teacher, just as she is a unique human being. At the moment she begins her teaching career, she confronts a new beginning—one that is, like motherhood, liable to make profound differences to her future (Zumwalt, 1984).

While Tracy develops a singular sense of herself as person and professional, she shares with other new teachers the challenges connected to dealing with students, parents, and administrators. She focuses on classroom management and control, stretches her understanding of what goes into a good lesson, figures out what serves as the best approach to the curriculum she must teach, and learns the myriad ways in which students learn. Down the road, she faces hurdles associated with gaining tenure in a school system and deciding whether to leave a particular school, move into administration, stay in the classroom, or leave the profession entirely.

Teachers go through patterns of change throughout their entire careers. These patterns have been richly documented throughout the educational research literature (Berliner, 1986; Carter, Sabers, Cushing, Pinnegar, & Berliner, 1987; Hargreaves, 2000; Hollingsworth, 1989, 1994; Huberman, 1993; Kagan, 1992; Levin, 2003; Levin & Ammon, 1996; Reiman & Thies-Sprinthall, 1998; Richardson, 1996; Rust & Orland, 2001; Ryan, 1986, 1992; Zeichner & Tabachnick, 1981; Zeichner, Tabachnick, & Densmore, 1987). As your career proceeds, you might want to investigate more deeply others' experiences of these patterns of development. At the moment, it is understandable that your main concern is the first stage of Survival.

Like many new teachers, Tracy might conceive of teaching as an occupation relying on solo performances. New teachers do need to think on their feet in front of an "audience," gain expertise through trial and error, and succeed or fail with little or no support from other teachers. They are often forced to improvise when schedules change, when students have difficulty with challenging material, or when they themselves simply have not prepared adequately for class. Many teachers complain about the isolation of their jobs. At some level, teaching is a solo performance, but to see it only in this light is to miss the opportunities for communal problem solving that sustain good schools and strong teachers.

Today, changes have occurred in some school districts in recognizing the importance of collaborative school cultures, especially for beginning teachers. Mentoring and induction programs within schools or networks attracting teachers from diverse schools (e.g., the National Writing Project, the Coalition of Essential Schools, or Wellesley College's Seeking Educational Equity and Diversity) have become more common. Other arrangements, such as team teaching and curriculum collaboration, which are found in many middle schools, can serve to mitigate teacher isolation.

Nevertheless, as a new teacher you will need to work out the ways in which you will shape your practice and succeed at work. Teacher preparation should aim at developing the capacity to respond intelligently and reflectively to the demands of teaching, both on an individual and a collective basis. Such preparation will bolster the rational and emotional abilities necessary for becoming a resilient, effective, and committed lifelong teacher (Zeichner & Liston, 1996).

AN INQUIRY-ORIENTED APPROACH
TO LEARNING TO TEACH

In her first few years on the job, Tracy must, as she says, "come very far, very fast." Indeed, she is working hard to do this. Many of the skills she acquires in her first job will transfer to her next teaching position; this will make the transition to a new environment easier. Yet, these gains will only occur if Tracy stays in teaching long enough to assimilate the many facets of knowledge and skill necessary to do this work well. The sad truth is that one third of all new teachers today abandon their careers within the first 5 years of teaching. In urban areas, one half leave teaching within the first 3 years (Ingersoll, 2001). In an age of elevated expectations, standards, and accountability for all K–12 students, their teachers, and teacher educators, it has never been more important that talented young people remain in teaching.

Few would argue against having high standards for American education. Nor would most people quibble with the notion that teachers need to bear responsibility for what occurs in their classrooms. Nevertheless, the use of high-stakes testing (i.e., examinations that determine whether a student will pass a grade or graduate from school) concern many educators. Tests, even the best ones, offer only a snapshot version of a student's performance on any given day. Despite their scientific pretensions, high-stakes tests are arguably not the best, and certainly not the only, form of student assessment. Certainly, holding teachers strictly accountable for student performance on such tests flies in the face of the complexity of real school environments. Ironically, one effect of holding new teachers responsible for high-stakes testing outcomes might be to drive new teachers out of teaching, or at least out of teaching in urban schools, where results tend to be poorer than in suburban schools. Nevertheless, such consequences of the high-stakes testing regimen might be an unintended by-product of this new age of accountability.

In this book we adopt an inquiry-oriented approach to these issues because such an approach enhances teacher capacity for thoughtful decision making (Tabachnick & Zeichner, 1991). We regularly stop the narratives from new teachers to pose questions to readers. We acknowledge that different readers will come to different answers, depending on their own beliefs, values, and backgrounds. This is not to say that anything goes. As we stress repeatedly throughout subsequent chapters, solid research exists for drawing conclusions about a set of principles constituting "best practice" in teacher education and teaching. You should invest time and effort in mastering this body of knowledge that is undoubtedly being taught in your teacher education courses. This book serves as a supplemental text that should help you make the links between what you are learning in your teacher education courses and the specific, concrete demands of teaching contexts. The chapters that follow will allow you multiple opportunities for exercising the analytical capacities and deliberative decision making that good teacher education nurtures. In each section, we also emphasize the need for communal consideration of the topics presented. This pattern of engagement is one you should sustain throughout your teaching career.

The narratives that follow should not be viewed simply as good stories. They are important tools with multiple uses. First, they help unearth preconceived, perhaps erroneous, notions about teaching that you are carrying into the profession. Dislodging these preconceptions and holding them up to the stark light of critical analysis will help you develop a richer understanding of the profession (McEwan & Egan, 1995). Second, these stories will help you consider—early in your career—the real-life demands made on teachers today. The stories here might be sobering, perhaps even depressing. However, the resilience of young teachers in the face of these challenges is as impressive as the difficult circumstances in which many of them work. We are inspired by the clever and creative ways in which they negotiate the challenges they face. We hope that you, too, will be stimulated to think proactively and intelligently about your future in teaching, that you will stay the course, and that you will become a mature, highly competent, lifelong, and proud teacher.

A Vision of Best Practice in Teacher Education

We assume most of you are enrolled in teacher education programs that strive to build the attributes of effective teacher preparation into their framework. We believe that such preparation includes an emphasis on curriculum that combines theory and practice, integration of substantial fieldwork with challenging academic coursework, opportunities for systematic reflection on one's preparation, attention to learning theory, developmental psychology, and the sociocultural dimensions of schooling and students (Levin, 2003). We see the "good teacher" as one who embodies the dimensions of caring and competence, who brings knowledge and expertise to teaching, including both disciplinary knowledge and professional understanding; who is resilient and flexible in the face of professional demands; who is disposed to being a lifelong learner; and who maintains an ethical stance toward this work. We also assume that many teachers who fit this description will go on to become teacher leaders (Wasley, 1991), individuals who eventually find themselves in the position of promoting other teachers' professional growth.

An Inquiry-Oriented Approach

Real dilemmas drawn from teachers' lives during their first years as professionals help those preparing to be teachers to consider the contemporary educational scene in all its complexity. Such intellectual exercises move teacher thinking from naive to more sophisticated ways of reasoning about the profession (Sprinthall & Thies-Sprinthall, 1983). Most teacher education programs provide ready-made socialization for the "communities of practice" (Wenger, 1998) that good schools enact. With the support of mentors and teacher educators, such communities offer significant avenues for guided reflection on the common problems faced by new teachers. Thinking about teaching as an inquiry-oriented activity from the beginning of teacher education nurtures a lifelong orientation to the occupation. Such an approach recognizes and validates the knowledge requirements and rational decision-making demands that shape the occupation today (Tabachnick & Zeichner, 1991). As beginning teachers become mature teachers, they activate these capacities regularly.

A Collaborative Approach

By promoting communal reflection so that it becomes a deeply habituated routine of teachers' lives, this book addresses the isolation felt by many new teachers. *Communal* suggests the need to break through this isolation through shared problem solving. By reading—and listening, in a sense—to the voices of beginning teachers as they struggle with the complex demands of teaching today, you can hear, ponder, discuss, and begin to make sense of the issues involved in urban and suburban teaching across the country today. In fact, you will discover that remarkable similarities exist across the experiences of many new teachers in disparate places. You will realize that the choices new teachers face about career, pedagogy, and school are common. Discussing these narratives in teacher education classes, within teacher-support groups, or with networks of like-minded teachers getting together in person or online will provide a rich experience of collaboration. Whatever form your communal reflection takes, we hope it becomes habit-forming.

In sum, this book is designed as an invitation for teacher education students and beginning teachers to engage in deep consideration of issues for which no simple, obvious, or "right" answers exist. As a highly situated activity, the act of teaching presents dilemmas that might seem different or familiar depending on your own social and geographic location. We are confident that the range of material contained here will amply demonstrate the competence, caring, and resilience of new teachers today. These narratives suggest that if new teachers such as these remain in the profession, especially in urban areas, reasons for optimism about the nation's educational future do, indeed, exist.

NARRATIVES IN THE FIRST PERSON

If the existence of gossip columns, soap operas, paperback novels, and Internet chat rooms is any indication, people are interested in people, what they do, and what they say. We spend a great deal of time during our daily lives talking, gossiping, complaining, and relating narratives about the people we know and have only heard of or know about. We continue to find personal narratives interesting even after we have known the characters for a long time. Each new chapter gets folded into a narrative that develops a pattern, sometimes linear, sometimes recursive, but always dynamic and engaging when we are invested in the characters. The best narratives might be the ones that please us, but the ones that dismay us, appall us, or infuriate us can fascinate equally well.

Humans are storytelling animals, and the narratives we tell ourselves and others are the chief ways we make sense of the world. The educational community has come to view narratives as one of the best ways to develop an understanding of the situation of teachers and their careers (Clandinin & Connelly, 2000). Narratives that draw on authentic conversations with real students and teachers provide a rich way of making meaning, as oral historians, sociologists, anthropologists, and qualitative educational researchers have long known. As one scholar put it, "Authentic conversation, with its embedded personal narratives, is a powerful yet challenging way to make sense of experience; to remember, reinterpret, and reorganize personal and social knowledge; to give and receive the support we all need to sustain ourselves and pursue our own visions and ideals" (Clark, 1995, p. 142). Narratives told in the first person, as in oral history, life history, and narrative inquiry (Tabachnick & Zeichner, 1991), all get at the uniquely autobiographical aspects of teaching in ways that other forms of research often overlook.

The fascination with narratives has made the research for this book a particularly pleasurable experience. We are grateful for the generosity of the new teachers who shared their experiences of teaching with us. These narratives provide an excellent teaching tool for probing and rehearsing the complex issues embodied in the process that has been called "composing a teaching life" (Vinz, 1996, p. xii). We believe that stories represent a fundamental structure of human cognition, a template that cuts across disciplines and cultures in framing human experience (Clandinin & Connelly, 2000; Van Manen, 1990). Most of all, we find stories to be a powerful way of engaging the complexity of teaching in an age of accountability.

The approach to the narratives here is, as we stated at the outset, descriptive. We mean by this that narratives help to open up a dialogue with prospective teachers about important school issues (Darling-Hammond & Hammerness, 2002). In this regard, the book presents what is in the lives of new teachers rather than trying to lay out what new teachers' attitudes and thoughts should be. In encountering the stark realities of new teachers' lives, some readers might be dismayed, or even discouraged, about the work of teaching. However, we are confident that ample evidence exists in these pages not only of the stress and strain of contemporary school cultures and their demands on teachers, but of the ways in which resilient, creative, and intelligent teachers negotiate those demands, at least in the short run. Sadly, whether the new pressures associated with accountability exacerbate the problem of teacher retention, especially in urban areas, remains to be seen.

We have tried to make the excerpts from the interviews lengthy enough to provide solid and stimulating material sufficient for engaging your consideration of the persons and problems presented in each vignette. Undoubtedly, individual responses to these vignettes will vary. You should recognize that there is no right or wrong answer to the dilemmas presented by these narratives; they serve, instead, as real-life examples of the conundrums confronting many new teachers, especially those working in middle and secondary schools in urban areas.

These narratives come from scores of young people who have entered teaching in the New York metropolitan area. This area includes teachers in poor urban neighborhoods, in middle- or working-class residential areas, and from the many suburbs surrounding the city. Most of the individuals profiled here were enrolled in teacher education programs—undergraduate, graduate, and alternative routes—at several public and private colleges in New York where the authors have worked.

A wide range of ages and backgrounds characterize the group of teachers to whom we have listened. Some come from privileged backgrounds and received their own schooling in affluent, mostly White middle- and upper middle-class elementary and high schools. Some of these individuals attended private, elite colleges. Others grew up in the city; indeed, they might be the first or one of the first persons in their families to have attended college. They have pursued their education entirely within public institutions.

Most of those we interviewed are White, and this lack of diversity in the teaching corps is a problematic reality of the profession these days. Some are first- or second-generation immigrants for whom teaching is an honored profession, reflecting the higher status accorded teachers in other parts of the world compared with here in the United States. Others come from affluent families for whom teaching as a profession might be seen as a step down from the career options perceived as higher among our participants' families. Ages range from 20s to 40s; most are women. A large percentage grew up in the northeastern United States, but at least 2 of our participants came from farms in the midwestern United States, and as New York is a destination for young people, more than a few participants come from places other than the northeastern United States

Despite being situated in one metropolitan area, we believe that the teachers whose voices are featured here are fairly representative of teachers in urban and suburban areas nationwide. A strong case can be made that today in the United States, rural teachers increasingly face the issues presented in this book and that education students and new teachers in rural areas would be well served by this book. Some of our interviewees teach in the wealthiest suburban communities in the United States; others work in residential neighborhoods in, or close to, New York City that contain large numbers of first- and second-generation immigrants; many teach in the poorest, urban schools.

We have come to understand that the experiences of our interviewees in various urban and suburban schools in the New York area are not terribly different from those in many other regions of the country, except perhaps for the fact that the issues presented are intensified in poor urban schools more than in wealthier communities and districts that simply have more money and resources. Interestingly, we have found that rural teachers also voice many of the same issues as those discussed by our interviewees from urban and suburban settings.

The narratives draw on the voices of new teachers who have entered the profession with little or no professional preparation, who came into teaching under various emergency licensing procedures. The stories include those of new teachers inducted within the "boot camp" model found in the New York City Teaching Fellows, an intensive program of coursework and full-time teaching analogous to many similar programs found in large metropolitan areas today that struggle each year with hiring enough teachers to staff classrooms. All in all, a wide range of teacher preparation models are represented among the book's many interviewees.

Most of these narratives are personal and not public ones, even though proper procedures or protocols were followed to protect the participants of our research. For instance, these protocols demand that we disguise the original names of our participants, as well as the specific neighborhoods, districts, and schools in which they work. These protocols are designed to protect the rights of interviewees as research participants, and, because much of the ground covered here is so intensely personal, we have ensured that individual identities are disguised to preserve their privacy. Above all, we are grateful to our interview participants for the time they have spent in sharing their experiences with us, a generous acknowledgment of their commitment to the importance of teaching and preparing the next generation of teachers.

Some narratives were recorded during summer breaks from the teaching life and others during the stress and strain of teaching in the months from September to June. What comes across is generally not the reflection and distance that derives from looking back on life experiences, but instead the immediacy and pressures faced by practitioners as they attempt to develop manageable modes of practice. These qualities are strengths of the narratives, offering a set of vivid, intense representations closer to snapshots than moving pictures. Many of the interviews lasted several hours and ranged widely over personal and professional experiences. Had we talked to some of these individuals even the very next day, perhaps we would have received a different picture of lives in action. Taken holistically, however, the viewpoints expressed here are consonant with much of the new, emergent data about what teachers are experiencing today (see, e.g., the work of the Harvard New Teacher Project, at www.gse.harvard.edu/~ngt).

In this book, we do not focus on longitudinal data—that is, how these new teachers' thinking about their profession and practice develops over time. Nor are the brief teacher stories contained here truly case studies in the sense of developing deeply and extensively a small number of exemplars of a teaching issue. Instead, we use a wide variety of teacher voices to get at the range of challenges and issues new teachers confront in their classrooms. These narratives have been plucked from their larger contexts, but we are faithful to their words in presenting these excerpts. The picture that emerges from these interviews is, above all, an honest and trustworthy one. This portrait should not make prospective teachers or teacher educators apologetic, defensive, or negative about the field, but should underscore the necessity of preparing forthrightly for the hard work that is necessary to succeed.

Additionally, this book is not intended to "prove" something about teaching, except perhaps how demanding, complex, and challenging it can be. The book does not aim at offering a set of research conclusions that would satisfy the kind of audience its authors face at educational conferences. Instead, the book is directed—frankly and personally—to teacher education students, beginning teachers, and others interested in teaching. It has been structured in a manner that reflects this intention. Nevertheless, the book rests on solid research, both our own and that of others within the educational research community. As we move into the middle parts of the book, however, we showcase the teacher narratives. In those chapters, we keep the citations to a minimum so as not to intrude on the highly personal space these stories create.

These new teacher voices provide an intimate engagement with the daily, highly contextualized, and autobiographical experiences of new teachers. Their stories touch on their families and friends, divulge what happens when they close the classroom door and start teaching, and candidly set out the struggles they face in the highly politicized world of education today. Many are not the type of story that would be readily shared with others in public forums, perhaps not even with other teachers, administrators, parents, or certainly students. We know from our own experience that these are, however, just the sorts of conversations about teaching that take place when teachers settle down to "teacher talk" with colleagues they deeply trust (Clandinin & Connelly, 1996). We are honored to have witnessed these testimonials concerning new teachers' lives in teaching.

Despite our own concerns, we found our interview participants to be anything but reticent about sharing their stories, even with a tape recorder set in front of them. Most commented that they found the process beneficial, especially in providing them with a forum to make sense of their work with someone who would "get it." Their sentiments reinforced our view that conversations of this sort need to be held, and held regularly, among future teachers as well as among teachers already working in schools. Teacher educators and administrators can help provide the space for these conversations to happen—with mentors, colleagues, and friends—in nonthreatening, informal settings. Where such opportunities are not regularly provided, prospective and new teachers often find their own spaces for such dialogue—in school lunchrooms, teachers lounges, offices, cars, restaurants, and bars. Our experiences suggest that teachers yearn for and profit from an opportunity to produce such narratives and thereby reflect deeply and systematically on their experiences, especially over time.

We acknowledge the difficulties that doing this sort of exercise presents in conventional teacher education settings, especially in classrooms with large numbers of students, grades to be given, a fixed set of weeks in the term, overworked teacher educators, and the boundaries of professional relationships to be maintained. Nevertheless, creating seminar-like settings for exploring the issues presented here might provide an early experience of concentrated, critical teacher reflection that can serve as a model for analogous practices later on.

Scholars who use interviews as a means of research come to realize that "teacher talk" is not just a matter of listening to teachers complain. Instead, these exchanges create a relationship between the one speaking and the one listening, one that rests on shared concerns, communal space, and taking the risk of honest biographical introspection (Connelly & Clandinin, 1988). Such dialogues can lead to positive outcomes; in fact, without them, solutions are rarely found to the ongoing challenges of teaching.

Thus, we have found our own conversations with new teachers to be invitations into relationships, which we value tremendously. We recognize the trust that our conversational partners have placed in us—faith that we will respect their narratives, travails, disappointments, and achievements as serious professional concerns. We have also learned that witnessing such reflection provides a powerful antidote to the frustrations we sometimes experience in our own work as teacher educators. Listening to narratives, hearing fresh insights, and recognizing our own forgotten pasts have all provided a sense of the good work that teachers do in getting to know young people, whether it be by means of teaching them about citizenship, writing a poem, analyzing a piece of evidence, or reading a novel. Teachers and teacher educators recognize that the satisfactions of seeing students learn, whether those students are 15, 20, or 35, can go a long way toward nurturing attachment to a demanding yet ultimately very rewarding career.

GROWTH AND DEVELOPMENT
IN THE "BRAVE NEW WORLD" OF TEACHING

Middle and secondary schools are distinctive cultures demanding unique considerations from teacher education students about how to handle the challenges associated with the first few years of teaching (Grossman & Stodolsky, 1995; McLaughlin, Talbert, & Bascia, 1990; Siskin & Little, 1995). This book's focus on new teachers working in middle and high schools sets it apart from the many other books focused on new teachers in elementary school environments. Still, many experiences of teaching can be considered crossover topics that pertain to both the elementary and secondary levels. Issues around the choice of teaching as a career, "having a life" in the early stages of teaching, and dealing with school administrators and parents are common ones faced by teachers in both sorts of institutions, as are dealing with diverse student populations, dealing with administrators, and crafting lessons in an age of increased accountability.

In recent years, secondary schools have been the targets of energetic efforts at restructuring and reform, especially given their unique features, large size (Cochran-Smith & Fries, 2001; Gordon, 2003), and "shopping mall" character (Powell, 1985). These reform efforts began in the 1980s and have continued over the last 20 years. In many cases, the aims of restructuring have been to make the new, smaller institutions more personal, even caring places in which more students graduate and perhaps even go on to college.

Many educators fear that the positive results of the school restructuring movement are being undercut, perhaps even undone, by high-stakes testing. High-stakes testing has resulted in slippage backwards toward the higher dropout rates small schools were designed, in part, to remediate. We have also found that the pressures of high-stakes testing on fragile urban educational environments might cause some new teachers to question their commitment to inner-city schools (Costigan, 2003; Crocco, 2002). These teachers might not leave teaching, but they might leave urban teaching because failure rates on these tests are often higher in urban schools. Whether a teacher creates possibilities out of the challenges produced by high-stakes testing can only be answered on a case-by-case basis.

As noted already, research into new teachers and their development demonstrates that the intense interactions between personal beliefs and values, combined with professional experiences and school contexts, shape new teachers' lives (Levin, 2003). Along the way, teachers not only educate students, but also educate themselves, coming to understand themselves better generally as persons as well as teachers. The process should also be understood as a process of cognitive development that occurs over time but can be nurtured by certain forms of adult learning (Sprinthall & Thies-Sprinthall, 1980, 1983). However, in the pressure-cooker climate of many schools located in metropolitan areas, faced with the repercussions of new mandates associated with the age of accountability, some teachers might find that development short-circuited by a focus on test preparation as the sole focus of their professional lives.

Traditionally, new teachers become knowledgeable about the craft of teaching through a series of fits and starts. They make progress, stall, and might even regress momentarily in their forward movement. They might feel that they have matured, but then they experience whiplash-like moments where they question whether they've learned anything at all. To the degree that high-stakes testing and the culture of accountability in schools preempts teacher decision making, we question whether this traditional rendition of teacher learning and career development still holds.

Over time, the experiences associated with traditional teacher development contribute to gradually expanding professional knowledge, with growth commonly registered as a set of epiphanies, or "A-ha! moments," as they are sometimes called. This conventional rhetoric of evolution in the teaching life might be too dramatic, even counterproductive to the degree that it implies a passive, involuntary process. Instead, teacher development from the stages of survival and consolidation on to renewal and maturity of teaching is very much a deliberate, active, and engaged process. Teacher growth only comes about as a result of dealing intellectually and proactively with resistances and problems (Zellermayer, 2001), working through knots in thinking (Wagner, 1987), relying on other professionals who form part of one's reflective community, and incorporating both failures and successes into the cognitive maps of teaching. Unless teachers reflectively engage with the problems in their career (Zeichner & Liston, 1996), they can scarcely expect to grow as persons and professionals. As we will see later in this book, finding a supportive school culture that will allow you to reflect on your success and failures and grow as a teacher is essential for development.

Educational researchers emphasize the fact that teaching is also a sociocultural practice. By this we mean that understanding teaching develops by means of interactions with administrators, students, parents, and other teachers. Recognition of the sociocultural dimensions of all learning experiences has been one of the key lessons associated with the "cognitive revolution" of the last 20 years (Bransford, Brown, & Cocking, 1999; Moll, 1990). This insight highlights once again the situated nature of teaching. Learning about teaching gains much from the particular environments in which the lessons are learned and the people encountered there. The situated or sociocultural character of this learning experience reflects the inherent communal nature of the teaching–learning phenomenon but also contributes to the messy and contingent nature of these processes.

It would be hard to underestimate the importance of teacher growth and development over a career. As a foremost authority on teachers' development puts it, "for teachers, what goes on inside the classroom is closely related to what goes on outside it. The quality, range, and flexibility of teachers' classroom work are all closely tied up with their professional growth—with the way that they develop as people and professionals" (Hargreaves, 1993, p. vii). Another scholar captures the interplay of personal and environmental factors in teaching when he calls teaching a "complex intellectual activity played out in equally complex social settings" (Griffin, 1999, p. 7). In sum, the quality of the context in which teaching activities unfold can be a critical determining factor in the ability of teachers, both new and mature, to capitalize on the possibilities for their own ongoing growth and development.

GOOD TEACHING AND GOOD TEACHER EDUCATION

In this book, we stress the importance of school cultures and school leaders in providing space for teachers to share aspects of their work and puzzle through the perennial problems they face. Sometimes, you will find such environments ready-made; that is, schools that already exude an air of mutual collaboration and reflective inquiry when you walk through the front door (Tabachnick & Zeichner, 1991; Zeichner & Liston, 1996). However, you might also find the need to "custom make" such environments, thereby creating your own space for such possibilities. Quite often, teachers use their own initiative to start groups that meet regularly to talk about an issue, to read and discuss books, or simply to get together socially for mutual support. Another alternative might be utilization of online resources like chat rooms offering virtual experiences of such communities of practice. Learning informally from one's peers or through more systematic investigations of one's own practice according to the ideas associated with "action research" provide important avenues into reflective inquiry. Over the short and long haul, capitalizing on opportunities or creating possibilities for such sharing can help sustain, build, and enliven a career leading to maturation as a teacher.

Many teacher education programs are structured in a fashion that takes the sociocultural dimensions of teaching seriously by promoting what we have referred to previously as communities of practice (Wenger, 1998). In other words, teacher educators promote collaboration and communal problem solving and structure time for these activities. Doing teacher education in this fashion helps prepare student teachers for working in environments in which collaboration is valued. Such support is important throughout the teacher education process, but it is essential in dealing with the new challenges of teaching associated with this age of accountability.

We should note explicitly that we do not believe teacher education gets washed out (Zeichner & Liston, 1987; Zeichner & Tabachnick, 1981; Zeichner et al., 1987) once new teachers graduate and take their first jobs. Instead, quality teacher education offers the best route to producing excellent teachers and for sustaining new teachers in their work during the critical first years in the field and beyond.

The hallmarks of this book—its emphasis on inquiry, collaboration, and reflection—are also the foundations of good teacher preparation programs. We take it for granted that teaching requires a strong knowledge base in subject matter and education, but becoming a teacher is, as should be clear at this point, about a great deal more than subject or content knowledge. Good teacher education can help develop the personal dispositions necessary to put knowledge and skills to good use. These dispositions include developing habits that are attuned to the ethical and relational issues of teaching as well (for more on this subject, see Noddings, 1984). During the first few years of teaching, a full repertoire of capacities will get called on for success in classroom teaching (Levin, 2003). Teachers who can engage challenges with such a repertoire will be those best situated to survive and indeed, flourish, during the early, critical years of professional formation.

In the pages that follow, we hope you will identify with, engage with, sympathize with, and respond to the voices of others like Tracy. Although new teachers face enormous challenges in this age of accountability, they also have found real possibilities for creating meaningful and satisfying work. As teacher educators for many years, our purpose here is to open up a dialogue between you and these new teachers. Although the narratives of the new teachers featured in this book emanate from their own situatedness in a major metropolitan area, we are confident of their broad appeal. We hope these stories will stimulate rich discussion of significant professional issues common to the complicated world of teaching today. Remember, there are no right answers to these questions!

REFERENCES

Berliner, D. C. (1986). In pursuit of the expert pedagogue. *Educational Researcher, 15*, 5–13.

Bransford, J., Brown, A., & Cocking, J. (1999). *How people learn: Brain, mind, experience, and school.* Washington, DC: National Academy Press.

Carter, K. (1990). Teachers' knowledge and learning to teach. In W. R. Houston (Ed.), *Handbook of research on teacher education* (pp. 290–310). New York: Macmillan.

Carter, K., Sabers, D., Cushing, K., Pinnegar, P., & Berliner, D. C. (1987). Processing and using information about students: A study of expert, novice, and postulant teachers. *Teaching and Teacher Education, 3*, 147–157.

Clandinin, D. J., & Connelly, F. M. (1996). Teachers' professional knowledge landscapes: Teacher narratives—narratives of teachers—school narratives—narratives of schools. *Educational Researcher, 25*(3), 24–30

Clandinin, D. J., & Connelly, F. M. (2000). *Narrative inquiry: Experience and story in qualitative research.* San Francisco, CA: Jossey-Bass.

Clark, C. (1995). *Thoughtful teaching.* New York: Teachers College Press.

Cochran-Smith, M., & Fries, M. K. (2001). Sticks, stones, and ideology: The discourse of reform in teacher education. *Educational Researcher, 30*(8), 3–15.

Connelly, F. M., & Clandinin, D. J. (1988). *Teachers as curriculum planners: Narratives of experience.* New York: Teachers College Press.

Cook-Sather, A. (2001). Translating themselves: Becoming a teacher through text and talk. In C. M. Clark (Ed.), *Talking shop* (pp. 15–32). New York: Teachers College Press.

Costigan, A. (2003, February 18). *Finding a name for what they want: A study of New York City's Teaching Fellows.* Presentation given at the Association of Teacher Educators Distinguished Research in Teacher Education Award, Jacksonville, FL.

Crocco, M. S. (2002, February). *Accountability and authenticity: Beginning teachers in the social studies*. Paper presented at the conference of the American Association of Colleges of Teacher Education, New York.

Darling-Hammond, L., & Hammerness, K. (2002). Toward a pedagogy of cases in teacher education. *Teaching Education, 13*(2), 125–135.

Gordon, D. T. (Ed.). (2003). *A nation reformed? American education 20 years after A Nation at Risk*. Cambridge, MA: Harvard Education Press.

Griffin, G. (1999). Changes in teacher education: Looking to the future. In G. A. Griffin (Ed.), *The education of teachers: Ninety-eighth yearbook of the National Society for the Study of Education* (Part I, pp. 1–28). Chicago: University of Chicago Press.

Grossman, P., & Stodolsky, S. (1995). Content as context: The role of school subjects in secondary school teaching. *Educational Researcher, 24*(8), 5–24.

Hargreaves, A. (1993). *Changing teachers; changing times: Teachers work and cultures in the postmodern age*. New York: Teachers College Press.

Hargreaves, A. (2000). Four ages of professionalism and professional learning. *Teachers and Teaching: History and Practice 6*(2), 151–182.

Hollingsworth, S. J. (1989). Prior beliefs and cognitive change in learning to teach. *American Educational Research Journal, 26*, 160–189.

Hollingsworth, S. J. (1994). *Teacher research and urban literacy education*. New York: Teachers College Press.

Huberman, M. (Ed.). (1993). Research on teachers' professional lives. *International Journal of Educational Research, 13*, 343–466.

Ingersoll, R. M. (2001). Teacher turnover and teacher shortages: An organizational analysis. *American Educational Research Journal, 38*, 499–534.

Kagan, D. M. (1992). Professional growth among preservice and beginning teachers. *Review of Educational Research, 2*, 129–169.

Levin, B. B. (2003). *Case studies of teacher development*. Mahwah, NJ: Lawrence Erlbaum Associates.

Levin, B. B., & Ammon, P. R. (1996). A longitudinal analysis of four case studies. *Teacher Education Quarterly, 19*(4), 39–57.

McEwan, H., & Egan, K. (Eds.). (1995). *Narrative in teaching, learning, and research*. New York: Teachers College Press.

McLaughlin, M. W., Talbert, J. E., & Bascia, N. (1990). *The contexts of teaching in secondary schools*. New York: Teachers College Press.

Moll, L. (Ed.). (1990). *Vygotsky and education: Instructional implications and applications of sociohistorical psychology*. Cambridge, England: Cambridge University Press.

Noddings, N. (1984). *Caring*. Berkeley: University of California Press.

Powell, A. (1985). *The shopping mall high school: Winners and losers in the educational marketplace*. New York: Houghton, Mifflin.

Reiman, A., & Thies-Sprinthall, L. (1998). *Mentoring and supervision for teacher development*. Reading, MA: Addison Wesley Longman.

Resnick, L. (1987). *Education and learning to think*. Washington, DC: National Academy Press.

Richardson, V. (1996). The role of attitudes and beliefs in learning to teach. In J. Sikula, T. J. Buttery, & E. Guyton (Eds.), *Handbook of research on teacher education* (2nd ed., pp. 102–119). New York: Simon & Schuster Macmillan.

Richardson, V., & Placier, P. (2001). Teacher change. In V. Richardson (Ed.), *Handbook of research on teacher education* (3rd ed., pp. 905–947). New York: Simon & Schuster Macmillan.

Rust, F., & Orland, L. (2001). Learning the discourse of teaching: Conversation as professional development. In C. M. Clark (Ed.), *Talking shop* (pp. 82–117). New York: Teachers College Press.

Ryan, K. (1986). *The induction of new teachers.* Bloomington, IN: Phi Delta Kappa Educational Foundation.

Ryan, K. (1992). *The roller coaster year.* New York: HarperCollins.

Sadker, M. P., & Sadker, D. M. (2000). *Teachers, schools, society* (5th ed.). New York: McGraw-Hill.

Shulman, L. S. (1986). Those who understand: Knowledge growth in teaching. *Educational Researcher, 15*(2), 4–14.

Siskin, L. S., & Little, J. W. (1995). *The subjects in question: Departmental organization and the high school.* New York: Teachers College Press.

Sprinthall, N., & Thies-Sprinthall, L. (1980). Education for teacher growth: A cognitive developmental perspective. *Theory Into Practice, 29,* 278–286.

Sprinthall, N., & Thies-Sprinthall, L. (1983). The teacher as adult learner: A cognitive-developmental view. In G. A. Griffin (Ed.), *Staff development: 82nd yearbook of the National Society for the Study of Education* (pp. 12–35). Chicago: University of Chicago Press.

Tabachnick, B., & Zeichner, K. (1991). *Issues and practices in inquiry-oriented teacher education.* New York: Falmer.

Tom, A. R., & Valli, L. (1990). Professional knowledge for teaching. In W. Houston (Ed.), *Handbook of research on teacher education* (pp. 373–392). New York: Macmillan.

Van Manen, M. (1990). *Researching lived experience.* New York: State University of New York Press.

Vinz, R. (1996). *Composing a teaching life.* Portsmouth, NH: Boynton/Cook.

Wagner, A. C. (1987). "Knots" in teaching thinking. In J. Calderhead (Ed.), *Exploring teachers' thinking* (pp. 161–178). London: Cassell.

Wasley, P. A. (1991). *Teachers who lead: The rhetoric of reform and the realities of practice.* New York: Teachers College Press.

Wenger, E. (1998). *Communities of practice: Learning, meaning, and identity.* Cambridge, England: Cambridge University Press.

Zeichner, K., & Liston, D. P. (1987). Teaching student teachers to reflect. *Harvard Educational Review, 57,* 23–47.

Zeichner, K., & Liston, D. (1996). *Reflective teaching: An introduction.* Mahwah, NJ: Lawrence Erlbaum Associates.

Zeichner, K., & Tabachnick, B. R. (1981). Are the effects of university teacher education washed out by school experience? *Journal of Teacher Education, 32,* 7–11.

Zeichner, K., Tabachnick, B. R., & Densmore, K. (1987). Individual, institutional, and cultural influences on the development of teachers' craft knowledge. In J. Calderhead (Ed.), *Exploring teachers thinking* (pp. 21–59). London: Cassell.

Zellermayer, M. (2001). Resistance as a catalyst in teachers' professional development. In C. M. Clark (Ed.), *Talking shop* (pp. 40–63). New York: Teachers College Press.

Zumwalt, K. K. (1984). Teachers and mothers: Facing new beginnings. *Teachers College Record, 86*(1), 138–155.

Chapter 2

High-Stakes Teaching

In 1996, a blue-ribbon panel of scholars, governors, and policymakers, named the National Commission on Teaching and America's Future (NCTAF), was convened to discuss the state of education in the United States today. Their work, contained in *What Matters Most: Teaching for America's Future* (NCTAF, 1996), underscored the importance of quality teachers and good teaching in improving the performance of America's public schools. This report emphasizes the fact that what teachers know and can do is an important influence on what students learn.

According to NCTAF, the long term success of school reform rests on preparing and retaining good teachers and creating conditions in which teachers can teach well. Having high standards for schools and holding schools and teachers accountable for the performance of students is only one part of the equation. Increasing the capacity of teachers to perform at high levels and providing them with the necessary resources and environments in which they can meet the new demands of teaching are crucial. Unfortunately, in some states, teachers have not been given the support necessary to bring about the needed changes. An emphasis on accountability and an expectation for increased teaching capacity has not been combined with an investment in new resources. This has intensified pressures on teachers as never before. For this and other reasons, concerns have been registered over a so-called teacher shortage that appears to be caused by an exodus or turnover of new and experienced teachers.

Much ink has been spent on documenting and analyzing this phenomenon. Ingersoll (2002a, 2002b) at the University of Pennsylvania has done extensive research on the subject. His investigations of comprehensive, national statistical data indicate that the problem is not so much a matter of teacher recruitment as it is of teacher retention. The challenge to keep teachers, especially highly qualified ones, in teaching looms largest in urban areas. Nevertheless, problems with teacher turnover undercut the efficacy of schools outside cities as well. Keeping highly qualified teachers in all schools, rich and poor, urban, suburban, and rural, large and small should be a priority for the American system of education today. Recognizing the contribution of strong teacher preparation to creating highly qualified teachers is also important.

As we will see later in this book, many factors enter into the decisions made by beginning teachers concerning where to teach. Each time a teacher chooses to take a position in a particular school district, he or she steps onto ground that masks long, hidden roots. The historical, political, and economic roots of the American public school system are a complicated mix of state and federal factors, yielding an idiosyncratic picture that is quite different from the more centralized approaches to education in Western Europe and other parts of the world. This chapter provides an introduction to an important set of contributing factors to the contemporary shape of schooling: the effects of educational reforms over the last 20 years, including the standards and accountability movement, and the problems of teacher recruitment and retention.

The purpose of this book is to explore the effects of the accountability movement on the practice of new teachers. Heightened calls for the accountability of schools and teachers came to be implemented in the last decades of the 20th century on a state-by-state basis through an approach that relied heavily on high-stakes testing. States differed in the scope, nature, and character of the tests used to hold teachers and schools accountable; clearly some tests were better than others and some states demanded more frequent testing of students. Nevertheless, the pressures associated with this testing regimen in many states held the potential for driving good teachers out of urban teaching where student failure rates were higher, and perhaps out of teaching completely. High-stakes testing thrust an even larger wedge between working in city and suburban schools. In other words, high-stakes testing created a situation that left many urban schools at even greater risk of having a less able teaching force.

Schooling has always been a highly political enterprise, and it is no less so today. Teachers need to be attuned to the politics impinging on their lives as teachers—whether it be high-stakes testing, vouchers, bilingual education, or the very legitimacy of public education in a democratic society. The issues laid out in this chapter show no signs of going away. Thus, thinking them through on an individual and group basis is an essential element in intelligent adaptation to the teaching life today.

THE PRESSURES OF ACCOUNTABILITY

Since the 1980s, globalization, neoconservative ideologies advocating free market solutions to public problems, antiunionism, and the rise of religious fundamentalism, among other factors, have all contributed to the increased politicization of the U.S. educational system. Schools in this country, and especially textbooks used in these schools (Ravitch, 2003; Zimmerman, 2002), often seem a pawn in the broad-based culture wars dividing many "liberals" from "conservatives." At least as measured by its willingness to support increases in school budgets, public support for public schools seems to have eroded. At the same time, teachers and schools are being held responsible for addressing a host of intractable social problems. Many parents and politicians across the nation see education as an institution aimed at remedying something missing, lacking, or just plain wrong—not only in students' lives but in society as a whole. Besides teaching children literacy, numeracy, science, and social studies, schools must address poverty, nutrition, interpersonal conflict, teen pregnancy, alcohol and drug abuse, and general alienation from the social values of the United States (Clark & Florio-Ruane, 2001). Schools face increased responsibilities as well as accountability with decreased public funds and support.

At the end of the 20th century, public opinion polls showed politicians and the public held conflicting beliefs about public education: Many expressed widespread support for local schools but also held the notion that schools in another city or state had "gone downhill." The latter sentiment reflected the ongoing drumbeat of bad news about education since the issuance of the report called *A Nation at Risk* by the National Commission on Excellence in Education (1983). This publication galvanized an educational critique that had been building for years among those dissatisfied with the nation's public schools. *A Nation at Risk* held that decline in the quality of American schools had brought about slippage in the country's ability to compete in a globalizing economy. The report was issued on the heels of what was termed a period of "malaise" during the late 1970s under President Jimmy Carter and a subsequent call for national renewal symbolized by the election of President Ronald Reagan.

Twenty years later, it is unclear whether the original diagnosis contained in *A Nation at Risk* or its prescriptions for change were on the mark. Many scholars today debate whether changes prompted by the report have had a positive effect on American education (Berliner & Biddle, 1995; Goodlad, 2002; Gordon, 2003; Olson, 2003b). Many conservative politicians and policymakers called for greater "choice" in American education following the report; that is, they wanted more options across the board: for parental choice of public school, for availability of vouchers to pay for private schools, for alternatives to regular teacher certification for prospective teachers, and for greater variety in the kinds of schools, including magnet schools, theme schools, elite academies, and even single-sex schools. New initiatives such as school management by private corporations and the proliferation of fast-track routes into teaching have also emerged as efforts to improve American education.

In urban areas, widespread experimentation with downsizing schools and creating new, smaller schools emerged as a prominent feature of school reform. Teacher collaboration, literacy efforts, site-based management, and greater parent involvement—have all taken their place in urban schools as reforms with a large impact on teacher work. Likewise, the middle school movement has transformed many former junior high schools into middle schools, with teams of teachers working together on interdisciplinary curriculum, in block-scheduled time periods, and with small cohorts of students whom they get to know well over several years.

Many of these changes have actually strengthened local control and choice within public education. At the same time, other reform initiatives have taken a markedly different path. The standards, accountability, and accreditation movements of recent years, including the No Child Left Behind legislation of 2001, have all pursued educational change through greater centralization and control. Some observers believe that these efforts are intended to undermine taxpayers' support for public education. By creating a sense that schools have "failed" to deliver an excellent education for all students, school choice and vouchers become attractive alternatives garnering greater public support. The result, of course, would be to take students and tax dollars out of the public school system at a time when the standards and accountability movement demanded greater rather than fewer resources.

Probably no reform has had a broader and deeper effect on urban and suburban schools alike than high-stakes testing. High-stakes testing refers to the comprehensive examinations in school subjects that have the potential of determining whether students pass a grade or receive a high school diploma. As we will see in subsequent chapters, teachers entering the profession today, especially those working in underresourced settings with students who bring learning and linguistic challenges to schooling, typically face formidable hurdles in meeting the demands associated with high-stakes testing.

THE INTENSIFICATION OF TEACHING

One undeniable result of the trend toward heightened accountability for schools, students, and teachers has been the "intensification" of demands placed on teachers (Hargreaves & Fullan, 1992). This intensification pertains to school administrators as well. Accountability pressures have had the effect of depersonalizing teaching, making it more stressful for practitioners, and increasing dropout rates. In some districts and states, rewards in the form of cash bonuses are given for teachers and administrators who produce better test scores for their schools. As a result of such pressures, even seasoned practitioners are leaving the profession at alarming levels, especially in urban areas where the needs for excellent teachers are greatest (Ingersoll, 2001, 2002a; Tye & O'Brien, 2002). Some experts place the blame for the high level of teacher departures from schools on this intensified climate, one of several unintended consequences of high-stakes testing in the schools (Kohn, 2001; McNeil, 2000; Sacks, 1999).

In schools across the country, teachers today are held responsible for doing more and doing it faster than ever before. If they fail in this effort, negative consequences accrue—for districts, schools, students, and untenured teachers. In some states, parental choice means that parents can take their children out of these "failing" neighborhood schools and put them in other public schools. In other places, legions of new "Teach for America" rookies focus heavily on literacy and numeracy skills at the expense of other subjects such as science and social studies.

Many teachers today who work in the so-called failing schools find themselves teaching standardized curriculum with scripted, "teacher-proof" lessons provided by textbook publishers and test preparation companies. Even teachers working in wealthy districts have seen their work culture eroded. Their professional judgment has been hemmed in by new strictures prompted by performance standards, assessment rubrics, and learning objectives, imposed by different education authorities. In certain cases, teachers believe these new requirements bring welcome structure to a decentralized national school system. In other cases, teachers feel that efforts at standardization have been misguided or at least overdone. They find that these measures undercut the creativity and autonomy they associate with working as educational professionals.

Whatever point of view you bring to this controversial issue, it is clear that teachers today are being inducted into a profession in which standards and accountability have become the norm. This simply was not the case 20 years ago. Clearly, the external pressures on teachers have reached a peak in the last 10 years. Moreover, these changes show no signs of going away. The trend toward centralization reflects a distinct departure from past educational history in the United States when the individual teacher had considerably more autonomy.

Until the 1980s most states had no exit exams for high schools. New York has, however, been different in this regard for decades. Its state-prescribed curriculum in major school subjects and Regents exams for academically able students have both existed since early in the 20th century. Yet previously, a Regents diploma was not required for graduation and only a small percentage of graduating seniors took the exams and opted for the Regents diploma. Secondary students had the option of passing the much simpler Regents Competency Tests (RCT), a minimum competency exam, for purposes of graduation. Now, the RCT has been abandoned and all students must pass a number of Regents exams. Failure to pass these tests means failure to receive a high school diploma. Some scholars fear that high-stakes tests are raising the dropout rate in urban schools markedly. Nearly all would concur that the tests have increased pressures on teachers.

This picture is not unique to New York but is common across the country. In many subject areas, such as reading, math, science, and social studies, tests are now given at early ages. In social studies, for example, New York currently requires tests in the 5th, 8th, 10, and 11th grades. In other states, pressures around literacy and numeracy tests have virtually eliminated instruction in social studies and science at lower grade levels, and art, music, and electives on the secondary level. This new regime of testing has produced a major departure from past patterns of curriculum and instruction at the elementary and middle school levels, where standardized achievement tests were more diagnostic than determinative of school placement, and at the secondary level where tests were used to separate middle and high-achieving students rather than raising the overall bar on graduation requirements.

Whatever the level, a general pattern of intensification of work pressures has dramatically altered the climate for teachers across the country. The race for higher test scores drives day-to-day decision making in classrooms and schools to an unprecedented degree. This process occurs even at schools in which students do fairly well on these tests. This is because testing is considered by many to provide a benchmark of quality in schools; thus, higher test scores are always desirable. In some communities, scores are believed to influence property values. With all this at stake, it is hardly surprising that some teachers find the pressures around tests to be acute.

At the same time, a growing consensus has emerged that good teachers have a powerful impact in the classroom (Darling-Hammond, 1999; NCTAF, 2003). Put simply, who teachers are matters greatly in terms of student performance (Darling-Hammond, 1998). Many scholars in the educational research and teacher education community believe the process of interaction between teachers and students is the essential factor in how people develop as teachers and how well students learn.

Disagreements do exist, however, about how to create good teachers. One camp believes that quality teacher education programs provide the only acceptable route into teaching (Darling-Hammond, 2000a). Another contends that alternative routes into teaching, such as Teach for America, provide adequate preparation (Ballou & Podgursky, 2000) and that bright teachers actually need little or no preparation in learning how to teach before stepping into classrooms.

Much public policy remains driven by the notion that teachers and students are interchangeable parts in a factory-like system. In this system, controlling costs and raising productivity are the best paths to educational reform (Weiner, 2000). Such an approach to education erodes rather than enhances quality. The processes of teaching and learning cannot be short-circuited by means of workplace efficiencies offering questionable economies. In the end, investment in human capital (i.e., developing the capacities of committed teachers) will produce the greatest return on investment.

In the chapters that follow, this book offers poignant reminders of these realities. You will encounter the autobiographical voices of many talented new teachers facing this intensified educational climate and their strategies for coping and succeeding despite its myriad demands.

TEACHER TURNOVER AND TEACHER SHORTAGE

Both the popular press and the media regularly report news of a teacher shortage. This shortage is manifesting itself nationwide but is particularly acute in urban school districts (Gewertz, 2002). New York City is a case in point. By the beginning of the 2002–2003 school year, 50% of all teachers were uncertified. The city needed 10,000 new teachers (Park, 2003), roughly 12.5% of the workforce. The situation in New York City is symptomatic of the acute shortage of teachers across the country, especially in urban areas (Mezzacappa, 2003). By 1999, the United States was losing roughly 200,000 teachers yearly (Feiman-Nemser, Schwille, Carver, & Yusko, 1999). One scholar characterized the problem in this way: "The United States faces a crisis of extraordinary proportions in terms of the anticipated need for teachers. It is estimated that half of the teachers in the nation will leave teaching in the decade that began in 1996" (Griffin, 1999, p. 12).

As we have noted already, the problem is not necessarily one of supply, although pipeline issues do play a role in certain subject areas. Overall, schools of education graduate annually more than enough teachers to meet the demands associated with teacher retirement, with the exception of three problem areas: math, science, and bilingual education. The problem, then, is not so much one of recruitment as it is of retention of teachers (Ingersoll, 2002b; NCTAF, 2003). Ingersoll explained that the so-called shortage of teachers is actually an exodus of qualified teachers. Those leaving teaching outnumber those entering the field by a factor of three to one. This explains the characterization of teaching as a "revolving door profession" (NCTAF, 2003; Ingersoll, 2002b). According to one report, "almost a third of America's teachers leave the field within 3 years of beginning teaching, and almost half leave after 5 years. The problem is worst in low-income communities, but it exists across all sectors of education and in all communities" (American Association of Colleges for Teacher Education, 2002, p. 1).

The turnover rate in high-poverty areas is almost twice that of low-poverty areas (NCTAF, 2003). Most of these departures occur early on in the teaching career. A number of factors contribute to the exodus from urban environments. According to the research conducted for this book, as well as other studies of urban schools, these factors include high-stakes testing, disruptive and chaotic teaching environments, poor leadership, and the low status of teaching as a profession. Interestingly, the teachers we interviewed did not primarily cite low pay as a reason for leaving, although low pay is always a factor in understanding teaching as a career. The modest level of teacher compensation in cities does play a role in the overall satisfaction with urban teaching as compared to the better paying suburbs.

Little national research has investigated whether teacher attrition can be linked to particular school characteristics. Recent work (Ingersoll, 2001, 2002b) has, however, examined the causes contributing to teacher turnover in general across the country. As one might expect, teachers leave their jobs due to retirement, layoffs, school closings and reorganizations, family or personal reasons, in pursuit of other jobs, or dissatisfaction with their work. Those who cite job dissatisfaction mention low salaries, weak support from school administration, poor student motivation and discipline, and lack of teacher influence over decision making. Still, this negative portrait is balanced by a National Education Association (NEA, 2003) study of public school teachers. This report indicates that if they had to do it again, a majority would choose teaching as their career.

One of the lessons Ingersoll drew from these data is the importance of providing support for new teachers. Clearly, teacher collaboration can contribute to teacher satisfaction. Ingersoll also counsels greater latitude for teachers in decision making. This underscores the importance of creating spaces in which teachers can use their rational skills in dealing with the challenges they face. Overall, teachers' working conditions, construed broadly, play the most important role in their decisions about whether to stay or to leave the profession. Attending to working conditions and treating teachers as professionals will contribute to retaining them in schools. Committed, knowledgeable, and well-prepared teachers with scope for autonomy and creativity will help improve schools.

Politicians, educational leaders, and the media have all taken note of the teacher turnover issue (Olson, 2003a; Thomas, 2002). In contexts where teacher shortages are extreme, the "solution" to the problem of teacher turnover has often relied on cheaper and faster ways of recruiting new teachers, almost certainly a means of continuing the revolving door of teaching. Advocates for improved working conditions and better salaries for teachers seem to have few supporters in positions of power these days.

Despite efforts to solidify the professional status of teaching, this movement faces an uphill battle against vested interests favoring teachers who are low-paid, temporary, easily replaceable workers.

At the turn of the 21st century, 130 bills were pending nationwide to implement programs to recruit teachers through alternative routes to certification (Laitsch, 2001). Some of these programs focus recruitment on college graduates, some on career changers, and others on retired military personnel. In each case, the demands of inducting such individuals into the profession and sustaining them throughout their time teaching differ markedly as do their retention rates. Some of these programs ask for a multiyear commitment; others require just a summer (Cholo, 2003).

By 2003, 45 states had authorized alternative paths to teacher certification. Twenty-five of these state programs were "structured" in one way or another (Blair, 2003). Taken together, these approaches place greater emphasis on the speedy recruitment and placement of new teachers in high-needs areas (Kanstoroom & Finn, 1999) than on reforming teacher education, licensing, or schools (Ballou & Podgursky, 2000; Darling-Hammond, 2000b). New federal rules, however, do require that teachers enrolled in alternative route programs receive high-quality professional development before and during teaching. Such professional development is linked directly to the standards and assessment movements and involves intensive supervision and mentoring (Edwards, 2003). These latter aspects represent a growing acknowledgment, even within quick-fix approaches to teacher shortage problems, that teachers need more than content knowledge to be successful as long-term teachers.

Some alternative route programs, such as the New York City Teaching Fellows (NYCTF) program, are based on the Teach for America model. In brief, this program typically involves an intensive "boot camp" summer workshop, a commitment to teach for a minimum of 2 years in troubled schools under the guidance of mentors, financial incentives or a free master's program, and reduced-credit education coursework. Great debate exists about the effectiveness of such alternative route programs as compared with regular teacher preparation (Darling-Hammond, Chung, & Frelow, 2002), but such programs seem to be here to stay—at least in the near future. Evidence does exist, though, that beginning teachers in alternative route programs are asking for more help and mentoring than is being provided. In other words, individuals in alternative route programs are themselves asking for the kinds of assistance typically provided within regular teacher education programs (Costigan, 2003).

Although finding a solution for teacher turnover is complex, the effects of the problem can be clearly grasped. Teacher turnover brings with it a high cost, draining both personnel and school finances and disrupting the creation of knowledge-centered and learner-centered communities. These disruptions affect minority students and low-income districts dispropor- tionately (NCTAF, 2003). Teachers today enter the teaching profession in many urban areas through regular or alternative programs, sometimes without any preparation at all, a situation that disadvantages their students. If they stay in the profession more than a couple of years, they might even continue to develop through their 4th, 7th, and 10th years (Rust & Orland, 2001). According to a June 2003 report issued by the New York State Edu- cation Department, the retention rate for NYCTF participants has ranged from a low of 62% for those who entered the program in 2000 to a high of 90% for those who began in 2002. Future research will need to determine whether these individuals remain in teaching, especially urban teaching, beyond the 2-year commitment they make when they enroll in the pro- gram, and whether they have become effective teachers.

Evidence suggests that it takes at least 2 years before new teachers come to understand teaching to a degree that they find satisfying (Rust, 1999). Today, we recognize better than we did 20 years ago that teacher education is an ongoing, career-long process, with stages of development throughout the career (Huberman, Grounauer, & Marti, 1993; Levin, 2003). Such de- velopment can only occur if a new teacher stays in the profession long enough to capitalize on the opportunities for learning essential to growth and development as a teacher. Inculcating such dispositions toward profes- sional development is a crucial component of any good teacher preparation program. Recent evidence suggests that the vast majority of teachers partic- ipate in ongoing professional development work throughout the year, with about a third pursuing such opportunities in the summers (NEA, 2003).

TEACHER QUALITY

Although a person's intelligence, ability to use words, and desire to teach is important, so, too, is that person's ability to relate well to children and ado- lescents. Personal characteristics, of course, are not the only ones contribut- ing to good teaching. We stress the autobiographical aspects of teaching because life history does play a role in making the decision to teach. Life his- tory and social context influence the decision to teach, as recent research confirms. In fact, some parents discourage their sons or daughters from en- tering teaching (Boles & Troen, 2003). Today more than ever, many men and people of color also avoid teaching careers. According to data from a 1999–2000 representative national data sample compiled by the National Center for Education Statistics, 74.5% of public school teachers were female and 84% were White, non-Hispanic (NCES, 2003).

In education literature, "teacher quality" refers to the preparation a per- son receives in becoming a teacher. This preparation includes deep under- standing of the subject matter to be taught, appropriate methods for teaching this subject matter, and the ability to remain reflective about teaching as new challenges emerge. A long-standing myth exists in this country that teachers are born and not made (Britzman, 1986). Such a viewpoint obviously leads to a different place than the argument found in this book—that strong and deep teacher preparation is essential to developing good teachers.

Mythologies abound when it comes to teaching. Another one that often circulates is that "anyone can teach" or "those that can't (do x, y, or z), teach (x, y, or z)." As with all mythology, some kernel of truth might be present in the aphorism. For example, in the first case, it is certainly true that those born with abundant intelligence, empathy, and willingness to teach might become better teachers than others. However, this is no different from saying that certain body types are better suited for becoming gymnasts and others for becoming basketball players. Certain traits are necessary but not sufficient for becoming a high-quality teacher. Even those with intelligence, empathy, and a strong desire to teach generally need professional preparation to succeed, especially those working in schools with the most disadvantaged populations.

Over the course of a lifetime, the most important factor in developing a teacher's highest quality work is informed appreciation of what constitutes excellent teaching in the classroom. Today we know a great deal about what these elements look like. Grafting those elements onto a particular classroom context is the work of a good teacher. For example, such practice includes what has been called "culturally responsive pedagogy" (Ladson-Billings, 1995, p. 46). Tailoring curriculum and instruction to the needs of one's students plays a significant role in defining good practice. Good teaching can be characterized by a set of general principles, but implementing those principles in the classroom depends a great deal on the particularities of students, school, and curriculum. In high-quality teaching, the need for well-informed professional judgment is acute.

Flexibility exists in the ways good teachers enact the principles of good teaching, as it does in other professions. Still, teaching is not for everyone, and leaving teaching is not shameful. Those who enter teaching must sustain the vocational desire to do what teachers do, and to do it better and better as time goes by. A steep learning curve lies at the heart of teaching because teaching is a complex intellectual activity (Griffin, 1999). If high-quality teaching is to be sustained, then teachers need to grow in their ability to teach and their knowledge of subject matter. This provides a strong rationale for finding a place in which you can grow as a teacher and gain support from your peers in the process.

For most of the 20th century, however, teaching was not seen as professional work. Instead, the perspective on teaching emphasized the behaviorist and technical approaches to the work. Educational "experts" talked about "teacher training" rather than "teacher education." Teaching was described as a set of skills, a "bag of tricks," or a few techniques. These characterizations made teaching sound more like a formula than an art (Calderhead, 1987; Clark & Yinger, 1987; Mayher, 1990), and discounted the professional knowledge necessary for doing it well.

The historical reasons for this characterization of teaching are complex. Behaviorists and some social scientists sought to prove that education is a science that could be reduced to a set of fixed laws and principles. Out of such thinking came past efforts at devising a "teacher-proof" curriculum, resting on the notion that formulas and scripts for teaching produce higher levels of learning. Like the standardization movement of today, teachers are seen simply as delivery vessels for lessons: Who they are, as well as who their students are, and the interactions between them are only incidental factors in learning. Even less respectful of the intellectual demands of teaching are those who see it as a bag of tricks. This viewpoint claims that teaching is mostly about knowledge of subject matter. If a teacher has a PhD in chemistry, for example, he or she will make an excellent teacher. Although content knowledge is necessary for good teaching, it is not sufficient for quality work. Thus, different frameworks concerning teaching and learning lead to different conclusions about how to improve the educational enterprise.

Other factors, also rooted in history, have created other social constructions of teaching. Universal compulsory education emerged in this country due to the demands associated with creating an educated electorate for a democracy. This approach to schooling became the norm throughout most of the country during the 19th century. In the early decades of the 20th century, public education was challenged by the vast numbers of immigrants entering schools. Providing compulsory education for a growing population was an expensive proposition, so states looked for ways to contain cost. Bureaucrats gradually replaced male teachers with female teachers, especially as the bar was raised from a few years of schooling to 8, 10, or 12 years. Women worked for significantly less pay than men. By the turn of the 20th century, as high schools became required and new laws forbade child labor, school teaching had become a heavily feminized profession (Hoffman, 2003).

During the early decades of the 20th century, educational leaders sought to contain costs by calling on efficiency experts. These individuals' expertise lay in improving industrial and commercial productivity by making workers able to produce commodities faster and more efficiently. Educational leaders asked these experts to address the problems associated with a new massive public education system struggling with educating millions of first-generation Americans while retaining costs in communities that were largely averse to levying high taxes (Kliebard, 1995). From these efforts arose the "factory model" of schooling whereby students, metaphorically speaking, moved on a conveyor belt from subject to subject, much like a Model T Ford on an assembly line. In other words, days were spent moving students through a course schedule segmented into 40-minute blocks of time. To paraphrase one industrialist, "the man who put on the bolt didn't tighten the screw," or in an educational sense, "the woman who taught American history didn't teach writing or reading."

To deliver curriculum in 40-minute sound bites or "periods," curriculum was divided into subjects, and subjects into sequences of courses. Students amassed Carnegie units, which reflected their acquisition of the requisite course time to be granted a diploma. Good teaching was viewed as a set of atomized scripts or behaviors that good teachers could be quickly trained to do, through normal schools and later in colleges. In New York City, the basic format for instruction came to be known as the *developmental lesson*, with exact specifications of the numbers of minutes teachers should spend on each prescribed segment of the lesson's development. In many ways, these approaches can be interpreted as early efforts to teacher-proof schooling, and this mechanistic approach to teaching continues today.

Such conceptions of teaching not only live on today both in political and public misunderstandings, but these misconceptions are all too often found in the minds of people who want to teach. It is not surprising that prospective teachers share in the national mythology concerning teaching. Despite the best efforts of organizations like the NEA and other professional organizations, many Americans fail to grasp the nature or demands of teacher work. Dispelling misconceptions within the American public is important for gaining greater understanding and support for the hard work teachers do. However, dispelling misconceptions about the work demands of teaching is critical for educating future teachers. Only with this understanding will prospective teachers be committed to putting in the hard work necessary for success.

DANGER SIGNS ON THE EDUCATIONAL HIGHWAY

The current culture of high stakes testing, standards, and accountability in the United States is a reflection of old ways of thinking about teaching—that is, teaching as a set of technical behaviors, where a one-size-fits-all approach to curriculum and assessment suits all the needs of a vast and complex country. The 2001 No Child Left Behind Act falls within this tradition, with its emphasis on high-stakes testing and threatened losses in federal aid if schools do not meet the benchmarks for passing these tests. Despite its promise to provide a "highly qualified" teacher for every American school child by 2006, educational researchers and journalists have raised concerns in two areas. One concern questions whether adequate funding exists to carry out the goals contained in the legislation. The second concern addresses the manner in which the law's provisions impact poorer districts differently from affluent districts that have greater resources to meet the new standards contained in the legislation ("Editorial: The Educational Sell-out," 2003; Winerip, 2002).

For almost half a century, educational researchers have argued that a mechanistic approach to teaching and learning can inhibit learning and disadvantage students, particularly poor students. Scholars have also acknowledged that student success in schools sometimes rests on tolerance for boredom, which does not reflect well on some of what occurs there. Other scholars have commented that a certain measure of success in schools, avoidably or unavoidably, depends on the willingness to work on unrewarding, unchallenging tasks seen, at least by students, as meaningless and disconnected to real life (Coleman, 1965). For decades, many adolescents have sadly judged schooling to be of little relevance to their life goals (Csikszentmihalyi & Schneider, 2000; Goodman, 1960). Such portraits of disaffection persist today, with many adolescents professing little interest in or love of learning as it takes place in schools (Johnson, Farkas, & Bers, 1994). Despite these reactions to schools, parents, teachers, and policymakers often insist on very traditional means and ends regarding schooling. They seem to assume that students should learn and teachers should teach in the same ways they encountered in their own educational experiences (Johnson, Immerwahr, & Farkas, 1994).

Whatever else might be said about accountability efforts in schools, it seems safe to say that high-stakes testing has probably not done much to enhance a greater love of learning in students than their parents. It is also questionable whether such educational reforms have enhanced future teachers' desires to be in classrooms. As we have discovered in our research, love of students and love of subject matter motivate most beginning teachers—not a love of testing. In fact, new teachers cite assessment as the bane of their existence; as we will see in the teacher narratives, they decry the inordinate attention assessment testing is given in their everyday lives of schooling.

In arguing against the new culture of accountability in schools, we are not arguing that assessment should play no role in schooling. Indeed, we understand the importance of accountability to a system of public education. Moreover, we believe that assessment—diagnostic as well as evaluative types—done regularly and authentically, should play a larger role in our educational enterprise. This viewpoint is supported by much of the current scientific research about how students learn (Bransford, Brown, & Cocking, 1999). This body of research emphasizes the importance of providing frequent feedback for students so they can redirect their efforts if they are not succeeding or on the right track. Such knowledge does not support the trivial, reductive tests used regularly in many states today.

Oversimplified technical solutions, scripted lessons, and lock-step instruction have, unfortunately, become the rule for teachers in underperforming schools (Hargreaves, 2000), and they have also become a significant factor in schools that are viewed as successful. These approaches loom as yet another form of teacher-proofing the curriculum, one more in the long line of cheap fixes for the problems of urban schools. Unfortunately, the limited scope offered in these programs for teacher decision making and their often spurious scientific pretensions have the potential of driving out the kinds of teachers necessary to improve achievement in urban schools.

However, a few recent beacons of the importance of the teacher, rather than testing, might signal that the tide is beginning to turn away from using tests as the chief lever for improving education in this country. New understandings, grounded in solid research, about the importance of quality teachers to the process of school improvement and student achievement point policymakers in another direction (NCTAF, 2003). Only by recognizing that the process of educating teachers involves significant intellectual and financial resources will this nation create quality schools for all its students.

REFERENCES

American Association of Colleges for Teacher Education. (2002). NCTAF shifts focus from supply to retention: Symposium paves way for new report. *AACTE Briefs, 23*(11), 1, 3.

Ballou, D., & Podgursky, M. (2000). Reforming teacher preparation and licensing: What is the evidence? *Teachers College Record, 102*(1), 5–27.

Berliner, D., & Biddle, B. (1995). *The manufactured crisis: Myths, fraud, and the attacks on American public schools*. Reading, MA: Addison-Wesley.

Blair, J. (2003, January 9). Skirting tradition. *Education Week, 22*(17), 4.

Boles, K. C., & Troen, V. (2003). Mamas, don't let your babies grow up to be teachers. *Harvard Education Letter, 19*(5) 1–3.

Bransford, J., Brown, A., & Cocking, J. (1999). *How people learn: Brain, mind, experience, and school*. Washington, DC: National Academy Press.

Britzman, D. (1986). Cultural myths in the making of a teacher: Biography and social structure in teacher education. *Harvard Educational Review, 56*, 442–456.

Calderhead, J. (Ed.). (1987). *Exploring teachers' thinking*. London: Cassell.

Cholo, A. B. (2003, July 21). "Summer fellows" learn lessons teaching in a city. *Chicago Tribune*. Retrieved July 21, 2003, from www.chicagotribune.com

Clark, C., & Florio-Ruane, S. (2001). Conversation as support for teaching in new ways. In C. Clark, *Talking shop: Authentic conversation and teacher learning* (pp. 1–15). New York: Teachers College Press.

Clark, C. M., & Yinger, R. J. (1987). Teacher planning. In J. Calderhead (Ed.), *Exploring teachers' thinking* (pp. 84–103). London: Cassell.

Coleman, J. (1965). *Adolescents and the schools*. New York: Basic Books.

Costigan, A. (2003, February 18). *Finding a name for what they want: A study of New York City's Teaching Fellows*. Presentation given at the Association of Teacher Educators Distinguished Research in Teacher Education Award, Jacksonville, FL.

Csikszentmihalyi, M., & Schneider, B. (2000). *Becoming adult: How teenagers prepare for the world*. New York: Basic Books.

Darling-Hammond, L. (1998). Teachers and teaching: Testing policy hypothesis from a National Commission Report. *Educational Researcher, 27*(1), 5–15.

Darling-Hammond, L. (1999). Educating teachers for the next century: Rethinking practice and policy. In G. A. Griffin (Ed.), *The education of teachers: Ninety-eighth yearbook of the National Society for the Study of Education* (Part I, pp. 221–257). Chicago: University of Chicago Press.

Darling-Hammond, L. (2000a). Reforming teacher preparation and licensing: Debating the evidence. *Teachers College Record, 102*(1), 28–56.

Darling-Hammond, L. (2000b). Teacher quality and student achievement: A review of state policy evidence. *Education Policy Analysis Archives, 8*(1). Retrieved September 12, 2003, from http://epaa.asu.edu/epaa/v8n1

Darling-Hammond, L., Chung, R., & Frelow, F. (2002). Variation in teacher preparation: How well do different pathways prepare teachers to teach? *Journal of Teacher Education, 53*(4), 286–302.

Editorial: The educational sellout. (2003, March 15). *New York Times*, p. A16.

Edwards, V. (Ed.). (2003, January 7). Quality counts 2003: "If I can't learn from you." *Education Week*.

Feiman-Nemser, S., Schwille, S., Carver, C., & Yusko, B. (1999). *A conceptual review of literature on new teacher induction*. Washington, DC: National Partnership for Excellence and Accountability in Teaching.

Gewertz, C. (2002, September 11). City districts seek teachers with licenses. *Education Week*. Retrieved September 11, 2002, from www.edweek.org

Goodlad, J. I. (2002). Kudzu, rabbits, and school reform. *Phi Delta Kappan, 84*(1), 16–23.

Goodman, P. (1960). *Growing up absurd: Problems of youth in the organized system*. New York: Random House.

Gordon, D. T. (Ed.). (2003). *A nation reformed? American education 20 years after A Nation at Risk*. Cambridge, MA: Harvard Education Press.

Griffin, G. (1999). Changes in teacher education: Looking to the future. In G. A. Griffin (Ed.), *The education of teachers: Ninety-eighth yearbook of the National Society for the Study of Education* (part I, pp. 1–28). Chicago: University of Chicago Press.

Hargreaves, A. (2000). Four ages of professionalism and professional learning. *Teachers and Teaching: History and Practice, 6*(2), 151–182.

Hargreaves, A., & Fullan, M. (1992). *Understanding teacher development*. New York: Teachers College Press.

Hoffman, N. (2003). *Woman's true profession: Voices from the history of teaching* (2nd ed.). Cambridge, MA: Harvard Educational Publishing Group.

Huberman, M., Grounauer, M., & Marti, J. (1993). *The lives of teachers*. New York: Teachers College Press.

Ingersoll, R. M. (2001). Teacher turnover and teacher shortages: An organizational analysis. *American Educational Research Journal, 38*, 499–534.

Ingersoll, R. M. (2002a). *Out-of-field teaching, educational inequality, and the organization of schools: An exploratory analysis*. University of Washington, Center for the

Study of Teaching and Policy. Retrieved March 16, 2003, from http://depts.washington.edu/ctpmail/PDFs/OutOfField-RI-01-2002.pdf

Ingersoll, R. M. (2002b). The teacher shortage: A case of wrong diagnosis and wrong prescription. *NASSP Bulletin, 86,* 16–31. Retrieved March 16, 2003, from www.principals.org/new/bltn_teachshort0602.html

Johnson, J., Farkas, S., & Bers, A. (1997). *Getting by: What American teenagers really think about schools: A report for Public Agenda.* New York: Public Agenda.

Johnson, J., Immerwahr, J., & Farkas, S. (1994). *First things first: What Americans expect from the public schools.* New York: Public Agenda.

Kanstoroom, M., & Finn, C. (1999). *Better teachers, better schools.* Washington, DC: The Fordham Foundation.

Kliebard, H. (1995). *The struggle for the American curriculum, 1893–1958* (2nd ed.). New York: Routledge.

Kohn, A. (2001). *The case against standardized testing: Raising the scores, ruining the schools.* Portsmouth, NH: Heinemann.

Ladson-Billings, G. (1995). Toward a theory of culturally relevant pedagogy. *American Educational Research Journal, 32,* 465–491.

Laitsch, D. (2001, August). How states are responding: Legislation enacted in 2001. *Policy Perspectives: Examining Public Policy Issues in Teacher Education, 2*(6).

Levin, B. B. (2003). *Case studies of teacher development.* Mahwah, NJ: Lawrence Erlbaum Associates.

Mayher, J. S. (1990). *Uncommon sense: Theoretical practice in language education.* Portsmouth, NH: Boynton/Cook.

McNeil, L. (2000). *Contradictions of school reform: Educational costs of standardized testing.* New York: Routledge.

Mezzacappa, D. (2003, March 12). Teacher attrition sapping urban schools. *The Philadelphia Inquirer.* Retrieved March 16, 2003, from www.philly.com

National Center of Education Statistics, U.S. Department of Education, "School and Staffing Survey." Washington, DC: Author.

National Commission on Excellence in Education. (1983). *A nation at risk: The full account.* Portland, OR: U.S.A. Research.

National Commission on Teaching and America's Future. (1996). *What matters most: Teaching for America's future.* New York: Author.

National Commission on Teaching and America's Future. (2003). *No dream denied: A pledge to America's children.* Washington, DC: Author.

Olson, L. (2003a, January 8). Quality counts reveals national "teacher gap." *Education Week.* Retrieved March 14, 2003, from www.edweek.org

Olson, L. (2003b, March 5). Task force casts doubt on *Nation at Risk* accomplishments. *Education Week.* Retrieved March 17, 2003, from www.edweek.org

Park, J. (2003, January 9). Deciding factors. *Education Week, 22*(17), 17–18.

Ravitch, D. (2003). *The language police: How pressure groups restrict what students learn.* New York: Knopf.

Rust, F. O. (1999). Professional conversations: New teachers explore teaching through conversation, story and narrative. *Teaching and Teacher Education, 15,* 367–380.

Rust, F., & Orland, L. (2001). In C. M. Clark (Ed.), *Talking shop* (pp. 82–117). New York: Teachers College Press.

Sacks, P. (1999). *Standardized minds: The high price of America's testing culture and what we can do to change it*. Cambridge, MA: Perseus Books.

Thomas, K. (2002, August 22). Teacher shortage is more a matter of "keeping them." *USA Today*, p. 7D.

Tye, B. B., & O'Brien, L. (2002). Why are experienced teachers leaving the profession. *Phi Delta Kappan, 84*(1), 24–32.

Weiner, L. (2000). Research in the 90s: Implications for urban teacher preparation. *Review of Educational Research, 70*, 369–406.

Winerip, M. (2002, February 19). A school left behind by new federal standards. *The New York Times*, p. B7.

Zimmerman, J. (2002). *Whose America? Culture wars in the public schools*. Cambridge, MA: Harvard University Press.

Going Further
and Checking It Out

These first two chapters have dealt with the educational research concerning learning to teach. The most important set of themes emerging from this research is the developmental nature of the profession. Teaching is knowledge work and people work. Growth in ability in both domains occurs over a long period of time. Early difficulties in one area or the other do not necessarily presage long-term trouble. As most teacher education programs underscore, taking time for reflection and ongoing professional development is critical to the growth process.

Another important theme in these chapters has to do with using reflection and professional development to analyze and consider teaching practice. Reflection can be solitary or communal. Professional development can be self-selected and subject specific, sought out during the summer months away from teaching, or it can occur on a schoolwide basis, preselected by administrators and provided for all teachers simultaneously. In either case, providing a forum for collaborative discussion of the challenges facing teachers helps relieve the solitary nature of teaching and helps teachers deal rationally and reflectively with the challenges they face every day. Some of these issues are subject specific and others confront all teachers in one school setting.

Keep in mind that teaching is complex, messy work. Also keep in mind that no easy solutions exist to the issues raised in subsequent chapters. The new teacher stories profiled here represent an honest assessment of the contemporary realities of schooling, especially in urban areas. One of our purposes in writing this book was to provide a faithful representation of what the lives of new teachers are like today—in an age of accountability, inadequate resources, and growing racial segregation within the nation's schools. We hope you will consider joining the ranks of urban teachers, but we want you to be well prepared to do that. Reading this book will contribute to both ends.

1. Because this book is based on the words of teachers, consider how important personal stories, voices, narratives, or vignettes are in your own life. How do you use stories to make sense of others' lives—your friends, families, acquaintances, or public figures? How much is your understanding of yourself "the stories that I tell myself about myself"? What are the defining stories of your life, and how did they shape you, create you, and make you the person that you are? What are the hallmarks, epiphany, or "A-ha! moment" stories of your life?

2. Consider how much contemporary culture values the stories of people. Does American society as a whole value the stories people are willing to tell, or does it silence and devalue people's experiences? Consider your own experiences in schools, hospitals, business, or other institutions. Do these "cultural systems" value who you are, what you have to say, the voice that you have, or the stories you want to tell? Or do public and private institutions tend to silence you? Do they not allow your "voice," or your telling of your story about who you are?

3. Investigate the symptoms of the "age of accountability" in your own community's schools. First, get a clear sense of what high-stakes tests are being required in these schools. Then, talk to teachers who are at different stages of their careers, from Survival to Consolidation to Maturity. Ask them their views about how their work has changed as a result of the high-stakes testing regimen in your state.

4. Make a list of the unique challenges and opportunities that teaching provides for people. What are the benefits of choosing teaching as a career? What are the disadvantages? Consider teaching from an autobiographical, economic, cultural, professional, or social perspective, and come to some conclusions about the benefits and challenges of teaching.

5. Look into the online archives of a major educational professional organization or news outlet, such as the NEA, the American Association of Colleges of Teacher Education (AACTE), the Association for Supervision and Curricular Development (ASCD), or the National Council for the Accreditation of Teacher Education (NCATE). Investigate their views on what constitutes teacher quality and what the "hot-button" issues regarding new teachers have been in their publications over the last 2 to 3 years.

6. Interview 10 people who are not teachers about their views on teaching as a profession, specifically regarding proper preparation and the daily demands of teaching. Be sure to find individuals who are different in background, race, gender, and class and analyze what is similar and different in their perspectives. Also, ask them

about their own educational experiences and question them about how these might have informed their views.

7. How well do you believe that someone with a college degree—perhaps yourself—is prepared to teach? Is a strong background in a content area or subject the best preparation to teach, or do you need additional assistance or education to be prepared to teach in schools in the United States?

8. Do you agree with the maxim, "Those who can, do; those who can't, teach"? Do you feel that teaching is a low-status profession? To what degree do you believe that teaching is as complex as practicing law or medicine? Why do you think many Americans hold teaching to be a low-status profession? What does such a conception say about the way our culture values, or devalues, the lives of children and their education?

9. How much do you want to replicate the "learned behaviors" of teaching that you experienced as a younger student? To what degree are you open to new understandings of the role of teacher or of the teaching practice? Do you find the conception you now have of teacher, teaching, and learning adequate? Do you believe that you need to go beyond the conceptions you now hold about teaching and learning?

Part II

TEACHING AS AN AUTOBIOGRAPHICAL ACT

INTRODUCTION

Making the choice to become a teacher involves moving toward a certain kind of work as well as moving away from other options. Secondary-level teachers often exhibit what might be called a "double consciousness" (borrowing from W. E. B. DuBois) about their desire to teach. They talk both about wanting to work with young people and their love of subject matter. Many, although not all, have positive memories of their own schooling. They wish to create similar experiences for their students. Even those with negative school experiences recognize the value of a good education and want to provide that for their students.

A recent report on American public school teachers by the NEA (2003) highlighted their positive views of this career. In 2001, the average teacher in American schools had 15 years of experience. Nevertheless, almost one quarter of the teaching force began full-time teaching within the last five years. The teachers profiled in this report indicated they spent long hours at their jobs and invested an average of $443 of their own money each year to meet the needs of their students. Nevertheless, the majority confirmed that they would choose the career again.

Despite the pull toward teaching, many of those we interviewed have wrestled with their career choice. The reasons are many. First, some found that their aptitude and inclinations led them in divergent directions, so they had difficulty selecting one career path. Second, many judged the status of teaching in the United States to be low by comparison with other professions. Third, a few had heard many stories of burnout. Fourth, some perceived that teaching would involve financial sacrifice. Finally, several mentioned a very

47

personal reason: the negative reactions they got from family and friends when they first mentioned interest in a teaching career. Those close to them had candidly reacted to this announcement by stating that teaching would not make the best use of their educations.

The reasons behind these career conundrums, our research revealed, are influenced by gender, class, and race. Some men might find the female tilt of the profession unattractive. Prospective teachers from secure financial backgrounds might be less concerned about the pay scale. A few individuals might find the lack of a career ladder in teaching problematic, whereas others are not concerned about that feature at all. Fewer and fewer people of color enter teaching today than was the case many years ago, perhaps as a result of widening opportunities in other careers.

Today, national standards for certification of teachers and accreditation of teacher education programs have been raised, especially since the No Child Left Behind Act promised a "highly qualified" teacher for all children. Thus, teaching as a career choice generally involves greater investment of time and money than it once did. A growing number of states require bachelor's degree, master's degree, and ongoing professional development to maintain a teaching license. In fact, more than half of today's teachers hold master's degrees, according to the NEA study. This number will most likely grow in coming years. The accountability movement has already called into question the system of lifelong tenure in some states. Raising the bar for teacher credentials and in-school performance is a priority for many new reform initiatives today because teacher quality is presently seen as the most important element in improving student achievement. Still, demanding higher credentials without considering the costs to teachers by way of preparation is a formula for continued shortages in critical areas.

In the following chapters, you will meet a variety of teachers—some of whom have graduated from teacher preparation programs, both undergraduate and graduate, and others who have entered teaching through an alternative route. We concentrate here on the many issues involved in deciding to become a teacher, the difficulties in "having a life" as a new teacher, and the move into the classroom for the first time. In each chapter, we focus on relationships—with the family and friends who react to the decision to teach, and with the colleagues, both young and old, who shape the social environment of the school. All have advice to give the novice, some of which sends various negative messages about the profession. These teachers bring high ideals into their careers. Whether they can maintain these ideals in the face of new teaching realities remains to be seen.

REFERENCE

National Education Association. (2003). Despite long hours, low pay, teachers love their profession [press release]. Retrieved August 28, 2003, from home.nea.org/newsreleeases/2003/nr030827.html

Chapter 3

Vocation? Profession?
Or Just A Job?

The requirements for becoming a teacher today represent an enormous change from the early 20th century. At that time, a bit of high school and some "normal school" preparation fulfilled the mandates for teaching credentials. By midcentury, states required bachelor's degrees for teachers, but exemptions from these rules occurred when cities or states experienced a crisis in filling teaching positions. Facing such a crisis in the late 20th century, at least one state allowed teachers to work with only a high school diploma as their preparation. Although clearly an aberration, such situations reflect the struggles of this nation to come to terms with a desire for compulsory public education and the costs associated with this stance. Today, many teachers hold advanced degrees, although exceptions occur, especially in urban areas.

From the early history of the United States, education has had a pragmatic function along with its religious, humanistic, and civic ones. Increasingly in this country, education came to be viewed as essential to preparing individuals for their roles as citizens of a democracy and productive workers within a capitalist system. In the 19th century (Winterer, 2001), classical education became less favored, even within the academic programs of many elite colleges. By the 20th century, vocational education and "life adjustment" programs supplemented the traditional humanities, classical languages, sciences, and the arts, especially for students not training to be teachers, ministers, or professors.

In the early republic, teaching was a male profession. By the late 19th century, teaching had become "women's work" (Carter, 2002). The feminization of teaching occurred for a variety of reasons. Figures like Catharine Beecher and Emma Willard promoted the notion that women's "natural affinities" for children would make them more nurturing of children than men had been as teachers (Biklen, 1995). At that time, not coincidentally, states struggled to find the necessary financial resources to meet the demands of compulsory education laws, growing population, and the expanding popularity of high schools (Perlmann & Margo, 2001). Thus, women were attractive workers for the expanding teaching force because they were typically paid about half of what men made as teachers.

Throughout the 19th century, more women gained formal education as female academies, female seminaries, and normal schools increased in number. Graduates of these institutions sought to put their educations to work. Many women, like Jane Addams, founder of the Chicago settlement Hull House, struggled with the decision about how to put their educational preparation to work in their lives. In her book, *Twenty Years at Hull House*, Addams (1999) recounted the crisis she faced after graduating from Rockford Female Seminary. She wanted to work but her options as a woman were quite limited in the late 19th century. Although many of her peers went into teaching, Addams chose to begin her lifelong work with immigrants by establishing a settlement house in Chicago that functioned as a school and social welfare organization.

Women teachers often continued their careers until they married and began their own families. Once married, they were typically forced out of their jobs because most school districts did not allow married women to teach. Consequently, a good number opted to remain single or lived in companionship with other women to avoid giving up their teaching positions (Blount, 2004; Crocco, Munro, & Weiler, 1999). Many such women, like Elizabeth Almira Allen, first female president of the New Jersey Education Association, used their independence to travel around the world numerous times and to fight for the rights of other teachers for tenure and pensions.

With the spread of high schools in the early 20th century, educational leaders had to reconsider curriculum offerings to accommodate the range of students now enrolled. In the past, most students attending high school were planning on going to college and the high school curriculum served as preparation for the college curriculum. Beginning in the early 20th century, high schools moved toward newer curricular offerings such as social studies. Social studies included study in areas such as community civics that were designed to prepare students for the demands of citizenship. Vocational education offerings became commonplace.

During the 20th century, the proportion of female teachers grew steadily. However, this growth was slower at the secondary level and in administrative positions. Today's teaching force is predominantly female (75%) and overwhelmingly White (84%). According to a report from the NEA (2003), the proportion of male teachers is at a 40-year low. Many male teachers, along with minority teachers, cite low pay as the reason they will not stay in teaching. To the degree that teaching "tipped" long ago toward the reality of being a female profession, it becomes even harder to recruit at least some men into a workforce dominated so greatly by the other gender.

The career patterns of men and women in teaching seem to differ. Many women today interrupt their teaching careers—temporarily or permanently—once they begin their families or have an additional child. It appears that many men use teaching as the first step in a career ladder into administration. Men still form a substantial proportion of elementary school principals, outnumber women as high school principals, and greatly outnumber women as superintendents of schools. The demands of having a life and raising a family fall unevenly on men and women. The difficulties and costs of child care contribute greatly to this imbalance. Few young families today have the support of relatives living nearby with the time available for extended commitments to babysitting. Such factors put pressure on some new teachers to move out of teaching for financial reasons where the costs of housing are quite high.

A major reason teaching has had difficulty establishing itself as a true profession in this country is the fact that most teachers are women. Further feminization of teaching is a cause for concern among teacher researchers. These scholars have called teaching a profession at risk (Grossman, 2003), given its lopsided gender profile and trends toward reduction of entry-level requirements in some places experiencing acute teacher shortages.

By contrast to the United States, many European and Asian countries pay teachers better, a token of their greater respect for the profession. Citizens of these countries view teachers as professionals and encourage them, at regular intervals, to take extended time off to retool skills and knowledge. These nations provide what we call in this country a sabbatical. In the United States, this option is available to college professors, a small number of private school teachers at elite institutions, and a very limited number of public school teachers.

The reasons for this differential treatment are many, but it seems clear that some societies view teachers' work as important because it contributes to the cultivation of learning and cultural transmission. These functions are more highly valued in some other cultures. As a result, teachers' status and pay reflect this valuation.

Today's demands for a highly qualified teacher in every classroom are laudable; all children, rich and poor, deserve highly qualified teachers. Still, such calls do not take into account the additional expenses incurred by teachers, such as special education teachers, who must now engage in additional preparation to meet new demands, even highly legitimate ones. At some level, every new teacher does a cost–benefit analysis concerning the choice to become a teacher. As standards for entering and remaining in the profession rise, many teachers are calculating whether the additional levels of preparation are justified in terms of their lifetime compensation. Without support for efforts to gain additional preparation or retool their skills, teachers might simply decide that the level of investment is not worth it and leave the profession entirely.

A recent report indicates that as a result of teacher shortages nationwide, "more than 50,000 people who lack the training required for their jobs have entered teaching annually on emergency or substandard license" (NCTAF, 1996, p. 15). Ultimately, schools must hire teachers to fill classrooms. Whether such emergency hires undercut efforts to improve the professional profile of teachers is a cause for great concern. Likewise, what the long-term effects of the highly qualified teacher mandate for every classroom remain to be seen.

When *A Nation at Risk* was published 20 years ago (National Commission on Excellence in Education, 1983), the authors predicted widespread teacher shortages, especially in areas like math and science. Shortages do exist in these areas, but the problems go beyond math and science. Retaining as well as recruiting excellent teachers in all subject areas and in all communities remains difficult. Although we do not wish to devalue those who teach for only a few years, stability is widely seen as a virtue in personnel matters. Constant turnover in schools, as in offices and other institutions, raises costs and undermines the quality that often comes with continuity. Likewise, in schools, much value derives from teachers getting to know students over a period of several years. Much attention has been given to the problem of firing bad teachers, but the larger problem lies in recruiting and retaining excellent teachers to improve the performance of all this nation's children, especially those in poor schools in urban areas. Compensating them in line with their academic preparation and the pressures they face in today's schools should be a high priority for the nation's leaders.

FRIENDS AND FAMILY

When a young person announces his or her decision to become a teacher, some family members react positively and proudly to the announcement. Often these families see teaching as a leg up into the middle class, as an honorable family tradition, or as a valued contribution to the knowledge industry or helping professions. Sometimes, family and friends privately or publicly judge teaching to be just the "right" sort of career for a woman who wants to marry and raise a family. Others focus on summer vacations and, rightly or wrongly, assume that teachers have more time on their hands than those working in other fields.

Unfortunately, though, many parents and friends also question such a decision (Boles & Troen, 2003). They ask why the investment in college tuition shouldn't translate into more lucrative and highly regarded work (for a systematic analysis of the costs of learning to teach, see Liu, Kardos, Kauffman, Peske, & Johnson, 2000). From our research, it seems clear that young people from certain social classes and ethnic backgrounds often encounter resistance from their parents to the choice of teaching. It is important not to overgeneralize reactions along demographic lines. However, one thing does seem clear. Students who enter teaching often give serious consideration to other careers first. They recognize the opportunity costs in lifelong wages that the choice of teaching entails. This is especially true in regions of the country like the Northeast where the costs of living, especially home ownership, are high.

Acquiring the expertise associated with becoming a teacher and staying afloat as a teacher is expensive, time-consuming, lifelong work. Parents sometimes assume that the investments they have made in their children's education will lead to a high-status career with significant prestige and income potential. Upward mobility is part and parcel of the American dream. Cultural lore dictates that each succeeding generation should surpass their elders' career achievements. By comparison with these aspirations, professional parents might see the choice of teaching as downwardly mobile. Likewise, lower or middle-class parents might see teaching as a disappointing choice because they hoped their offspring would become a doctor, lawyer, or business executive.

Given such attitudes, announcing one's decision to choose teaching can be, in certain circles, like telling family and friends that one is becoming a nun, joining the Army, or enrolling in the Peace Corps. Friends might see the decision as noble but also as naive and self-sacrificing. This might be especially true if a young person has settled on teaching as a career, rather than as a temporary interlude of community service, as the Teach for America program is widely viewed. In this case, friends and family see the choice simply as a strategic and generous stopover on the way to more serious professional commitment. In other cases, newcomers to the United States might be disappointed that their children are not entering business, finance, medicine, or law so that they, too, can get ahead in this "land of opportunity." Of course, these negative reactions do stand side by side with positive ones many parents express at their offspring's decision to follow their passion into teaching.

Responding to the Issues

1. Are any members of your family in this field? What have they told you about teaching? How have your friends responded to the news that you will become a teacher?

2. If you are in a graduate program for teacher education, how many of your friends from college were going into teaching after graduation?
3. What do you think are the chief reasons people go into or steer clear of teaching as a career today?

TEACHING MOTIVATIONS

The young people interviewed for this book opted for the teaching life because they want to make a difference. Again and again, we heard them say that they believe they can do this best through teaching. Many of them also express an attraction to the intellectual excitement of work that provides them an opportunity to be lifelong learners. These individuals are secondary school teachers, it should be emphasized. The research literature has portrayed secondary school environments, cultures, and teachers as distinctly different from elementary schools and their practitioners, although surely these differences can be overdrawn (Siskin & Little, 1995; Talbert, McLaughlin, & Bascia, 1990). We recognize that the motivations of most teachers involve some combination of love of schools, learning, and students.

The prospective teachers we interviewed often expressed a strong commitment to working in urban areas. Nevertheless, we know that other student teachers commonly voice their fear of working with students different from the ones with whom they attended school. In each group, probably a fair number see teaching as a stepping stone to other educational careers. Their short- or long-term goals might include educational administration, policy, publishing, software sales and development, or college teaching. In this respect, they reflect the pattern anticipated for their generation; that is, a sequence of jobs over the life span rather than one linear and lifelong career path.

A few examples of the motivations and pathways to teaching of some of these individuals will give a taste of the stories that follow. This brief sample highlights four social studies teachers, but in the pages that follow, teachers of other secondary subjects are also introduced. Each of these individuals enrolled during the same year in a prominent teacher education program in New York City, but their stories were each distinct, reflecting the different ways in which teachers come into teaching today and the variety of motives impelling them to pursue this line of work.

George took his undergraduate degree in history at a large school upstate. A somewhat disinterested student in high school, his academic career had caught fire in college because he found himself loving his history courses. Although he toyed with the idea of law school or going immediately into a doctoral program in history, he ultimately decided to teach for a few years and then see how he felt about his tentative commitment to teaching.

He enrolled in a teacher certification program with a master's degree and secured his first teaching job in a suburban district close to where he had grown up. He was very clear about the fact that although he enjoyed working with young people, it was his love of history that had brought him into teaching.

After taking an undergraduate degree in psychology, Susan enrolled in a PhD program in that field with the intention of becoming a university teacher and researcher. Halfway through the program, she discovered she really enjoyed teaching much more than research. She made the decision to terminate her work in psychology with a master's degree. She then enrolled in a master's program with teacher certification. After graduation, she took a job teaching humanities at a small middle school in Chinatown. She had to take some extra courses in social studies to meet the certification requirements of the field and enjoyed them. However, she was clear that it was her love of children and the connections made through teaching that had brought her into the profession. Susan was married during her master's program and planned to have a baby sometime within the first few years of her teaching career.

Martin had studied religion as an undergraduate. Both Susan and Martin worried about their content preparation for the challenges of teaching social studies. Like Susan, Martin took extra courses to round out his background in history, even though he had done significant work in ancient and medieval history as a religion major. After graduation, Martin took a job at a high school where students must apply for admission. He quickly became involved with a variety of extracurricular activities that were academic and competitive in nature. Martin enjoyed the life of the high school and all it had to offer.

Yael was an immigrant to the United States who became imbued with a love of country and patriotic desire to "give back" to her adopted land. An enthusiastic individual, she wanted to teach at the middle school level where she could teach American history and work with energetic and creative middle school students. She ultimately secured a job at a middle school with several thousand students at an outer borough quite a distance from her apartment in Manhattan. Like Susan, she married shortly after graduation from the program and planned to start a family within a few years.

Numerous studies have been done of the reasons people go into teaching. No set of right or wrong motivations characterize this decision. What is interesting from a sociological standpoint, however, are the reasons teachers cite for entering teaching and the reactions they receive to these announcements. Together, such stories situate teaching into its cultural niche, as an altruistic endeavor that often seems to need justification by bright, highly educated young people, especially in major metropolitan areas of the United States where a competitive, get-ahead ethos pervades society and where women today have so many other career options.

A recent book on the subject of teaching takes as its title *Teaching as the Learning Profession* (Darling-Hammond & Sykes, 1999). This word choice reflects the fact that the body of expertise required to become a teacher spans knowledge in several domains. Pertinent subject matter includes disciplinary content, learning theory, developmental psychology, pedagogy, curriculum and assessment, and the history and philosophy of education. Knowing something about how to apply educational technology in classroom settings also must be added to this lengthy list of requisite competencies shaping effective teaching.

More and more, educational experts point not only to knowledge and skills, but to certain dispositions as necessary for becoming an effective teacher. These dispositions focus on the capacity for reflection and personal growth. From the outset, some teachers seem to recognize the need to stay current in their field and exploit the opportunities that present themselves. Others actively seek out extraordinary opportunities such as the Fulbright Scholars or National Endowment for the Humanities programs, the Gilder Lehrman Summer Institutes in history, the National Writing Project, the Teaching American History grant program, the Seeking Educational Equity and Diversity program sponsored by Wellesley College, or any number of other summer offerings available to teachers. Participants gain much from refreshing their knowledge and skills in the context of meeting and working with teachers from all around the country. When school starts again in the fall, their revitalized enthusiasm for teaching gets communicated to students who also benefit from both their teacher's enhanced knowledge and modeling of love for learning.

Responding to the Issues

1. What has motivated you to take up the teaching life?
2. Is there any "right" set of motivations for going into teaching? What are the most common reasons, in your experience, for making this choice?
3. Why do so many women and so few men choose teaching?

NEW YORK CITY METROPOLITAN SCHOOLS

In exploring the motivations in teaching of this group of idealistic young teachers, we find that many of them are attracted to urban teaching, but an equal number of them are somewhat fearful of working in city schools. We explore this topic in more depth toward the end of the book, but at this point, we introduce some of the features of this metropolitan area, which has enormous variety in the teaching situations found there.

New York City itself is a school district with over 1 million students, many of whom are poor and immigrant students (Freedman, 1991; Kozol, 1992, 1996, 2001). Other districts in which these beginning teachers work include portions of New York, New Jersey, or Connecticut. Many of the school districts found nearby are radically different from those of New York City. The suburban communities surrounding New York City contain some of the most affluent towns in the United States. Many of their school districts are quite small, containing only a few elementary schools, one or two middle schools, and a single high school with fewer than 2,000 students. Taxes can be quite high in these communities, some of which pride themselves on having the best public schools in the country. In many cases, this reputation is justifiable. Their high school campuses resemble college campuses. Quite a few teachers at the secondary level have doctoral degrees or advanced master's degrees. Some even have public relations directors who ensure that the news coming out of the district office provides a steady drumbeat of good news and high achievement.

By contrast, the New York City public school system has a long reputation of having a formidable—indeed hostile—bureaucratic system, with dysfunctional schools, unruly and even dangerous students, and an unwieldy governance system. We found that even if parents of our prospective teachers did not question the decision of their child to become a teacher, they were often puzzled by the choice to teach in New York City. They expressed concerns about their children's safety and their ability to teach effectively in what they perceived as a hostile work environment. In some cases, we found that even the new teachers schooled in the city themselves chose to teach elsewhere. Not surprisingly, they were attracted by the higher salaries and what they perceived as more favorable working conditions in the suburbs.

One rather singular feature of the New York City scene over the last 15 years is its diversity of schools. The New York City Board of Education has been a leader, along with Chicago, in the establishment of new small schools. Across the city, scores of these schools have been established as part of the "school restructuring movement" (Crocco & Thornton, 2002). Funding for small schools has come from the city and state, of course, but has been supplemented by major funding from the Annenberg Foundation in the early 1990s and the Bill Gates Foundation in the early 21st century.

Research indicates that small schools have positive effects on student achievement by creating environments in which students, who otherwise are at risk of dropping out, remain in school, graduate, and attend college at rates not equaled by those attending large schools of over 2,000 students in the same city. Fewer disciplinary problems exist at small schools as well, undoubtedly due to the greater degree of students' sense of "belonging" in these more personal environments. Not all, but many, new teachers interviewed for this study opted to take their first job in such schools, which are often suffused by a commitment to interrupting the high correlation between low socioeconomic status and high rates of alienation and dropping out from New York City's public schools.

When some of our interviewees began their jobs in these schools, many of the schools did not have to teach a Regents curriculum or give their students Regents tests. The schools had received waivers from New York State when they were first established that allowed them to graduate students through a process of what was called *portfolio assessment*. Over the course of 4 years of high school, students prepared portfolios of their work in major subjects, demonstrating the fashion in which they had met state requirements and their growth in understanding of subject matter. In some schools, students took oral exams related to their portfolios in front of panels of teachers, just as doctoral students defend their dissertations in front of professors on their examining committees.

In recent years, however, small schools lost the battle for avoiding Regents exams through use of portfolios. These schools today must administer Regents exams in major school subjects (Crocco, Faithfull, & Schwartz, 2003). Teachers at small schools, like others around the state (Grant, 2000), believe that imposition of the Regents requirements has circumscribed their flexibility with teaching and curriculum. As we explore more fully in subsequent chapters, many of these teachers now feel they must "teach to the test."

The demands imposed by high-stakes testing are being felt in schools across the nation. However, in no setting are these demands felt more acutely than in urban schools, where the challenges of fundamental literacy in the English language for all students can be considerable. Teachers at small schools, however, are the most disturbed by these changes. What attracted them to urban teaching in the first place was the opportunity to create in such environments an atmosphere of caring and concern along with one of flexibility in curriculum that would capitalize on their students' interests and keep them in schools. The new requirements undercut these possibilities significantly and threaten to elevate the dropout rates at small schools until they are in line with those at large schools.

MAKING THE MOVE INTO TEACHING

The stories of new teachers in this book represent a mixed bag of experiences—some positive and some negative. We focus on stories dealing with their decision and declaration to become a teacher. We explore how they try to fit this demanding work into their personal lives. In making the transition into teaching, these young individuals struggled with many issues. These are presented in subsequent chapters through their own, often eloquent, and always heartfelt words. The dilemmas they confronted once they made the decision to become a teacher were numerous. Among them were the following: whether to stay in New York City or take a job in the suburbs, how to master the content in their field, how to deal with classroom discipline, how to meet the needs of all their students, and how to stay awake to get all this accomplished. All of them dealt with sleep deprivation.

As we noted, the individuals profiled here all had considered a range of alternative career possibilities: law, journalism, drama, international relations, business, and medicine. Again and again, however, we heard them say they wanted to "make a difference" in the lives of young people. Few of them talked about pay scales, except to gauge their relation to the task of paying off student loans or raising a family. Mostly, they were eager to find a first teaching position that would allow them to be the teacher they had been preparing to be. They worked hard at this goal throughout frenzied weeks of student teaching and requisite coursework. They then took their first teaching job after graduation only to discover that they were now working harder than ever before.

Speaking with them after their first year of teaching highlighted the pressures they felt in doing a decent job every day with 150 to 175 students, if they were working in New York City's high schools. At the same time, they tried to put into practice all that they had learned in their teacher education course about "best practices." They carved out a Friday night or a Sunday afternoon as their time of rest, perhaps catching a movie or running in the park. Mostly, their heads were spinning with the demands of their jobs. Chastened by the experiences of their student teaching placements, they knew they would not reach everyone. Yet they worked hard at connecting with students and struggling to help them pass the tests that would shape their futures, for better or worse.

Their stories are not representative, in a scientific or statistical sense, of all beginning teachers, we recognize. We believe, however, that they do a good job of illustrating the kinds of stresses, strains, challenges, and possibilities experienced by many beginning teachers. Do not be distracted by the differences between your own life history and those recounted here. Instead, listen for the commonalities inherent in these stories and your own hopes, dreams, and fears about being a new teacher.

Responding to the Issues

1. In what ways is teaching high school different from teaching middle school or elementary school, in your judgment?

2. Do you view teaching as a vocation or profession? Or do you see it as simply a job, like any other? Does this perception make any difference to your working life?

3. Do you think it is correct to assume that most men do not want to work in a female-dominated career? What might be done to improve the gender balance within the profession? How can teachers of different racial and ethnic backgrounds be brought into teaching? Do you think it is important to have a mix of backgrounds in the profession?

REFERENCES

Addams, J. (1999). *Twenty years at Hull House*. New York: Signet.

Biklen, S. (1995). *School work: Gender and the cultural construction of teaching*. New York: Teachers College Press.

Blount, J. M. (2004). Same sex desire, gender, and social education in the twentieth century. In C. Woyshner, J. Watras, & M. S. Crocco (Eds.), *Social education in the twentieth century: Curriculum and context for citizenship* (pp. 176–191). New York: Peter Lang.

Boles, K. C., & Troen, V. (2003). Mamas, don't let your babies grown up to be teachers. *Harvard Education Letter, 19*(5), 1–3.

Carter, P. A. (2002). *Everybody's paid but the teacher*. New York: Teachers College Press.

Crocco, M., Faithfull, B., & Schwartz, S. (2003). Inquiring minds want to know: An action research project in a New York City professional development school. *Journal of Teacher Education, 34*, 19–31.

Crocco, M. S., Munro, P., & Weiler, K. (1999). *Pedagogies of resistance: Women educator activists, 1880–1960*. New York: Teachers College Press.

Crocco, M. S., & Thornton, S. J. (2002). Social studies in the New York City public schools: A descriptive study. *Journal of Curriculum and Supervision, 17*(3), 206–232.

Darling-Hammond, L., & Sykes, G. (1999). *Teaching as the learning profession*. San Francisco: Jossey-Bass.

Freedman, S. G. (1991). *Small victories: The real world of a teacher, her students and their high school*. New York: HarperCollins.

Grant, S. G. (2000). Teachers and tests: Exploring teachers' perceptions of changes in the New York state testing program. *Educational Policy Analysis Archives, 8*(14). Retrieved May 10, 2003, from http://epaa.asu.edu/epaa/v8n14.html

Grossman, P. (2003). Teaching: From a nation at risk to a profession at risk? In D. T. Gordon (Ed.), *A nation reformed: American education 20 years after A Nation at Risk* (pp. 69–81). Cambridge, MA: Harvard Education Press.

Kozol, J. (1992). *Savage inequalities*. New York: Perennial.

Kozol, J. (1996). *Amazing grace: The lives of children and the conscience of a nation*. New York: Perennial.

Kozol, J. (2001). *Ordinary resurrections: Children in the years of hope*. New York: Perennial.

Liu, E., Kardos, S., Kauffman, D., Peske, H., & Johnson, S. (2000). *Barely breaking even: Incentives, rewards, and the high costs of choosing to teach.* Draft prepared by Harvard Project on the Next Generation of Teachers. Retrieved April 30, 2003, from www.harvard.edu/~ngt

National Commission on Excellence in Education. (1983). *A nation at risk.* Washington, DC: Author.

National Commission on Teaching and America's Future. (1996). *What matters most: Teaching for America's future.* New York: Author.

National Education Association. (2003). Despite long hours, low pay, teachers love their profession [press release]. Retrieved August 28, 2003, from home.nea.org/newsreleeases/2003/nr030827.html

Perlmann, J., & Margo, R. (2001). *Women's work? American schoolteachers 1650–1920.* Chicago: University of Chicago Press.

Siskin, L., & Little, J. (Eds.). (1995). *The subjects in question: Departmental organization and the high school.* New York: Teachers College Press.

Talbert, J., McLaughlin, M., & Bascia, N. (Eds.). (1990). *The contexts of teaching in secondary schools: Teacher realities.* New York: Teachers College Press.

Winterer, C. (2001). *The culture of classicism: Ancient Greece and Rome in American intellectual life 1780–1910.* Baltimore: Johns Hopkins University Press.

Chapter 4

"Having a Life" as a New Teacher

Americans live in a materialistic society. If popular culture is any indication, citizens of the United States value making money, acquiring material goods, and living a comfortable life above most other matters. In this, they are probably not different from the rest of the world. History suggests, however, that Americans might be more interested in the commodities associated with the "good life" than other societies. Since its establishment, this country has been fortunate in achieving a high standard of living. Some critics comment that the abundance of material goods has produced the contemporary syndrome of "affluenza," in which too much focus is placed on what we will have rather than what we will be as a nation.

Within such a cultural context, the so-called nurturing professions of nursing, teaching, or social work are not highly rewarded occupations. If salary is taken as a token of what the culture values, then teaching ranks lower than professional sports, entertainment, finance, medicine, and law. Even less skilled work (i.e., work requiring less educational preparation) often is remunerated at higher levels.

Teaching is often portrayed as idealistic work. Sometimes this seemingly benign view masks a cynical perspective. Those who hold this view think that teachers are those who want an easy life of summer vacations. Or, they believe that teachers are persons who cannot stand the pressure of other, more competitively oriented professions. Perhaps they believe that those who elect teaching simply are not talented enough to pursue other options. All this flies in the face of what our research shows. The teachers profiled in this book all had numerous other choices, and considered those choices carefully. Why they chose teaching over other choices but often hesitated on their way to this final decision is the subject of this chapter.

Historically, teaching has often been a step up into the middle class for second-generation immigrants, those from rural areas, or the working class. Additionally, as we have already noted, women of previous generations often had few other options beyond teaching, secretarial work, or nursing. As more and more women attended college in the 20th century, many of them pursued careers in teaching, even if only for a modest period of time.

Today, the workplace has expanded professional opportunities greatly for women and minorities. The information economy has opened a variety of new career options. Far more lucrative career choices exist for young people leaving college today. The burden of college loans often necessitates selection of jobs that pay well even if a young person is attracted to more service-oriented careers.

Clearly, most people do not choose teaching for financial gain, or for advancement to prestigious, glamorous, or powerful positions in society. Instead, they seek a profession that they find personally fulfilling and rewarding. Despite the negative stereotypes about teachers circulating in certain quarters of our culture, we found that many people enter the teaching profession with high ideals and noble goals.

When a person chooses to teach, he or she generally recognizes that this will entail financial sacrifice over the course of a career. This personal choice is often rooted in a desire to work closely with other people. Teaching obviously allows one to work with young people, to bring out the best in them, and to engage others' lives in ways that work in business and industry often do not allow. People who choose teaching appreciate that there are many nontangible rewards of choosing this career.

Coming to terms with what brings satisfaction in life and acting on this knowledge is an important aspect of adulthood. Many people who enter the teaching profession do so because they are attracted to the intrinsic rewards of the work, despite the fact that the extrinsic reward of the paycheck might be problematic, especially if they marry and have children.

What we discovered in our interviews with young teachers was that none of them saw monetary reward as their prime motivator in making a career choice. Again and again, these young people expressed incredibly idealistic sentiments about their motivations to teach. In a few words, they summed up their desires with the simple yet monumental declaration that they wished to "change the world." In the rest of this chapter, you will encounter stories of those who came early and late to this career. No one set of motivations is right and others wrong. Still, the commonality of expressed motives impressed us. Perhaps it will resonate with you as well.

THE FIRST CAREER CRISIS

John's story is not the traditional one of choosing to teach. He did not decide on this route during his time in college. Instead, he began work in a different field and then made a decision to leave the corporate world of sports and entertainment behind him. Here, he describes his reasons for making the switch:

> I didn't plan on being a teacher. My mom is a teacher and has been all the years of my life. It never appealed to me. When I completed my undergraduate work, I wanted to go into sports and entertainment. I began grad school with this goal in mind and worked at a local radio station doing promotions. It was exciting. I got to meet so many people and attend events all around the country. Promotions took up a lot of my weekends, however. That's one of the only downfalls to the business, besides breaking your way into real money, which I didn't see as a problem for me.

> After a year the fun stopped. Staying at a club till 4 A.M. was boring. I wanted so much more out of life. Eventually, I quit and pursued my Master's degree full time. I was fortunate enough to have the support of my family, but I knew I needed a job.

> I went back to the middle school that I graduated from and asked my old principal for a job. At least, I thought I was going for a job. I didn't know it was more like a career. I had no idea that she'd actually hire me. But as it turned out, they were just about to fire a Phys Ed/Health teacher. I walked in at just the right moment. How hard could it be? I played basketball all through college and that wasn't so tough. Playing basketball with 12-year-olds would be easy. Health? I'd follow the book.

> That's what I thought.

> I got thrown into the world of lesson plans, staff development, parent–teacher conferences, standards, chalk, calling parents, making up calendars, making up notices, making up games, making up health facts … I didn't really know what to do and it all seemed to go so fast that I didn't have time to do it right. At least that's what it felt like.

> Besides actually teaching, I had to get certified as a teacher. There were tests and forms and records that needed to be dug up from nowhere. I'd never been fingerprinted before in my life.

> Then there was my actual life. My friends couldn't understand why I didn't stay out late anymore. My girlfriend didn't understand why I slept late on weekends and took so many naps. I don't think I even understood what was going on. I worked from 8 to 3, Monday to Friday. Why was I still so tired? It's

because kids drain you, especially since I was teaching 300 kids a week. That's 300 different personalities, and more for those kids who have more than one. That's 300 different life situations and problems, talents, and dreams. Anyone who hasn't taught wouldn't be able to grasp this lifestyle.

But that was just my first year. I'm in my second year now and even though I'm still the newcomer, I am so much more laid back. I know what to expect and I think my entire body has adjusted to my career. My entire life has adjusted to my career. I'm a better teacher this year because I have time to think. I also have an established relationship with the kids at my school. Kids know me and respect me and I'm a lot more comfortable around them because when a situation comes up I can just handle it. I don't have to search for an answer and pray that it's right. I can even say that I really like most of the kids. They grow on you as the year goes on.

John's views reflect the themes introduced at the beginning of this chapter. He shared the not-uncommon view of teaching described there, expressed in his question, "How hard could it be?" He was quickly disabused of this notion but gradually managed to adjust to the demands of his new work. John's family, girlfriend, and social circle all needed to adjust, as did John, to the scarcity of free time in the life of a new teacher. In this respect, John's story is a familiar one.

"REPAIRING THE WORLD"

Energetic, enthusiastic, and reared within a family of educators in the Midwest, Claire had spent a year of college studying in India. There, she finally realized how important education was to her. Only gradually did she come to embrace the career option of teaching:

I'd always sort of known I wanted to be a teacher, but I just never really pursued it; it was always something more to kind of fall back on ....

Several years and a few jobs later, Claire had an epiphany. She realized that she did, indeed, want to become a teacher. Before she had even graduated from her master's program, a prestigious school district in Westchester County, New York offered her a position. This position would have paid quite well. In the end, however, she opted to accept a job at a very small, new high school in New York City. Claire's decision about which offer to accept was not surprising to those who knew her. In the course of an interview at the conclusion of her teacher education program, she talked a lot about her reasons for going into teaching, using language used by many progressive educators:

If you're concerned about society, especially in a democracy, then part of what's so important about that is that people participate, and for someone like me, it's important that my life has meaning in terms of shaping other people's lives…. I see it as my way of contributing to a better society. And doing that is trying to educate people in a way that makes them aware of their world, and makes them aware of why they are important as people, and it also tries to give them skills to be able to do what they feel they want to do to make our world a better place.

The president of the college of education from which Claire received her master's degree talked regularly about the mission of his school. In doing so, he used the Hebrew phrase *tikkun olam*, or "to repair the world." Claire had traveled far—literally and figuratively—in making her decision to become a teacher. Besides her desire to repair the world, or at least a small pocket of New York City, Claire also enjoyed working with young people. Looking back at her earlier life, she realized she had always been involved with children and adolescents through tutoring and volunteer work of one sort or another.

Interestingly, when Claire finally opted to enter the field, not everyone in her family welcomed the decision:

Some of my gene pool thinks that I shouldn't do it, just because there are lots of negative aspects of it. Some of them think it doesn't really matter, whatever else you have to pay, the rewards of teaching are great enough that that's what you need to follow. And the people that influence me the most are the people that taught me money doesn't matter as much; it's making a difference that matters, and it's the people that you are in connection with that matters. And so, all those kinds of things were just much more conducive to teaching than to any other career.

Consider the ways in which John's and Claire's stories converge or diverge with your own path into teaching. Acknowledging the challenges of making career choices is hardly surprising, because so many options exist for so many college graduates today. Highlighting hesitation about the choice of teaching is also unsurprising, given the uncertain status of teaching as a profession. A recent analysis of the reforms needed to professionalize teaching finds this picture all too common, noting how many top-notch students forego teaching for other careers (Troen & Boles, 2003). Think about what is drawing you to the field and what concerns you as you complete the following exercises.

Responding to the Issues

1. In choosing teaching as a career, what steps or considerations were part of your decision-making process? Looking back, was this a deliberate process of consideration or a drift toward the decision? How do you think your decision-making process will affect your commitment to the field?
2. What aspects of a school's structure, culture, and philosophy will be most central to your job search? Have you considered the distinctive cultures of different grade levels; for example, middle school as opposed to high school? Have you visited various schools to experience how each has a different feel and culture?
3 Have you talked widely with people who work in education about the daily demands of their jobs? What are the satisfactions, demands, and challenges that they have experienced in their careers?

THE EMOTIONAL LIFE OF TEACHING

Caring is a term that entered the lexicon of requisite teaching dispositions in large measure due to the work of philosopher of education Nel Noddings. Noddings published a book by that name in 1984. More recently, another popular writer on the teaching life, Hargreaves (2001), highlighted what he called the "emotional geographies" of teaching. In this article, Hargreaves argued that teaching is emotion-laden, as well as technical and intellectual work. How could it be otherwise? Teaching centers on interaction with people. Therefore, emotions are never far from the surface of the work.

Of course, the caring dimensions of teaching are precisely what bring many people into the field. If a person is motivated to make a difference, it goes without saying that he or she feels caring for others will be part of the job. Noddings (1984) described caring as "largely reactive and responsive. Perhaps it is even better characterized as receptive" (p. 19). She posited caring as an ethical ideal with many applications, but particular ones within the context of schools. She dealt at some length with how caring might be enacted within the teacher–student relationship. In general terms, she explained, "[c]aring involves stepping out of one's own personal frame of reference into the other's. When we care, we consider the other's point of view, his objective needs, and what he expects of us" (p. 24). More concretely in terms of the demands of teaching, she noted, "The one caring as teacher, then, has two major tasks: to stretch the student's world by presenting an effective selection of that world with which she is in contact, and to work cooperatively with the student in his struggle toward competence in that world" (p. 178).

Any caregiving work, such as teaching, can be exhausting. When teachers carry a sizable "caseload" of 150 students or more each term, the demands of teaching can wear even young teachers down. Getting to know so large a cohort, much less learning how to care about them can be a challenge when so many young people are involved. In some school settings, caring can run amuck, when the needs of caring outstrip a teacher's capacity to respond.

In secondary schools, the ethical goal of caring might be even harder to carry out than in elementary schools, where teachers spend more time each day with their students than simply one 40- or 50-minute period. The new teachers most attuned to caring gravitated away from large, impersonal high schools. A number of them opted for jobs in middle schools, where the opportunities for getting to know students are often greater. Many also selected smaller, restructured schools, where caring is central to the expressed ethos of the school. In small, restructured schools, the teaching load is smaller than it is in traditional high schools. At the same time, the expectations for teachers' involvement with students in these environments have been raised considerably. Teachers teach courses in their field, but they also advise students about academic and personal issues. They might see the same students for 2 years in a row. All in all, these measures allow teachers to get to know their students far better than is traditionally the case.

The emotional demands of teaching, as distinct from the content, lesson planning, and administrative chores, can be incredibly draining for new teachers (Tickle, 1991). As we will see, the demands of caring cut across all schools to some extent, whatever the district, age level, philosophy, or administrative style. Occupations that focus on service to others are generally going to be more taxing emotionally than those involving sitting in an office and facing a computer all day. Nevertheless, in certain settings, the demands associated with caring can be acute. Getting a handle on what can and cannot be done in responding to students' needs is an important adaptive skill for young teachers.

In addition to motivational issues related to teaching, this chapter focuses on the emotional demands of teaching, both inside and outside school. The stories are sobering. In each case, idealistic new teachers were hard pressed to establish boundaries in their jobs, a problem that could produce highly negative consequences if left unaddressed over several years. One teacher we interviewed decided to leave teaching precisely for this reason, an early case of burnout. Teachers surviving beyond the first few years learn that establishing boundaries between their professional and private lives is essential to remaining afloat as a teacher.

In Hargreaves' (2001) article, he included a discussion of the sometimes tough work of coping with parents. Rarely is this a topic that prospective teachers contemplate when they consider their motivations to teach. That is why we include it early in the book, even though it might fit more appropriately in the next section. Over the last decade, educational reformers have called for more parental involvement in schools. This trend is undoubtedly a positive one in many regards, but dealing with parents as a young teacher can be daunting. Phoning the parents of high school students can be difficult for a whole host of reasons. Hargreaves was correct in highlighting the many dimensions of the emotional life of teaching. This work is not just about working with kids, but with their parents, your colleagues and administrators, and increasingly, the public.

In this chapter, we explore a few options young teachers have in dealing successfully with parents. Keep in mind that parents' support can be of great help to you at any stage in your career. Figuring out how to make parent support work for you is an important task. For starters, keep in mind that these are parents of your students, not your own parents!

Responding to the Issues

1. What discussion has there been in your teacher preparation program for dealing with parents?
2. Has there been any discussion of the public relations aspect of schooling today? Public education has an "image" problem in many communities today; some school districts have even hired public relations liaisons to help with their community relations. What types of proactive steps might public school teachers and administrators take to ensure good relations with the communities in which their schools are situated?

TALES OF COMMITMENT AND CARING

Susan worked in a middle school where most of the students were from families of Chinese immigrants. This shaped Susan's work in ways that she both expected and did not expect. Let's consider the multiple demands found in this passage that are being made on Susan's commitment to caring for her students:

Most days, the kids—and this is really one of the issues that I've struggled with a lot, and I really want to address more next year—were with me all the time, and I feel like more than anything, that's what drained me. Because they're middle school kids, and one has to have them with you so much of the time, it's just crazy. If I stayed till six, there would be kids there until six, a lot of times, and longer even. They were there all the time. And they would say, "Well, we just want to do homework, we have nowhere to go." And it's true, the parents are new immigrants; they work in the garment district. They work crazy, crazy hours and they don't have any after school things to go to and they have nowhere to go. And so, they would beg to stay in class and do homework or something. So, you know at first, I guess as a new teacher, you're like, oh, of course you can stay, why not. And you let them stay, but then you don't really get a lot of work done when they're there.

Later in the conversation, Susan had more to say about this topic:

I think that someone could have warned me about this. I went into teaching more because of wanting to connect with kids and wanting to really nurture them and stuff like that. I think it might have helped if someone had said, you know, you're going to [need] to set boundaries and really be very specific about the boundaries. You just expect that you're going to be very tired and that you're going to need time to yourself … because the thing with kids is, once you've sort of let them take over your life and they are there all the time, it's much harder to step back, and then all of a sudden say, no you can't be here all the time.

Quite rapidly, Susan confronted a set of demands she had not fully antic-ipated. When she interviewed for this position, she was attracted to the com-mitted and caring faculty. However, she had not fully comprehended what this translated into on a daily basis:

All the teachers are there; all the kids are there. I mean, not all the kids, but a lot of the kids are there until late; tons of kids everywhere. So anyway, I'd stay there late. At the beginning of the year, I could be there very late, until eight some nights … One thing you discover when you're teaching is that, at least for me, it's emotionally and physically draining … What surprised me is how hard it is just to be on for so much of the time, and how much of a drain it is. It is one thing when you're student teaching, when you have breaks and you're doing it with someone else, and you work really hard on that one lesson or those lessons you're going to teach, but then you have a break from it. It's not constant. I guess I didn't realize just how much of a drain it would be on me emotionally and physically. I would be catatonic when I came home; I wouldn't want to talk to anyone. There was a period when I didn't even want to talk to my husband because I had talked all day long and the last thing I wanted to do is talk more, so I just wouldn't talk. I'd be dead quiet and he'd say, "What's happened to you?"

Within months of taking this job, Susan found herself thoroughly exhausted. All schools make enormous demands on the energy levels of their teachers, but here the demands were even greater than the norm. Her situation raises some critical questions to consider at this time.

Responding to the Issues

1. Is this issue of setting boundaries something that teachers can appeal to administrators for help in dealing with?
2. What role should administrators have in maintaining a cadre of teachers that do not overextend themselves?
3. How does a teacher who has started the school year with a lax set of procedures rein things in and establish some boundaries for his or her students' behavior?
4. What role do you think mentor teachers can play in easing the adjustment of new teachers into their work?

"DON'T WOMEN HAVE CAREER OPTIONS OTHER THAN TEACHING THESE DAYS?"

Clarissa is an African American woman who attended private schools and graduated from an Ivy League college. Clarissa did not start college intending to teach, but gradually, through a series of experiences working with youth, found she enjoyed the work and began to consider the option of teaching. At first, her parents found it hard to accept her decision:

I don't necessarily think that my parents are a hundred percent sold on teaching. [W]hen I told them that I [was considering] teaching in a public school, in New York City, they were like, what happened? My mom is sort of on the fence about it…. Maybe they see some danger involved in it, and they also just see that it is a lot of work and teachers tend not to get enough respect and prestige and pay that other professionals do.

As Clarissa's student teaching experiences developed, she returned home to find that her friends and family's opinions on teaching were changing, for they began to ask her questions about her work:

[T]hey have seen how excited I've been about becoming a teacher, and how invested I am in my forthcoming profession. [So], they're starting to ask me a lot of questions about my kids and what my day is like and everything; I think they're pretty much excited for me.

African American women of the past who sought professional work had few career options beyond teaching and nursing. Throughout most of the 20th century, teaching was a high-status profession in the African American community, even though remuneration, especially in the South, was low. Nevertheless, teachers commanded great respect in the community and teachers tended to be women. Clarissa believed her parents wanted her to pursue medicine or enter the world of finance, as her brothers had. Gradually, family and friends came to understand Clarissa's decision as right for her. She was energized and excited about the work she was doing. She felt strongly that having African American teachers in the classroom was important for young people of her community:

Just looking at the experiences that I had in a predominantly White school and the access that I had to a good quality education has motivated me. Then, to look at the students [in the cities where I have worked], they didn't know that Black students went to college ... that definitely provides me with a good enough reason to be a teacher. And the students I've worked with have mostly been non-White, and they're surprised that I don't have my own children, or that I went to college, that I am getting my master's degree.... So, I certainly think that is a huge reason why I wanted to be a teacher. I think that just my presence in the school is important ... that it's important for Black students and Latino students to be able to see teachers of color in places of authority, and especially where they may not necessarily have those kinds of role models in their own communities.

Another one of the new teachers also encountered resistance to her career choice. She confided that her father-in-law, a retired teacher, had strongly discouraged her from replicating his career choice. She chalked it up to his being "burnt out," but such reactions undoubtedly can take their toll. Lack of strong familial support and societal validation can dissuade some talented individuals from entering a field that will require a strong commitment if the work is to be done at a high level. As you consider your future, be sure to let your family, friends, and social circle know how important the choice is to you and why.

Responding to the Issues

1. In what sense do you see teaching in public schools as making a contribution to democracy and citizenship?
2. Think back to the influential teachers in your life: To what degree did you see them as role models? If you did see them in that fashion, in what respect were they role models for you?
3. Would you consider working in an urban school district? Why or why not? How important to you is teaching a diverse group of students?

NOVICES AND VETERANS: PERFECT TOGETHER

In the following selection, George explains what motivated him to choose teaching, at least, as he acknowledges, for a few years. Keep in mind that George was only 22 when he finished his master's degree and began teaching—closer in age to his students than to many of his colleagues. George found very few people his age in the teaching force at his school. To a certain degree this made him uneasy, but ultimately an informal mentor, closer to the age of his grandfather, brought him to an appreciation of the positive aspects of an intergenerational mix of teachers in a school environment.

Recent research suggests that working in a school with such a mix might be important in helping novices succeed at their work. Researchers associated with the Harvard Project on the Next Generation of Teachers (Kauffman, Johnson, Kardos, Liu, & Peske, 2002) found that three types of professional environments exist in schooling: those dominated by novices, those dominated by veterans, and those with a mix of ages and stages of work experience. In a "more integrated environment, where neophytes and their more experienced colleagues are continually communicating," new teacher growth might be better supported than in other settings (Viadero, 2003, p. 7).

George's story had other intergenerational elements. He had attended high school in Long Island and remembered those days as ones in which he gave somewhat indifferent attention to academic matters. However, he also remembered those days as ones in which he was consistently excited by his history courses. This might have been due to the influence of an uncle who taught the subject and the many family conversations around the dinner table concerning history. In college, George pursued a double major in history and political science and improved his academic performance considerably.

He thought about law and politics as careers as well as pursuing a doctoral degree in history. He talked about his decision-making process:

Well, I just loved history, and wanted to become a teacher. [But] the first thing I really wanted to do was go to grad school for history, and then maybe do some research, because I find that I'm a research-oriented person ... [But] I followed recommendations from family members that are in teaching, and they told me the best way to go is the fast route, which was getting my teaching degree, getting a job, and then re-evaluating my position after a couple of years. And, then the second thing that really influenced my being a teacher was the fact that I was a teacher's aide in college. I worked about four days a week, from seven to four, with kids from the Handicapped Children's Association. These were Head Start kids who would come in the class with all sorts of bruises, and all sorts of emotional problems, and it really turned me on to really wanting to help kids. I may not be the hero of the world, but at least giving them some sort of person to look up to, or at least someone that they can communicate with, because obviously they weren't really communicating with their parents or other family members too well. So, I think those two things really spurred me to become a teacher.

Despite the inspiration of his uncle, George found that his parents disagreed about his decision to teach:

Obviously from my uncle the teacher and my father, who is a very intelligent man, and loves history as well, he was really happy that I wanted to become a teacher, really happy that I wanted to have a role with kids in the classroom. My mother wasn't so happy. But my mother kept saying she wants the best for me, but she thinks that I won't make enough money as a teacher. And I do see that as being something that will happen, but I don't see this in dollar amounts, at this point in my life. I might see that later, but at this point, I do have affection for the kids and a love of history and it's the place I want to be. My mother really wanted to send me to law school because she thought I would become a really good lawyer. And my dad did want me to go to law school, but he's comfortable with anything that I want to do.

George reflects on the opportunity costs of his decision and its ramifications for his social life:

I'm a young guy, twenty-two years old, and a lot of my friends are living the fast life right now, either as stockbrokers or going to law school, or going to med school ... My best friend is very supportive of me, [but] my other friends—all they see right now are green dollars, all sorts of material possessions. So they don't really want to hear about my teaching too much. It's really

*my best friend that I talk about it with and a couple of people in the program
that support me. But other than that, there really isn't much conversation
about teaching.*

There's a poignant aspect to George's comments about his parents and
their differing expectations for their son's life. Nevertheless, coming to
terms with parental perspectives and carving out one's own path in sync
with or in opposition to those expectations is part and parcel of the transition to adult life. Clearly, in this setting, financial factors played a role in the
devaluation of teaching. George's primary concerns were not with money;
nevertheless, down the road, this situation might very well change.

George's mentor guided him through the challenges of his first few years
of teaching in a demanding school environment. Although this high school
was known for being a demanding place to work, it also provided George
with an outstanding professional development program, a strong department chair, and mentoring for new teachers. All these factors contributed
to George's success in the school. Even though he continued to nurture
dreams of getting a doctorate in history, he was gaining excellent preparation in learning to teach history through his work in this school.

Responding to the Issues

1. What do you value most in teaching?
2. Have you investigated the mentoring options provided in schools
   in your area for new teachers? Are mentors assigned to new teachers or do new teachers choose their own mentors? Are these paid or
   volunteer positions in the schools in your area? Look into this in
   schools in your area and get the answers to these questions.
3. What would you want a mentor to do for you during your first year
   of teaching?
4. What about the generational mix of these schools? What kind of
   generational mix would attract you to teach in a certain school?

REFERENCES

Hargreaves, A. (2001). The emotional geographies of teaching. *Teachers College Record, 103*(5), 1056–1080.
Kauffman, D., Johnson, S. M., Kardos, S. M., Liu, E., & Peske, H. G. (2002). "Lost at
sea": New teachers' experiences with curriculum and assessment. *Teachers College
Record, 104*(2), 273–300.

Noddings, N. (1984). *Caring*. Stanford, CA: Stanford University Press.

Tickle, L. (1991). New teachers and the emotions of learning teaching. *Cambridge Journal of Education, 21*(3), 319–329.

Troen, V., & Boles, K. C. (2003). *Who's teaching your children? Why the teacher crisis is worse than you think and what can be done about it*. New Haven, CT: Yale University Press.

Viadero, D. (2003, April 30). Hasty hiring, heavy duties found to plague new teachers. *Education Week, 22*(3), 7.

Chapter 5

From Noble Ideals
to Everyday Realities

A teacher education professor, who used to teach high school, relates the following story:

> I recently ran into Bob, a high school teacher and former colleague of mine. I asked him if he was still teaching at our former high school, the High School of Business and Industry. He told me that he had moved on to another, less well-functioning school in a poor urban neighborhood. "Why?" I asked, "Business High was a great place; you'd be hard pressed to find a better school."

Indeed, in those days, the High School of Business and Industry was an appealing place to teach. A magnet school, it drew students from all over the metropolitan area. The student body was incredibly diverse, and teachers were selected through a process of interviews by teachers, parents, students, and administration. The students, administration, and teachers wanted to be there. They created an ethos of shared values and shared purpose. In a nutshell, this educational community had produced what has been called the "good school" (Lightfoot, 1985).

The professor continued, "In any event, when I asked Bob why he left Business and Industry, I was surprised by his answer." Bob put it this way:

> *Why, just about everyone left after you left. You'd hardly recognize the place. The new principal told me, "Well, you know teachers are all interchangeable." That said it all to me. We were just gears in the machine. He cared*

79

about test scores and running a slick-looking school, but there was no com-
mitment to the teachers. The teachers all got frustrated with the lack of sup-
port, the lack of valuing us. Most left to teach in the suburbs. And, not just
because the pay is better there. There you get some respect. Me, I'm now at a
far more difficult school, but at least I'm appreciated.

As sad as Bob's story is, his experience reflects a view of teachers all too common among educational authorities, and, frequently, teachers themselves. This understanding of teaching goes something like this: Teaching is a craft that relies on a toolkit of techniques, to be sure, but not much more. Teachers' autobiographies, educations, and values matter little, or not all. In such schools, students' life stories, hopes, and aspirations also matter little or not at all. Teaching is simply about delivering a lesson. Learning consists of mastering a lesson.

This is an impoverished view of teaching, a technocratic one rather than a humanistic one. Such a view evokes the factory model of schools discussed earlier. Teachers are automatons who work on the assembly line of schooling. Students are widgets that get spit out every year, where maximum value is accorded to efficiency and low cost of production. Little attention is given to ethical and moral considerations of developing human beings with the potential of contributing to society as intelligent citizens of a democracy.

Teachers come to understand themselves, their values, and their students gradually across the span of their careers. However, the capacity to understand these elements depends on administrative leadership that nourishes these understandings within the structure of the school. The emphasis within the accountability and high-stakes testing movement over the last 20 years has produced administrative attitudes such as the ones just described above. Furthermore, this movement has created a deskilling process that has dramatically shaped what teachers do in their teaching (Grant, 2000; Segall, 2003). In other words, the accountability movement has contributed to shaping work content in line with this technocratic view of teaching. The character and ethos of schools change as a result. And some teachers hit the road.

This chapter gives voice to a point of view that believes that teaching is not an automated set of teaching skills and behaviors, but a profound autobiographical process of connections forged between teachers and their students. Once again, you will hear from those who are enrolled in teacher education programs at a variety of institutions, public and private. You will also encounter a number of stories from the New York City Teaching Fellows (NYCTF) program, which is based on the Teach for America model.

The NYCTF program recruits teachers with a strong academic background and significant work experience who are interested in teaching in troubled urban schools. After an intensive summer program, these individuals immediately begin to teach in "hard-to-staff" schools in poor neighborhoods. They continue with their education coursework while teaching full time. Thus, they have a unique insight into the experiences of teacher preparation, urban schooling, and the processes of becoming a teacher. Generally a bit older than those who went through the elite master's program, they are often, like John who we met in the last chapter, career switchers. They have been selected in a competitive program that has far more demand than slots available. Although they will work hard in their new schools, they are also getting a master's degree, compliments of New York City, along with their full teacher salary.

The following excerpts are statements taken from some of the NYCTF fellows on their first day of the summer induction into teacher education. Their comments speak to the sense of vocation and motivation that has drawn them into teaching:

- *A vacuum is created. Air rushes in to fill that space. I am here because I was pulled, like when you open a door or window, and a vacuum moving in this direction for a number of years. I've been wanting to make a change where I can make a change.*
- *I am here because I have reached another of the main points in my life where I want to jump off the train I am on, and take another one in another direction.*
- *A part of me has always wanted to teach. I enjoy the feeling of helping someone understand something they didn't before—and there are selfish reasons, too. There is the seductive attraction to the power of a captive audience!*
- *I am taking care of some unfinished business from my earlier years when I heard from so many people that I ought to be a teacher. Now I can say that I gave it a try, and not wonder about what could have been.*
- *I was clearly burnt out and stayed because of professional inertia that catches way too many people. It was safe, secure, and carried a steady paycheck. I worked, by the way, with reasonably professional people who were entertaining both on and off the job … but I was in a rut.*

THEORY TO PRACTICE

It is interesting to consider the initial theories many novice teachers bring to their work, especially those who have come to teaching through other work routes. Because they, as most Americans, have spent substantial portions of their life in schools, they have some understanding of what education is. Like traditional master's students, they express a desire to nurture and help young people.

Writing in his journal for one of his teacher education courses, Joseph provides his own theory of education. His ideas include concepts such as befriending, learning about life, and molding students. His care for students includes concerns for their vocational development and lifelong learning:

> *My concern is that I get a good grasp and knowledge of the material so as to make me a better teacher. My concern in education is that students are not just taught, but also "befriended" and guided in terms of learning about life, not just academics. I hope to be a teacher that will change the way young people think in many aspects so as to help them mold themselves into what they feel is their path.... Being a teacher and person, to me, is measured on the mark you leave on those around you—be that academic or social.*

Arnie, another NYCTF fellow, also focuses on having a relationship with his students.

> *A lyric came to mind from The King and I. It comes from a song Anna sings in the first act to the children and the concubines of the King as she begins her first class, "Getting to Know You." The one thought I want to always keep in mind is that I want to project to those students I have in my charge a desire to want to learn more about them so I can best meet their needs in the classroom.*

These teachers are not thoroughly naive, simply hopeful. They recognize there will be rough spots along the way. Arnie, like other new teachers, expresses his intentions in terms that are characteristically idealistic:

> *[I have an] anticipation of making mistakes, but hopefully they will be easy to correct. I anticipate chaos. I know I will not be as successful as I want to be in controlling [them]. I anticipate going home to celebrate after a long day. Even if the day was crazy and I feel like a failure, I will celebrate because it means the beginning of this journey. I'll be able to turn it out in a way that I can survive and also know my students will have gotten a lot out of being in my class.*

On entering the classroom, new teachers are often shocked by the immediacy of dealing with students. As their ideals confront the everyday realities of classrooms, teachers recognize that their aspirations might be harder to fulfill than they had anticipated. Indeed, the first year of teaching can be consumed with daily traumas, especially if the initial theories of teaching they carry into classrooms resemble the quintessentially American notion that "anyone can teach." Arnie had a particularly difficult introduction to classroom life:

The students were mean, nasty, spiteful, unremittingly obstreperous, un-ceasingly cruel, hyperactive, disobedient, snide, and a dozen other words that are too obscene for this journal to handle—and those were the better-be-haved ones! I got home tonight and poured myself a big glass of Scotch and asked myself, "What have I gotten myself into?" But after I chilled out, I real-ized every day is going to be different. There are some days when the stu-dents will be engaged and willing to participate in the class and cooperate with their teacher. There will be other days, unfortunately, like today. On bal-ance, there will be more of the former than the latter. I am still optimistic. To-morrow will be a better day.

Milder in tone, Bob expresses the harsh realities that surface in some high school classrooms to challenge his high ideals:

In my classroom, I am upset today. I have got to relax…. There are a few kids that I think are great. And two or three are going to be a problem. I just have to make sure that they stay a small problem. Plan for the day. Ignore the prob-lem. How can I? The "bad" kids take up so much time.

Natasha also acknowledges that the realities of the classroom challenge even experienced teachers. She recognizes that negotiating a way to interact with students can become an overwhelmingly important factor in teaching. Her views have been well supported as a feature of high school life by educa-tion scholar Linda McNeil (1988, 2000). McNeil's work offers sobering por-traits of the negotiations that are endemic aspects of high school life. The bargain runs like this, according to McNeil: "If you [the student] behave, then I [the teacher] won't give you too much work." Natasha recognizes that such negotiation will begin on day one of her independent teaching life that will come after she completes her student teaching experience:

I am immediately impressed by how unruly the students are. Even when Ms. Anderson (cooperating teacher) begins to speak, they fail to settle down. I observe her method of dealing with the students and decide that setting the tone for the first day will be crucial to my success in the fall. I have already purchased a book on classroom management recommended to me by friends who teach in another district.

As teachers enter their first year of teaching, they tend to focus on their troublesome, noncooperative, or disruptive students. They measure their practice against the bellwether of these students. If the problematic kids can be brought in line and taught, then good teaching for all can begin to take place. At the middle school level, the problem of classroom management can be acute, as Frank discovered:

My first bellwether was this kid, Dwayne. If Dwayne was bored he'd start sucking his thumb, and then he would be out of his chair, walking around the room. And I was like [saying], "If Dwayne is bored, that means the others will soon follow." At first I would address Dwayne, and have Dwayne do something for me, so that I would at least keep him busy. And then I would say, "OK, I think Dwayne's really bored ... let's move on to the next activity."

And at that point, it was making peace with the fact that out of 16–17 kids that day I really had three who were being real pains in my ass. The other 14 were sitting there waiting for the show to be over so they could go on. Maybe they were talking among themselves ... they were just killing time, saying, "[Sigh,] OK, whenever the teacher gets done fighting with those three, I know he'll be back to us, so we will just sit here." 'Cause they didn't get out of their chairs and just sat there. And I said, "This is something to know about these students!"

In schools with endemic management issues, certain key players in the classroom often hold inordinate power over the classroom climate. If new teachers can figure out who such individuals are, they can better control classroom dynamics. Some new teachers like Patrick are better with this than others. Here a mentor and friend writes about Patrick's ability in this regard.

It was very funny how he was able to recognize the classroom leader ... Patrick said, "I know when he comes in with his hat on, I am in for a rough day. This guy sets the rules for the rest of the class. So, I made him the class janitor." Patrick continued, "A lot of people will be upset with that, but he is so proud to be the class janitor.... And he goes around and he sweeps up and he reprimands the kids for being messy."

Later in the first year, most new teachers start to relax and develop what for them becomes satisfactory classroom practice. This is not to say that the problems go away entirely:

There are a few kids that do disrupt the class and it is literally hard to do any kind of a lesson. But if you do have a solid lesson that is getting them active—in getting them out of their seats to come up to the board—getting them hands-on, [then it's ok]. I'm trying to get them to do as much hands-on science as I can, and they're all partaking. The noise level in the class is loud, but it is good noise.

The framework for the NYCTF fellows, like the one used in the Teach for America program described in a book by Popkewitz (1998) on this subject, shapes new teachers in particular ways. Certainly, the experiences of the teaching fellows are more accelerated, and therefore more intense than those experienced by traditionally prepared students. Graduates of traditional programs get deep exposure to classrooms through student teaching. This experience allows for guided practice under close supervision by a cooperating teacher. By contrast, the teaching fellows had a "baptism by fire" into the challenges of urban schools. Even with the help of a mentor, their supervision was more spotty and irregular than what most teacher education students receive. In essence, the fellows were new swimmers thrown into the pool with a bit of preparation. They were encouraged to kick hard to stay afloat.

As all new teachers claim classroom space, understandably they become concerned with day-to-day survival. Ideals are shelved for a time, and their focus changes to strategizing about the day-to-day demands of teaching. The good news is that eventually most new teachers develop a teaching practice that is personally rewarding and beneficial for students. The bad news is that, at least for a time, their initial sense of ideals and values about teaching gets put aside in the rush of dealing with students, administrators, and the "time on task" that comprises the intensified world of teaching today. Provided with the space and time for reflection, they might recapture these ideals. Unfortunately, some teachers abandon the profession before they get to this place.

Responding to the Issues

1. How much do education students and new teachers' values matter? Are teachers primarily technicians who hand out material and deliver a product, or are they reflective practitioners who develop their teaching theories in practice?
2. What changes have you, or your colleagues, gone through already during your teacher preparation process? If you are not yet teaching, what experiences do you see on the horizon that will shape your views about teaching in new ways? Do you think the stories in this chapter are like those you will experience? Or, will your experiences be different? Why or why not?

TEACHING IS TOUGH WORK

One of the strongest themes emerging from our discussions with beginning teachers concerned the degree to which they found teaching to be demanding work. One graduate of an Ivy League university commented that his undergraduate career had not been as difficult as his student teaching experience. Those who do their student teaching at a professional development school often come to the same conclusion. Professional development schools are institutions that work closely with colleges of education in the preparation of future teachers. In such settings, student teaching becomes an internship experience in which teacher education students opt for greater responsibilities than are typical of conventional placements (Crocco, Faithfull, & Schwartz, 2003). Rather than taking on only one or two classes at the high school level, they might teach three classes, advise scores of students, participate in school governance, and carry out action research projects. Despite the hard work, these student teachers find the opportunity to interact as equals with experienced teachers to be a satisfying one and an excellent induction into the profession.

The preparation associated with teaching, especially in the first few years, can extend the workday well beyond hours spent in direct contact with students in classrooms, into the evenings and weekends. All subject matter has its own unique configuration of challenges. For example, teaching social studies seemed particularly demanding work for many of the new teachers interviewed. The content demands are high in terms of the breadth of knowledge needed at the secondary level. Likewise, using meaningful assessment activities requires that students do regular writing assignments. In both English and social studies, the task of correcting written work can be incredibly time-consuming.

Responding to the Issues

1. Given the fact that new teachers go through change during their first year of teaching, what means could new teachers use to give voice to their concerns, hopes, and evolving insights into teaching and learning?
2. Every teacher's lounge, it seems, contains burn outs, or people who have given up on teaching. Teachers go through a life-long process of change and development and some teachers do become disillusioned and disengaged. Why do you think teachers burn out? How inevitable is such burning out and disengagement? What stories can you tell of teachers who have remained in the profession and are engaged and happy in their work? What can you find out by talking to experienced and happy teachers about how to avoid burnout?

EPIPHANIES ABOUT THE DEMANDS
AND REWARDS OF TEACHING

One of the new teachers we interviewed was switching from teaching social studies to Italian. She felt the demands of teaching a foreign language were not as great as those in social studies. On the other hand, when we interviewed her a few years after she made this change, she complained that teaching a language was not as stimulating as teaching social studies. Over the course of her transition from teacher education program to teaching full time, she came to recognize how demanding teaching is as a career:

> It's funny because before the [teacher education] program finally started I thought that teaching would be, you know, an eight to three [job], and I would go home and that would be the end of it. But after one class, not even, I don't even want to say one, or maybe a couple of classes, I had an awakening. And the awakening was that the day is not going to end at three o'clock but you're going to work well into the evening and preparing lessons. And you're definitely a teacher full-time. If you see your students on the street, you're still their teacher. You still have that relationship to maintain, even though you're outside the confines of the school. But I've been used to that with other leadership roles I've had.

Ellen now recognized more accurately than she had earlier both the demands and rewards of teaching:

> Once I started to student teach I really became aware of what an enriching experience it was to teach, which I hadn't realized before. That just proved I wanted this profession. The satisfactions happened to be quite a few, occurring at a lot of times throughout my early teaching experience, like when the student's face would light up when I would prepare something and they would understand. And even better when they would come back a week later and talk to me about what I had talked to them about a week before, and just the power of that. I didn't know I could impart such, not just knowledge, but ideas. How they would retain them and really work with them in their own lives. That was really rewarding.

Different teaching subjects and grade levels produce different demand and reward structures. Elementary teachers, for example, generally work closely with their students all day, with only minor breaks. Science teachers have relatively long laboratory periods of hands-on engagement with students who need careful monitoring for safety reasons. English teachers have dozens of papers to correct. Social studies teachers need to master American and world history, civics, and economics, at least in New York state. All teachers spend considerable time planning their lessons, reviewing student work, and monitoring student progress.

Doing the job right means daily engagement with scores of children and adolescents; staying up-to-date in the field means investment of time in professional development outside of the classroom over the course of the career. The realities of contemporary society mean that a not insignificant proportion of students enter classrooms daily poorly fed, poorly clothed, undernurtured, and perhaps a great deal worse. Any profession in which individuals work with people as intensely as they do in teaching can produce stress. When children enter classrooms abused, neglected, dependent on drugs or alcohol, or unable to learn, the stress is magnified tremendously. Managing these demands is a pivotal task for beginning teachers. Likewise, it is important to recognize that one is running a marathon, not a sprint. Finding opportunities for refreshment, relaxation, and personal growth is very important. This is not to suggest cutting corners, but to emphasize balance. Deriving satisfaction from a job well done is a critical means teachers use to stay fresh in their work.

As you think about your first few years in teaching, be sure to consider what strategies you will employ to deal productively with the sometimes unrelenting requirements on your time and energy. We know that we have said this before, but it bears repeating. Recognize as well the support that can come to you as a new teacher in finding a place to work with a group of fellow teachers who share your vision of a learning community. Earlier we noted the difference such an environment can make. When such an environment erodes, teachers sometimes leave the school or abandon teaching altogether.

In considering your placements in student teaching and for your subsequent jobs, be sure to find fellow faculty who will join you in contributing to a high level of academic achievement in the school. Research shows how important these dimensions are to the overall quality of a school and the teaching life taking place there (Bryk, Lee, & Holland, 1993).

Responding to the Issues

1. The vast majority of teachers work in public schools. Do you have a commitment to public education? Why or why not?
2. What other kinds of schools might you find attractive to teach in? What draws you to those schools?

THE THREE MOST IMPORTANT THINGS IN TEACHING

Someone interested in boiling down a complex problem might ask a teacher this question: What are the three most important things in teaching? The answer might be like the one given to an old saw about real estate that goes like this: What determines a house's price? Location, location, location! If we had to answer the question about teaching in just three words, they would probably be: Reflection, reflection, reflection! However, we would have to add that reflection, a lot of reflection, is necessary but not sufficient to becoming a good teacher. Good teaching cannot be boiled down to 3, 5, or even 10 elements that represent a magic formula for the enterprise.

This section hammers home several important points. First, bringing a reflective stance to teaching is tremendously important in the first year on the job. How else can you figure out what you are doing right and wrong every day? Of course, finding the time to reflect will be a challenge, we admit. Formal or even informal mentoring programs in schools for new teachers can build the reflection process into your teaching just as it undoubtedly forms part of the supervision process associated with the student teaching placement.

Second, maintaining a reflective stance to teaching as you get beyond "staying afloat" in your early years is also tremendously important. After a few years of teaching, you will begin to consolidate the gains of the first years. Some aspects of your work will become routine. You will have a sense of having gained skills and knowledge that you never had before. Still, further improvement in your profession demands that you continue to challenge this sense of accomplishment by balancing it with recognition of the need for continued growth and learning.

Finally, reflecting about teaching remains important throughout one's career. Can anyone predict the cases in which "burnout" is likely to occur? Does it stem, for example, from too much reflection or not enough? Is it disillusionment or a lack of energy that produces this change? Many people enter teaching in part because they have enjoyed the learning process. Sadly, some teachers lose touch with this dimension of their profession and their persona.

This is a difficult problem that many school administrators confront regularly. Investing energies in keeping faculty alive is undoubtedly preventive medicine that might limit the need to deal with the problem of teacher burnout and teacher retention. Creating a culture in which teachers regularly retool skills and knowledge helps to promote an expectation that growth and development are lifelong processes. The alternative is to atrophy, an unfortunate state for teachers and students.

Clearly, the academic calendar provides regular and ample opportunity for refreshment and long-term planning. Such breaks also allow teachers to shed the frustrations and disappointments every year in any job inevitably brings. These times away from school also offer an opportunity to gain a modicum of satisfaction on doing a job not perfectly but tolerably well.

In subsequent chapters, we say more about structured programs of professional development. We bring the topic up early on in this book because it is so important. Engaging in "teacher talk" of a positive, reflective, and productive order can provide an occasion for intellectual revitalization and communal support. The motivations of love of subject matter and the desire to work with young people can often be lost sight of in the hurly-burly world of schools and the daily demands of teaching. When schools do not structure such opportunities into teachers' schedules, enterprising individuals turn to other venues. They meet in coffee shops, restaurants, and bars to make space for this reflection with their colleagues. Today's world of online communication can also provide such space, either through e-mail exchanges with colleagues from one's school or with like-minded people from around the country and around the globe.

Claire recognized the importance of finding a school faculty that shared her understanding of teaching. Claire's process of deliberation about the type of school in which she would take her first job was, like Claire herself, deeply thoughtful, well considered, and rational. Her job search was also ambitious because she had set a high standard for the kind of place in which she would work. Central to those requirements was the relationship of faculty to their work and each other:

> *And my ideal school would be where the teachers all see themselves as life-long learners, as intellectuals who are really craving whatever it is, whether it's more knowledge, whether it's greater understanding, whether it's just looking at things in a different way.*

Claire was actually working to create such a school in the place she had decided to begin her teaching career. Claire was a potent force in a small school and it was possible that she was going to succeed in shaping this place in line with her vision.

Responding to the Issues

1. Canvass the schools in your district. What are the models for professional development currently offered in each of these schools?
2. Talk to two or three teachers who are in their 50s who you believe are models of lifelong learners. Interview them about what keeps them motivated to pursue career development opportunities. Find out what kinds of options they have pursued. Develop a written statement synthesizing what you've found, a "formula" for staying alive as a teacher.

THE "DAILINESS" OF TEACHING

Teaching has a relentless quality to it. Day in and day out, scores of students present themselves, looking for guidance and learning under the tutelage of their teacher. This alone can provide its own unremitting pressure on a 25-year-old, unaccustomed to responsibility for so many other young people so many hours of every day.

Lesson planning and its constant demands loomed large in the issues with which our new teachers struggled. The following vignettes represent some of the particular challenges associated with lesson preparation and teaching schedules that struck the brand new teacher. As we have seen, Claire took her first teaching job at a new, small high school in New York City. She had turned down an offer from an affluent district to the north of the city because she wanted to work with a diverse mix of students.

In her teaching position, Claire wore a variety of hats as technology coordinator, humanities teacher, and advisor. At the end of her first teaching year, she reflected on the contrasts between her student teaching and her first job:

> *I look back at student teaching with envy ... I think the biggest thing I had holding me back was just time. In terms of using the methods and philosophies, there was plenty of room for that and I just didn't have time to develop it. I look back at student teaching with envy, when I would spend a whole weekend designing one lesson plan ... I was able to teach one class in the first semester and teach it again in the second semester, and that was great, because then I had a foundation and was able to refine it. I just felt so much of the time that I had these great ideas about how I should plan and how I should design a curriculum ... Now, a lot of times I am throwing things together and hoping they will work, or grabbing whatever I can find. That is always frustrating to me, just not feeling like I have the time to be able to give to planning the way I know I should.*

There is no denying the fact that the first few years of teaching are extremely tiring and stressful times. At the secondary level, two, three, or four preparations, five classes, and 150 to 175 students can leave a beginning high school teacher stretched to the limit. During that first year, the new teachers we talked to found themselves fortunate to get Friday night and one other weekend day and night as a break from the unrelenting pressures of preparation.

Claire's vignette highlights one aspect of the tug and pull of the beginning teacher. An extremely conscientious young teacher, Claire was torn between the admonitions of her teacher education professors about the "right" way to plan lessons and the time limitations of school life. Many practicing teachers succumb to the temptations of shortcuts and compromises. Even as early as their student teaching experience, they have witnessed their cooperating teachers doing little lesson planning. In this regard, student teachers forget the years of experience veterans bring to the enterprise. For many new teachers such as Claire, it is a constant struggle to find the time to "do it right."

The dilemmas of new teachers can be a lot like the lament of working mothers. Working mothers often complain that in "doing it all," they feel as if they are not doing anything terribly well. Coping with the dailiness of teaching is a major challenge of the early career years. Take solace in the fact that it does get easier with time.

Responding to the Issues

1. What role do you believe teacher preparation plays in the life of a teacher during the first few years of teaching? Later on in the career?
2. How can the theories and suggested practices found in teacher preparation programs be accommodated to the work of classroom teachers? For example, what areas of classroom practice do teachers have control over where they could enact the recommendations of their teacher preparation program?

DON'T SMILE UNTIL CHRISTMAS?

Jonathan entered his master's degree program right out of college in upstate New York. The son of two teachers, who heartily endorsed his decision to enter the field, Jonathan wanted not only to teach, but to work as close as possible to the town in which he grew up. He also knew he wanted a diverse mix of students. He was lucky in the end to find a position near where his parents lived at one of the larger, urban high schools in this mostly suburban county.

His first-year assignment called for teaching five sections, albeit at different ability levels, of Global I, the first year of a 2-year sequence in World History. As the child of teachers, Jonathan brought some sense of the demands of teaching into his teacher education program. Still, the realities of the first year took him a bit by surprise:

> *I knew it was going to be a really tough year in terms of how much work I was going to put in inside and outside of school. I knew it was going to be a very draining year physically and emotionally, and it was. I went in there fully—I mean the teacher education program itself was difficult so far as student teaching and coursework, and I just knew as a full-time teacher it was going to be more of the same. And, in a lot of ways, it was worse than what I experienced here in the master's program.... It was just day in and day out—and the tough thing is, even if you're not really ready for the next day, it comes*

anyway, and you have to stand in front of the classroom and just get ready. And that was something I struggled with. I mean, you go in there with a half-hearted lesson that you planned, maybe, and you don't want to do it, and you know, you just go home exhausted, and that was that. I knew that was going to happen, I really did, and it did happen.

What caught Jonathan by surprise was classroom management:

What I least expected was that I didn't realize how important classroom management is. I expected to go in there and be Mr. Nice Guy and Mr. Funny Guy and expect it to go well. You know, and it did for the first couple of weeks until they realized that you're kind of a doormat that they can kind of walk all over. Then I realized I need to get a lot stricter. My students even told me towards the end of the year that I really nailed it in terms of how to treat classrooms and students. That's what I least expected, that is, how important it is to set the proper environment in terms of everything. Just in terms of setting up classroom discussions and general classroom behavior rules for the classroom, which I guess is something I didn't realize how important it was. You know, I had some really great lessons that just wouldn't work because I had inefficient classroom management and that was probably what I least expected, how important that element is.

Somewhat later in the conversation, Jonathan returned to this theme, one of the most critical concerns of all beginning teachers. When asked what he would do differently as he approached his second year of teaching, he responded:

Two things: first, classroom management: Going in the first day, set down, "these are the rules; here's the way it's going to be." And I won't be "Mr. Nice and Funny Guy" first; I'll set lines. You have to do that. That's what I'm going to do differently. The other thing is that I want to mix up our lessons a bit more. I don't want to have so much lecture and discussion. You know, with how easy the [Regents] test is, now I realized that I'm going to get my students there no matter what, and no matter what I do. I could spend a week doing the Congress of Vienna and no one's going to do any worse on that exam.

After 1 year of teaching, Jonathan made some decisions about how he would do things differently the next year, especially in terms of test preparation and classroom management. Jonathan had already learned, through practice, some important lessons about what style of teacher he wanted to be. Happily, Jonathan was a reflective person, which led him toward some resolutions for the following year. After 3 years on the job, Jonathan earned tenure at his school. He recognized that the process of reflecting and reorienting his work had contributed to his success, as well as a strong teacher preparation program.

Responding to the Issues

1. Is there any place for a "Mr. Nice Guy" or "Mr. Funny Guy" in teaching? Should Jonathan totally disavow these personae in his classroom?
2. From what you have seen thus far, what are the biggest challenges you will face in dealing with classroom management issues?
3. Have you found schools in which teachers see professional development as an important part of their employment opportunities? How are the teachers in your field staying up to date with knowledge and skills?

HETEROGENEITY AND ACCOUNTABILITY

In her first year, Claire taught humanities, an interdisciplinary curriculum combining history and English, at her tiny school of less than 200 students. Extremely energetic, Claire welcomed the challenge of teaching dual subjects, advising, and managing a "Tech Team" of students who worked with her on computer maintenance throughout the week. She also believed strongly in faculty deliberation, which was a key feature of the school's decision-making approach.

As at many small schools in New York City (Crocco & Thornton, 2002), school administrators at Claire's school are few in number. Like other restructured schools, teachers are responsible for running the school through a consensus-based model. What this means is long hours (typically at least 2 hours each week) of faculty meeting time to give attention to what Claire calls the "burning issues" of the week.

At the end of her first year, Claire deemed her experience of teaching a success. She loved the school, her colleagues, and the students. Still, in the course of a long discussion that demonstrated her satisfaction about her school's scope for teacher autonomy, several areas of stress and frustration emerged. These problems represent those commonly voiced by beginning teachers, especially those working in smaller schools in urban areas.

Claire was concerned with her heterogeneous classes, where the range of skills, especially reading and writing, was quite broad. Even though her class size was relatively small (25) by comparison with the norm in New York

City (35), she still found it difficult to accommodate all her students equally well. Listen to her expression of concern on this score:

I just totally missed some of my students; I let them down ... I think there's a whole push for heterogeneous classes, which I fully support. But I don't think people know how to do it, and I think that there's a lot of teachers at my school that don't know how to do it. And I think that's a real weakness I have. If there are going to be heterogeneous classes out there, then you ought to be really skilled to work with that and make it successful, and you can't lose the high kids, and you can't lose the low kids, and everyone ends up teaching to the middle.

The work of Oakes (1985) has been important in raising the issue of tracking and its effects on the academic achievement of all students. Other researchers (Cohen, 1994) have argued for the need to build heterogeneous groupings into teaching situations. They call for mixed ability, race, and social status as necessary considerations in forming cooperative learning groups. Still others (Rubin, 2003) have noted the problems with such groups in racially charged and detracked school settings.

One of the points Oakes (1985) made is that tracking is correlated with race and class in America's schools. She argued that it produces academic underachievement for many students, and underestimates minority students' ability because of the nature of the testing instruments used to determine academic placement. Yet the practice of tracking persists in many schools. Claire's experiences might point to why support continues to exist for tracking among administrators, teachers, and parents. We return to this very important subject toward the end of this book.

Responding to the Issues

1. What were your own experiences with tracking?
2. What specific preparation have you received thus far, or will you receive in your teacher preparation that will assist you in coping with classroom management issues?
3. What does it mean to teach in a diverse school? How do you view the challenges and advantages inherent in teaching in diverse settings?

CRISIS AND REFORM

For the last 20 years, public education has found itself in a perennial state of crisis and reform. Although some prominent, progressive spokespersons in education, such as Meier (2003) dispute the diagnosis and the remedy, clearly the accountability regimen in the nation's schools rests on the viewpoint that American schools are in trouble. The No Child Left Behind Act of 2001 reflects this perspective, with its emphasis on literacy and numeracy, high-stakes testing, and accountability.

The approach taken by this act is one of two approaches to reform over the last 20 years (Cochran-Smith & Fries, 2001). One path has emphasized accountability measures through standards and high-stakes testing. The other has emphasized reform efforts such as school restructuring, enhancement of teacher capacity, and changes in teacher education. Each platform for change has produced different pressures on teachers, novices and veterans alike. These reforms have also altered the set of school types in which new teachers can choose to work, especially in urban areas. Thinking through what type of environment will be optimal for you is essential in preparing adequately for the brave new world of teaching.

Many individuals profiled here expressed their motivations to use careers in teaching to improve education, especially for poor students. It is not entirely clear whether the educational reform efforts of the last 20 years will in the end enhance their ability to accomplish this goal or undermine it. However, we obviously cannot talk about these reforms monolithically because the two types of reform move in contradictory directions.

One of the concerns we bring to this book is that reforms focused on accountability, especially when resources are not provided to support the new levels of accountability, might drive out the very individuals best positioned to effect positive change in urban education—well-educated, hardworking, and committed teachers. These individuals might find their scope for creativity and decision making so circumscribed that they feel less like autonomous professionals and more like automatons of the classroom.

Despite these challenges, most of the beginning teachers interviewed for this book expressed confidence about their ability to cope with these challenges, especially those who have completed comprehensive teacher education programs. Such preparation has been shown to produce a strong sense of self-efficacy as a teacher, which is an important attribute in teacher success and commitment over time (Darling-Hammond, Chung, & Frelow, 2002).

A key player in the reforms of the last 20 years has been NCATE. This organization joined forces with the standards and accountability movement as a means of elevating the qualifications and expertise of both beginning and advanced teachers. Guidelines promulgated by NCATE and other organizations, such as the National Board for Professional Teaching Standards and the Interstate New Teacher Assessment and Support Consortium, have brought about a relatively uniform vision of the knowledge, skills, and dispositions necessary to enter and advance within the educational profession.

These organization's initiatives have had tangible consequences for those preparing to be teachers and those seeking advancement. In some states, tenure and merit pay systems are aligned with these professional standards. As we look to the future, it seems clear that teaching in this country will continue to be shaped by the dual and contradictory impulses of the educational reform movement of the last 20 years.

In the midst of these cross-currents, one thing remains clear: The first few years are crucial to creating a teaching life that resonates with the inheritance of autobiography and development of skills, knowledge, and commitments so that a person remains in the profession. Keeping excellent teachers in schools, especially urban schools, should be a major national priority. The loss of excellence seen in low teacher retention rates represents a tragic waste of human capacity and talent, especially in schools with the most critical needs (Lankford, Loeb, & Wyckoff, 2002).

Virginia Edwards (Olson, 2003), editor of the educational newspaper of record in this country, *Education Week*, put it this way: "Studies show that when it comes to student achievement, effective teachers are more important than any other school ingredient." Closing the gap across all races, ethnic groups, socioeconomic groups, and regions clearly hangs in this balance.

As we move forward in this book, we present the voices of new teachers as well as those of people who have already been introduced. The new vignettes will bring you into contact more fully with the worlds of classrooms and schools today as experienced by novice teachers. We continue our approach to examining these stories in a manner that emphasizes the necessity of authenticity to autobiography and collaboration as important dimensions of satisfying work in teaching. Likewise, we continue our inquiry-oriented method of posing dilemmas based on these stories and questions related to them as the best means of grappling with the challenges of teaching. Our reading of the educational research (Darling-Hammond & Hammerness, 2002) and our own life experiences as teachers and teacher educators convinces us that this is the best way to prepare for the challenges ahead.

Responding to the Issues

1. Interview three teachers you admire about the issues introduced in this chapter. Select teachers who represent different levels of experience. Construct a set of topics to cover with them and spend an hour or so talking to them about these issues. Consider what, if any, developmental profile of lives spent in teaching emerges from these interviews and what lessons you can derive from these discussions.

2. If you could create a school, what would it look like? What value would you place on inquiry? On collaboration among teachers?

On diversity of student body? On lifelong learning for faculty and administrators? Would you emphasize the carrot or stick approach in getting teachers to buy into these goals? Why would you choose this path?

3. Lay out your career goals for the next 3, 5, 10, and 20 years. Brainstorm the possibilities; project yourself into your most desirable future. Consider who you are, what you value, and what you want to accomplish in your life. Graft those desires, values, and traits onto your goal planning and consider the steps you will need to embark on to meet those goals.

4. Select one or two of the stories told here. Develop the rudiments of the story into something that projects the action out 5 or 10 years. Explain your choices in elaborating the story's plot line in terms of what you can glean about the person's interests in teaching and what you know of the educational research about teacher growth and development.

5. Look into local press coverage of the demands placed on teachers due to the accountability movement. The circumstances are not unique to any one area of the country. For example, *The New York Times* reported the story of a Florida kindergarten teacher (Winerip, 2003) who was leaving her position due to the changes at her school related to accountability. What profile emerges of the choices teachers in your area are making?

REFERENCES

Bryk, A., Lee, V., & Holland, P. (1993). *Catholic schools and the common good*. Cambridge, MA: Harvard University Press.

Cochran-Smith, M., & Fries, M. K. (2001). Sticks, stones, and ideology: The discourse of reform in teacher education. *Educational Researcher, 30*(8), 3–15.

Cohen, E. (1994). *Designing groupwork: Strategies for the heterogeneous classroom*. New York: Teachers College Press.

Crocco, M., Faithfull, B., & Schwartz, S. (2003). Inquiring minds want to know: An action research project in a New York City professional development school. *Journal of Teacher Education, 54*, 19–31.

Crocco, M. S., & Thornton, S. J. (2002). Social studies in the New York City public schools: A descriptive study. *Journal of Curriculum and Supervision, 30*(1), 217–233.

Darling-Hammond, L., Chung, R., & Frelow, F. (2002). Variation in teacher preparation: How well do different pathways prepare teachers to teach? *Journal of Teacher Education, 53*, 286–303.

Darling-Hammond, L., & Hammerness, K. (2002). Toward a pedagogy of cases in teacher education. *Teaching Education, 13*, 125–135.

Grant. S. G. (2000). Teachers and tests: Exploring teachers' perceptions of changes in the New York State testing program. *Educational Policy Analysis Archives, 8*(14). Retrieved May 10, 2003, from http://epaa.asu.edu/epaa/v8n14.html

Lankford, H., Loeb, S., & Wyckoff, J. (2002). Teacher sorting and the plight of urban schools: A descriptive analysis. *Educational Evaluation and Policy Analysis, 24*(1), 37–62.

Lightfoot, S. L. (1985). *The good high school: Portraits of character and culture.* New York: Basic Books.

McNeil, L. (1988). *Contradictions of control: School structure and school knowledge.* New York: Routledge.

McNeil, L. (2000). *Contradictions of school reform: Educational costs of standardized testing.* New York: Routledge.

Meier, D. (2003). So what does it take to build a school for democracy? *Kappan, 85*(1), 15–22.

Oakes, J. (1985). *Keeping track: How schools structure inequality.* New Haven, CT: Yale University Press.

Olson, L. (2003, January 8). Quality Counts reveals national "teacher gap." *Education Week.* Retrieved January 8, 2003, from www.edweek.org

Popkewitz, T. S. (1998). *Struggling for the soul: The politics of schooling and the construction of the teacher.* New York: Teachers College Press.

Rubin, B. C. (2003). Unpacking detracking: When progressive pedagogy meets students' social worlds. *American Educational Research Journal, 40*(2), 539–573.

Segall, A. (2003). The impact of state-mandated testing according to social studies teachers: The Michigan Educational Assessment Program (MEAP) as a case study of consequences. *Theory and Research in Social Education, 31*, 287–326.

Winerip, M. (2003, May 28). The changes unwelcome, a model teacher moves on. *The New York Times*, p. B7.

Going Further
and Checking It Out

In Part II, you met a group of new teachers who faced common challenges related to the decision to become a teacher, to tell family and friends, to "have a life" as a teacher, and to deal with subject matter demands and classroom management. Accountability issues did not loom as large in the stories presented in Part II as they will in subsequent chapters. Certain aspects of teaching have not been altered by the high-stakes testing movement or the reform movement in education overall. Teachers in most school districts still teach approximately 180 days; many of them continue to have two or three "preps" each year; that is, two or three distinctive courses for which they must prepare each day. Classroom management issues still confront every new teacher who must adapt a style compatible with his or her own personality and in sync with the culture of the school in which he or she teaches.

Despite these constancies, some features of schooling have been dramatically altered by the age of accountability. Schools such as Claire's have lost the option of using portfolios as summative assessments for their students. Students such as those Claire teaches are at risk for greater numbers of failures on high-stakes tests than are those at the suburban school where she chose not to teach. Claire's ability to reflect, reflect, reflect withers away in the face of the demands she faces as technology coordinator, adviser, and social studies teacher.

Most significantly, perhaps, all the teachers portrayed in this book are well aware of the public pressures to make them accountable and the generally low regard in which teachers are held by some citizens of their communities. Public sentiment today, especially as reinforced by legislation such as the No Child Left Behind Act, seems to suggest that teachers are the problem, not the solution, to improving American education. Simplistic views of education promote the notion that federal mandates and school choice programs hold the key to improving American education. Instead, we believe that good teachers are the key to improving American schools. Retaining good teachers, especially in urban areas where the challenges are greatest, is, instead, the most important task facing policymakers and educational leaders at all governmental levels.

By discussing and debating the issues at the heart of these stories, you will be dealing with both theoretical and practical challenges for every new teacher, no matter where she or he is teaching, at least for the foreseeable future.

1. Devise a utopian portrait of what schools of the future might look like if full funding of expert educational recommendations could be carried out across the country. How would teachers' work be different in such settings?

2. Interview two teachers at a local school and two of your teacher educators about their career paths. What do they like and find frustrating about their work? What are their long-term career goals? What factors inform their decision making about staying in or leaving the positions they now hold?

3. Divide a teacher education class into three groups. Using newsprint or large-sized paper, have each person in each group draw their conception of (a) teacher, (b) classroom, and (c) learning. After the education students have drawn their pictures, place them together in three places in the room. Have an "art gallery showing" and have each group go around the room and view what they have created. Use the following questions as the basis for a discussion.

   a. What do the teacher pictures tell about our conception of teachers? How traditional is our view of teachers? Are they in front of the room? How are they standing? What are they wearing? How are the teachers relating to the students?

   b. What do the classroom pictures tell us about our understanding of our practice? Are the chairs in rows, or are there learning centers? If students are pictured, what are they doing? Are they passive or engaged in doing something?

   c. What do the learning pictures tell us about our understanding of learning? What types of learning are represented? Is in-school or outside-school learning depicted more? Does this learning take place with family and friends or in school?

   d. What are the similarities and dissimilarities among the three groups? Do teaching, learning, and classroom look alike, or is there a flow between the pictures? Or, are the pictures radically different? What do the various representations tell us about our understanding of teaching and learning? Which model is represented more, a traditional, teacher-centered model, or a progressive, student-centered model?

4. The middle school experience has been less defined and more variable a teaching and learning situation than common-branch elementary instruction, or secondary subject-based instruction. During the next week, ask people—parents, teachers, administrators, students—what they know about middle schools. Record your answers in a notebook. The brief interviews need only last a few minutes. The following questions and prompts can be used as a guideline:

   a. What do you know about middle school students? Do they act differently than elementary or high school students?

   b. Describe your own middle school experience. Are your memories as vivid as your elementary or high school experiences? Could you share a story (anecdote, vignette) about middle schools, about anything that you know about this experience?

   c. Why do you (or why don't you) teach in a middle school? Have you ever considered teaching at this level? Why did you choose to (or not to) teach at this level?

5. Make a list of the positive and negative aspects of the teaching life in terms of your own personality and interests. How will you deal proactively with what you construe as the difficult dimensions of this career? For example, how could you structure your time as a teacher to provide sufficient "down time" during the academic year so that you do not burn out from the workload of teaching? How will you use your vacations and summer time off to refresh yourself adequately so you are energized when you return to school? Will time off be an opportunity to do something totally different from intellectual pursuits or will it be a chance to immerse yourself once again as a student in your academic area of interest?

6. Poll your friends and family members for their views on teaching. Open a conversation with them about this career choice and let them help you reflect on the fit between teaching and your life goals. Hypothesize about the values that might inform the statements expressed here and whether they accord with the values that inform your own views about these matters.

Part III

ENCOUNTERING
CLASSROOMS AND SCHOOLS

INTRODUCTION

Many new teachers spend a very restless Sunday night. In all likelihood they are thinking of what happened last week, or what they might do in class on Monday morning when the bell rings, the kids pour into the classroom, the door is shut, and the lesson begins. In fact, new teachers spend a great deal of time thinking about their practice. While driving on the highway, and in supermarket checkout lines, they ponder, "How to get Juan to write?" or "How could I have handled that fight in the hallway better last Thursday?" or "How can I best present dividing fractions to a remedial math class?" The search for a satisfactory lesson is particularly acute for new teachers.

Margarita, a second-year teacher, recently told of her search for a satisfactory classroom practice: "Over the weekend, I spend every extra minute of my time—in the car, washing dishes, picking over vegetables in the market—thinking about what I will do on Monday with my kids." Another teacher once explained that the best ideas for the day's lesson came each morning in the shower, and in the slow ride up her school's elevator.

This part of the book focuses on what happens when new teachers enter the classroom, seeking to develop a teaching practice that they consider personally rewarding and beneficial for their students. However, many new—and many experienced—teachers tend to believe that once the classroom door is closed, and they are in front of the class, they alone are responsible for everything that happens. New teachers frequently come up with lessons and classroom practice based on what seems "doable," in other words, what will be accepted by their students. New teachers see themselves as solo performers, whether it be orchestra conductors, drill sergeants, or factory foremen. The solitary conception of this performance is understandable because many teachers today remain isolated from each other. For some, "teaching with the door shut" is a personal choice, and for others teaching in isolation is a reality simply because neither the time nor the opportunity exists to share thoughts with colleagues about teaching and learning in the classroom.

Marybeth, who is getting good support in her job, speaks of this situation:

> There are a lot of teachers who want to do their own thing, and don't want to bother with anyone. Don't really share materials or ideas. And I would find my experience much more difficult if that were the case with me. I can't understand how you can just do your own thing, and not share. I mean how are you to grow as a teacher?

Despite such situations, this chapter argues that for better or worse teachers are not really as isolated as they think. Although new teachers might or might not be able to share teaching practices with others, significant factors influence, shape, and sometimes control what is possible in the classroom. These outside factors not only influence classroom practice, but also contribute to how teachers see themselves as teachers. Some of these influences are obvious. For instance, the cultures and backgrounds of the students in a particular school might have a profound impact on how teachers learn to teach, as does the community in which the school is located, the physical condition of the school, and the type of support—or lack of it—from one's colleagues and administration. All these factors create a school culture that either empowers or disadvantages new teachers, and that greatly influences possibilities in the classroom. Put simply, every school is a unique and particular type of school, and every school has a set of healthy and unhealthy influences that mold how teachers teach and how students learn.

Other less obvious influences also lean on teachers as they develop their teaching practice. For instance, the rhythms and cycles of the school year, with its organization into semesters, holidays, and examination days are a strong reality that shapes how teachers conceive of possibilities in their teaching during the school year (Clandinin & Connelly, 1986). In addition, depending on where the teacher is situated in her or his career, she or he focuses on different aspects of teaching and learning. For instance, in the first few years of teaching, as new teachers move from career entry to career stabilization (Huberman, 1993), they tend to focus at different times on such concerns as student assessment issues, classroom management, the context of the school culture, curriculum and lesson designing, as well as getting, keeping, or changing a teaching position, or leaving the profession (Rust & Orland, 2001).

LOOKING AT NEW TEACHERS' CLASSROOM PRACTICE

The common thread among the themes presented in this part of the book is that they all concern factors that influence new teachers' classroom practices. New teachers are naturally absorbed with what happens, or will happen, in their classrooms. How a teacher thinks about what is possible in her or his classroom is influenced by a number of factors, from how that teacher views what is good teaching—and new teachers vary in this—to the types of lessons or views about student learning encouraged by the school in which a teacher works. Other factors include the level of autonomy and support provided to the new teacher, and the relationship the beginning teacher develops with his or her students, as well as the home cultures of students, their native languages, socioeconomic and geographical status, and many other influences.

As in past chapters, occasionally the coming chapters use short snippets of new teachers' longer narratives to focus on an important issue. In other cases, longer excerpts are featured. We hope that the combination of narrative types allows you to focus on issues of classroom practice, teaching, and learning in a multilayered and complex way. It is a mistake to avoid the complexity of classroom practice by pretending that delivering a lesson is only about learning objectives, formal lesson plans, student activities, and assessment. So much else comes into play once the door gets shut and the lesson starts.

The teachers in this chapter are mostly first- and second-year teachers; a few teach at the middle school level. Middle school education has, since its inception, been somewhat less well defined than either elementary school (common branch teaching) or high school (subject-based teaching). As an activity, you might try to have someone you know identify the difference between a middle school, intermediate school, and junior high school. Their fumbled responses quickly drive home the message that thinking has not been clear or coherent for these grades over the last 50 years.

Another reason to mention the middle school is that the current climate of accountability and high-stakes testing has produced middle schools that often look more like high schools, with intensified accountability for teachers and students. Although many teachers and parents think middle school students are different from high school students, in many ways both middle and secondary students share the difficulties of adolescence. As Tyler put it, "Some of my 12-year-olds are 12 years old, but many of my 12-year-olds are 18 years old!"

Once again, these new teachers come from a variety of backgrounds: Some come from an undergraduate teacher education program housed in a large, public university and others, from a master's program at an elite private university. Some are currently certified to teach on an emergency basis.

These individuals have begun teaching with only a college undergraduate degree in a subject discipline. Others have been recruited into the NYCTF program. They have had an intense summer teacher preparation program that launches them into full-time teaching while they pursue a master's degree program in education simultaneously. Some teach in poor urban areas and others in wealthy suburbs. Some are teaching at the high school level, some at the middle school level. Whatever their situation, they share common problems experienced by beginning teachers in classrooms and schools found across metropolitan areas in this country.

REFERENCES

Clandinin, D. J., & Connelly, F. M. (1986). Rhythms in teaching: The narrative study of teachers' personal practical knowledge of classrooms. *Teaching and Teacher Education, 2*, 377–387.

Huberman, M. (1993). *The lives of teachers* (J. Neufeld, Trans.). New York: Teachers College Press.

Rust, F., & Orland, L. (2001). Learning the discourse of teaching: Conversation as professional development. In C. M. Clark (Ed.), *Talking shop* (pp. 82–117). New York: Teachers College Press.

Chapter 6

Lessons, Kids, and Classrooms

Lessons come from many places. They can be stolen, borrowed, or remembered. They can seem to come from nowhere, an inspiration, if you will, or they can be literally provided by a script written by educational publishers or for-profit testing companies. Lessons can be based on what was remembered when teachers themselves were students, or they can be based on what was learned in educational methods coursework. Frequently lessons planned in the first years come up in the desperate search for something that is simply "workable" or "doable" and that will keep students engaged and focused on some kind of meaningful learning activity.

The following narrative is based on a lesson given on his first day by Theo. Later, Theo shared the story of his lesson to a group of education students, and Steve, a new teacher, borrowed the lesson, which seemed to be a good one. The question, however, remains that if a lesson looks right, or feels right, on paper, is it a good lesson? Frequently, new teachers feel they have to meet the style and content of lessons based on what the district, school, or administration wants. Good lessons then become ones that fit that framework. Sometimes, new teachers express their desire to teach a certain type of lesson, but complain that "They won't let me." Steve and Harris, his principal, show that even when "They let me," that does not solve the problem of what makes a good lesson.

Theo is a personable, former varsity football player, and a first-year high school teacher who was asked to present his experiences to a student teaching seminar. Theo related his tale of a highly successful first year and his thorough enjoyment of his work. Theo taught in a school that had been placed under administrative review because of its poor performance. Not surprisingly, the student teachers in the class asked him if he had been forced to teach in a certain way, particularly in light of the new more rigorous Regents tests. Theo responded by telling the class of his first day's experience in teaching.

The day before he was set to begin teaching, he was assigned a class of students who had failed the World History examinations. Taken off guard by this news, Theo told the student teachers he decided to have his students focus on a chapter about Ancient Egypt in a textbook. After the first day of class, he told them to read about hieroglyphics in their textbooks for homework, so that the second day's lesson could include an exercise having his students do translations of English words into hieroglyphics. The next day he had poster-sized newsprint "stations" set up around the room so that students could translate facts about ancient Egypt into English from hieroglyphs, and from hieroglyphs into English. Theo told the class of student teachers:

> *And when the principal came, he was really impressed about how interested the students were in translating the hieroglyphics. They were involved with learning and that seemed to be the key for the administration. I think if you know what you are doing, and if the students partake actively, why wouldn't an administrator love your lesson?*

Theo's lesson brings up some questions about the lesson production that became clear when Steve, a middle school teacher, borrowed Theo's idea during his first semester teaching. There is nothing inherently wrong with borrowing ideas for a lesson. In fact, good teachers borrow lessons all the time and most successful, experienced teachers are honored when others borrow from them. Adapting lessons to new audiences is important, however. Even more important is understanding what goes into a good lesson and why a borrowed lesson, or any lesson for that matter, worked or did not work.

WHERE DO GOOD LESSONS COME FROM?

Let's set the stage for this story: Steve is an enthusiastic beginning teacher who comes to a teaching career in his 40s after many years in business. He was hired by Harris, a novice principal himself, who was actively recruiting fresh, energetic teachers. Harris is concerned with good instruction in his school in an era of increased accountability and high-stakes testing. Steve recounts his tale:

> *When Harris entered my classroom, he saw students wandering around the room with pads of paper or notebooks in hand, looking at the walls. On the walls I had taped pages of newsprint with English letters and Egyptian hi-*

*eroglyphics written or drawn on them in magic marker. There was much
noise and the students were talking in pairs and in groups. The students
were looking at the English words and hieroglyphs, writing in their notebooks, and, then, writing on the newsprint taped to the wall. After about 20
minutes of this, I told the students to go back to their seats, and I asked them
what they had learned, and we discussed the differences between "picture
language" and "letter language."*

*When I asked the students what they knew about Egypt, they were pretty ig-
norant. They knew about "pyramids," "mummies," and that "The king was
named Pharaoh." Some of the African American kids stated that "Egypt was
a Black culture," and one activist-type kid mentioned that "Egyptians invented the airplane." I didn't know what to do, so I said, "Okay, open your
textbooks to page 349 and read the chapter in the textbook about the Egyptians. Maybe we can get some answers to our questions there."*

Steve further shared that after about 5 minutes of reading, the students,
with their uncanny ability to know when the bell is about to ring, began
packing their bags. As the bell rang, Steve shouted after the class, "Be sure
to answer the five questions at the end of class for homework."

Steve told us that he met the principal later in the day to talk about the
lesson. Harris focused on the activity that involved students reading newsprint on the walls, and he seemed pleased that the students were very engaged with the process. He asked what had led Steve into this lesson:

*I told him that the previous night's homework was to have the students trans-
late their names into hieroglyphics based on information in the textbook.
When they entered the room earlier in the day, after I had gotten them settled
down, I directed their attention to 10 pieces of newsprint on the walls, five in
English, five in hieroglyphs. The students were directed to go around the
room, translate the hieroglyphs into English, and vice versa. They were to
copy their translation into their notebooks. When they had done that, they
were to sign their name in hieroglyphs on the English newsprint, and in English on the hieroglyphs, and move on to the next of the 10 quotations.*

Steve explained that he felt the lesson was a success because the students
were so engaged in the translation activity, "and these were tough kids," he
added. In addition, the principal was impressed by the ability of this new
teacher to engage his students. However, neither Steve nor Harris could
clearly articulate how the highly enjoyable hieroglyphic activity prepared students for the upcoming state examinations, which seemed very much on the
principal's mind as he spoke with Steve. Indeed, Harris questioned how such
an activity "fits in" with the required social studies curriculum. Steve said:

We both sensed that there were some really good things going on in this lesson. There was reading and writing and the kids were very involved. It seemed to me basically a good lesson—though there were some problems—and I am glad that the principal came to see this lesson. I just wish that I was more secure in knowing why I was doing what I came up with.

As he began to reflect on the lesson and whether it had "worked" in his classroom, Steve found himself puzzled by several aspects. He was not sure how he should handle the comments about Egyptian culture made by his African American students. He felt especially uncertain how to respond to the assertion that Egypt had "invented" the airplane. He began to wonder whether borrowing a lesson from another teacher without thinking it through himself was the best way to go.

Additionally Steve felt the limits of his own content knowledge as a social studies teacher, especially regarding ancient Egypt and its significance to world history, as well as his ability to deal effectively with crucial pedagogical strategies linked to reading and writing difficulties for some of his students. Of greatest concern to Steve's principal was the issue of whether any aspect of the lesson had effectively prepared students for the Regents exam, which seemed to be the single most important yardstick of educational utility in his principal's eyes. Their shared lack of understanding behind the lesson's purpose and subsequent flow of activities produced problems when aspects of the lesson demanded modification with this new audience. It is that deeper level of understanding, the reflection that goes into the lesson planning process, that tripped Steve up even though his borrowing of Theo's lesson originally seemed like such a good idea.

Responding to the Issues

1. Although Steve borrowed a lesson, he saw it as potentially effective based on his current thinking about good teaching practices. What attracted Steve to Theo's lesson? Is this type of story a common one, in your experience? With lots of lessons on the Internet these days, how common is borrowing from this source?
2. Steve was clearly unable to bring any deep knowledge of Egyptian culture to the hieroglyphic activity. Thus, he was unable to facilitate a whole-class discussion concerning certain aspects of Egyptian history. What advice would you give Steve? What would you recommend he do in that same class the next day? How would you help Steve further develop lessons like this one? Or would you counsel Steve not to borrow lessons in the future?

3. The students' comments brought up sensitive issues about Africa and African American history that are deeply significant to some individuals. Steve simply did not respond to these statements because he didn't know what to say. How would you have handled the students' comments?

4. This lesson contains many elements (reading, writing, translating, group work, project-oriented learning) and crosses many disciplinary divides (history, geography, and linguistics). What, if anything, do you find appealing about the approach sketched out here? How much interdisciplinary curriculum have you had in your own education? What do you see as the potential pitfalls in teaching interdisciplinary curriculum?

5. How concerned should Steve be in his social studies lessons about covering the stipulated curriculum and preparing his students for state examinations? Are your state and local curricular mandates helpful or a hindrance to your developing practice? Are these arguments he can use with his principal when the principal complains that his hieroglyphic activities are not preparing students for the Regents tests?

CLASSROOM MANAGEMENT

We met Susan several chapters back. She teaches in a small urban middle school in lower Manhattan composed primarily of Chinese immigrants. When asked what she found to be the biggest challenge of her first year of teaching, her response was typical of those given by new teachers:

One challenge is figuring out how close to let myself get to these kids and how to deal with my co-teacher. She is new, too, and is, in some ways, very different from the culture of the school. She has taught 8 years already, and had come from a big public school in another city. And her mentality was much more of a traditional type teacher, which is "I don't do that ..." and a bit of "Are you crazy? The kids would ...." She had a lot of walls around her, in terms of, for example [saying,] "I'm the teacher, too bad." And she was really clear about not letting the kids get too close to her. And that was also true in terms of her classroom management strategy, not just strict, but just very much "this is the way it is, and those are the consequences." As a new teacher, I was definitely more on the side of trying to give so much of myself all the time, but I don't know if it was always best. And so, part of the way through the year, I was still trying to figure things out, how to be the kind of teacher I'd always wanted to be and how to live up to my ideals in terms of why I went into teaching in the first place, but still, not to the degree where it was taking too much out of me.

Somewhat later in the conversation, Susan comments further on these issues:

Everyone says to you when you're a first-year teacher, don't be too nice. You hear that, especially in middle school, "Don't be too nice, you go in there and don't smile for the first four months. And don't show your personality too much; just be very serious all the time." And of course, like most first-year teachers, you're [saying,] "Oh right, whatever ..." Of course, you don't want to be a pushover, and you set limits and you have rules and all that stuff, but I don't want to be serious all the time. So I showed a lot of my personality and told a lot of stories, a lot of personal stories, and funny things. The students loved coming to my class and they felt like it was really a warm place. A lot of people observed me and said, "The tone in your classroom is so wonderful. The kids feel so comfortable, and they can speak their mind without fear of being criticized and that's great." But in the classroom of my co-teacher, the kids are just like robots. You know she has them perfectly well behaved, but she doesn't smile and she's very stern and distant. And of course the advantage for her is that it's much less exhausting. Because she only has to say once, "Sit down," and they do it right away because they're scared of her, because she can be really mean. With me, they feel more comfortable so that has its advantages, but also its disadvantages because it's harder to rein them in a little bit, you know.

This passage highlights several dimensions of the classroom management conundrum. Teachers in one school sometimes have differing expectations for students and different styles of classroom management. This lack of consistency poses problems. One problem for new teachers is being perceived as "soft" on classroom management if veteran teachers are strict. If the opposite is the case, other problems arise. New teachers are often admonished, "Don't smile until Christmas." This bit of advice reflects the notion that in the long run it is easier for a teacher to start strict and loosen up a bit, then to start loose and later attempt to rein in students. Finding a classroom management style is an important but sometimes difficult challenge for new teachers. The question seems to come down to this: How do you manage a classroom in a way that allows you to find a satisfying teaching practice that creates the best conditions for students' learning?

Sometimes, the caring dimensions of teaching get challenged by the realities of working with cantankerous supervisors, lazy teachers, and belligerent students. Many, if not most, teachers enter teaching with a sense of devotion to their work and a genuine desire to reach out to children or adolescents, nurture them, and make a difference in their lives. Yet the realities of classrooms and schools with bell-driven schedules and a curriculum to be covered, as well as the pressures associated with dealing with scores of children every day, can drive those caring concerns underground. Frequently, new teachers drop their ideals and settle instead for managing and controlling a class, concentrating on their own survival more than student learning. Many teachers ultimately find a balance between getting to know their students and providing a safe, comfortable space for them and the necessity of setting rules, especially in large classes. Thinking about how you will deal with the balance between friendly and firm with students who might be only a few years younger than you is essential to developing as a teacher with a workable and successful set of classroom management strategies.

Responding to the Issues

1. Does classroom management only mean disciplining students?
2. Fairness is a really important issue to students. How will you work at treating all your students fairly? What set of principles, values, and guidelines will inform your approach to discipline?
3. Why would someone write a book on classroom management with the title *Don't Smile Until Christmas*? Discuss with others preparing to teach the types of advice they have been given about proper demeanor in the classroom, especially for young teachers.
4. What rules will you have for your students? What student behaviors do you see as negotiable and flexible, and what others are nonnegotiable and fixed? Will you include your students in setting up rules for behavior and language? What will you do if school behavior rules for students differ from what you see as healthy or good for your classroom? Will you hold yourself to the same rules of behavior and language as your students? If so, how? How will you go about introducing discussion of these rules into your classroom? Should these rules be democratically arrived at with your students?
5. Someone once said that to understand schools, you need to study the operation of prisons and the army. Is this a caricature or is there any truth to this assertion? What are your thoughts and feelings about hall and bathroom passes, or other mechanisms teachers use to control student behavior? What "army" or "prison" rules might you be tempted to adopt to control students' movement, language, and behavior? Do you think these rules are more necessary in large, urban high schools? Or are they equally important no matter where you are teaching?
6. Do you think you'll feel comfortable letting your "true" personality shine through when you begin teaching? Why or why not?

MANAGEMENT AND CONTROL ARE ABOUT MORE
THAN MANAGEMENT AND CONTROL

This section is also about classroom management. Sticking with the topic a little longer reflects the anxiety many new teachers bring to the subject. This section focuses on the issue from a slightly different vantage point and attempts to get across the notion that sometimes management issues are not what they seem.

Any new teacher who has spent time in the teachers' lounge knows that loads of "teacher theories" about education circulate in such places. Advice gets handed down from teacher to teacher as accumulated wisdom that is typically not part of formal education coursework or professional development seminars. The most commonplace teacher theory goes something like this: "If you can't control the kids, then you can't teach them anything." Similar to this is the notion that "If you lose control, you'll never get it back."

Such sayings illustrate that teachers, like it or not, must attend to the challenging task of managing and controlling students. Teacher educators and some experienced teachers offer a different understanding, stating that "98% of creating order in a classroom is having a good lesson." Yet new teachers typically do not agree with this. Creating an orderly teaching environment seems the first priority and one that must be tackled head-on, not indirectly through good lesson plans.

New teachers regularly talk about classroom management and student control as being the chief concerns they face in stepping into classrooms. Experienced teachers and some teacher educators appear reluctant to spend too much time discussing these topics. They see these discussions as trivial, overly negative, and so situation-specific as to defy easy formulation into general principles that can be addressed in teacher education courses. As a result, new teachers might not get as much discussion of these topics in their formal education coursework as they would like. Whatever discussion does occur in their program of preparation, it probably is still safe to say that this will be one of new teachers' chief concerns on their first day of teaching.

All the talk about classroom management and student control, particularly among new teachers is, however, slightly misleading. The words *management* and *control* seem to capture a deep desire on the part of new teachers to create a safe, orderly, and healthy learning environment. When new teachers use these words, they are capturing meanings that are more significant than they appear at first glance (Costigan, 2003). To put it succinctly, management and control mean much more than management and control.

Sarah is an articulate and energetic new teacher who enjoys teaching and has built up a close relationship with her students. She sees herself as a strict disciplinarian and looks unfavorably on one colleague who cannot control his class:

Classroom management is about how much you are on top of the kids. In the beginning he just let them get away with a lot of stuff. And he wasn't really on top of everything that's going on with them. Like when there was a disruption in the classroom he would kind of just teach through it and not really address anything, and I think—and this is my own opinion—students take advantage of him because he has an accent and they feel that they can get it over on him. It's unfortunate.

Another colleague picks up the problem of classroom management:

I've seen a hulking former linebacker quake in fear of a sixth-grade class, and a petite female teacher close to retirement put the fear of God into a class composed of assembled truants, chronic failures, and ex-convicts. And I am not making this up.

Very different sorts of individuals can all be successful with classroom management. Finding a personally satisfying mode of management is crucial. Not every style will work with every teacher. Beginning teachers tend to try different approaches. To develop their own style, they frequently pay close attention to their teaching neighbors, borrowing their styles to see if they will work for them. Michael speaks of a colleague on his educational team who is having trouble controlling his class.

His classes are chaos. We've tried to help him, but ... he's not really where the three of us are, he just really doesn't enjoy it. Like we really just asked him [about it], and he'll say, "I really don't enjoy the kids, I don't enjoy teaching them." He just finds it not a rewarding experience. And I'm sure June will be the end of his teaching.

Extensive conversations with new teachers reveal that management and control are words that are not only about disciplining and enforcing, but reflect larger concerns about how to create respectful and orderly environments in which students can learn. In many schools, this means looking outside the classroom because it is hard to have safe spaces in class if schools are not perceived as safe. In other words, classroom management issues are far more complex than just figuring out what sanctions to use if a student fails to turn in homework or acts up in class.

Sarah explains her ideas further:

Management is about having a relationship with the students. Even now, they could be talking when we're doing something, and I just can look at the student now, and they'll say, "I'm sorry," and they'll stop talking. Where in other classes they are wild, bouncing off the walls. So I think it's important to set up those ground rules from the beginning. And even with gum, when they come into my room [chewing gum], I'll say, "What's in your mouth?" and they'll say, "Oh, I'm sorry," and they'll go to the garbage can and throw it out. While in other classes there's a lot of discussion about it. I think it's a matter of staying on top of them from the beginning—and consistency. And with any kind of discipline it's consistency. Like with swearing, they know that I just don't want to hear that type of conversation. And that's pretty much it. It's just that they know what you are going to accept from them, and hopefully most of them will follow the guidelines.

Later in the conversation, Sarah gets even closer to giving this idea clear expression. It becomes clear that management means creating optimal conditions for learning in the classroom:

Management and control are creating a safe space where learning can take place. Because if you don't have the children at a point where they are concentrating and they are on the road to what you want them to be doing, if they are distracted and are talking to each other. In my classroom, no one is allowed to stand out of their seat without getting my permission.

Tyler, another novice, contributed his perspective on this subject:

We established ground rules in September, and we've been following them diligently. We contact parents constantly. We talk to the students and let them know the kinds of behaviors we are not going to accept. There are certain academic standards they're going to have to meet or they're going to be failing.

Tyler sees systematic attention to classroom management as part of healthy school cultures. In fact, management and control are necessary functions of what all caring teachers must do.

There's one team member who also is very involved. When I say to him, "One of the boys is bothering one of the girls." He'll respond, "Do you want me to sit on him?" I'll say, "Definitely. He's been giving me trouble, too, and we'll work on it together."

Tyler believes that establishing one's own approach to classroom management is central to developing one's overall teaching style:

Teaching is an art form. You have to learn to watch for certain things, and keep your eyes open for certain things. So when you're teaching a lesson, you're keeping your eyes open, surveying for negative situations before they happen. So management is extremely difficult, but you can never let your job down.

Juan uses a military metaphor, but is also concerned with creating a safe and orderly environment where learning can take place.

Teaching is like a strategy game, where you put certain troops in certain places, and I have to put certain students in certain places where I know they are going to do well, and learn well, and other students in other places where they are not going to get into trouble. So I am constantly shifting and moving them around, and constantly surveying, and constantly controlling my troops—you would say.

Another first-semester teacher, Ken, joked about this issue, a good way to relieve some stress about the subject:

Well, yeah sometimes I imagine my birth announcement [years ago], I can see what it says, it says, "Ken was born with classroom management skills. He's going to make a great teacher one day."

New teachers have much to say about classroom management because they are preoccupied by this subject. However, by the second or third year of their teaching, many have moved beyond this state of heightened concern, having developed a style and an understanding of what works and does not work in their classrooms.

Responding to the Issues

1. Research in the United States and in the former Soviet Union in the 1960s revealed that teaching in the former USSR was much more progressive than in the United States, which was overtly authoritarian. Researchers found it ironic that American schools seemed not to focus in any way on democratic practices in teaching students, but on control and authority (Bronfenbrenner, 1970). Why have authoritarian, teacher-dominated, and student-passive classrooms continued in many school districts?
2. What metaphors would you use for schools today? For your approach to classroom management? What opportunities have you had in your preparation for teaching of exploring your own theories related to what works and does not work in this area? How much does your own personal experience of schooling influence these views?

3. Is the authoritarian and hierarchical structure of schooling a desirable or workable model for education in the 21st century? Do teacher-dominated classrooms prepare students to participate in a democracy? Should teachers encourage democracy in the classroom? If they should, can they? How? Do approaches to classroom management differ according to the race, class, and gender of the students?

4. When new teachers speak of management and control, do they mean making students engage in certain behaviors? If not, what else does this mean?

5. Can students become responsible for their own learning, that is, self-motivated learners? Or, is a carrot-and-stick approach the only effective one to motivational problems? How can teachers engender in their students enjoyment, if not a love, of the subjects they teach? Is school learning inherently unpleasant so that children have to be forced to learn?

6. Students are learning all the time. In fact, children and young adults are hard-wired for learning (Csikszentmihalyi, Rathunde, & Whalen, 1993; Csikszentmihalyi & Schneider, 2000; Dewey, 1991). How can teachers create classrooms that reflect learning as it occurs in real life? Can students "do" history, math, and English, as historians, mathematicians, and writers do, or, does classroom learning have to be artificial and "learning about" subjects?

EDUCATIONAL COURSEWORK AND SCHOOL CURRICULUM

Recently a small group of new teachers were touring a small alternative middle school in New York City called Excelsior Academy. This new school has many of the benchmarks educators think should be important for all schools. Excelsior Academy was a part of a local community's planning, and neighborhood groups had input into its design. The school actively recruited dedicated teachers who were interested in the school's program, which emphasizes collaboration with parents, teachers, administration, and the local social structures. The hallmark of the academic program was to use local cultural institutions, such as museums, local theater and dance companies, and local historical societies and sites, as the center of hands-on, project-oriented approaches to learning. Students were arranged in "houses," and each teacher acted as a counselor to a dozen or so students. The school day was broken into large blocks where students could work on projects. Graduation requirements included a final multidisciplinary project and a presentation on the part of the students to assembled faculty, parents, students, and invited members of the local community (Meier, 1995).

The new teachers who visited this school found it immensely appealing. At the end of the visit, the principal fielded questions. One new teacher asked her, "You know, I'd certainly like to work here, but where did you get the ideas for all the good things that are happening in this school?" The principal answered, "Certainly not from my education courses. They were absolutely useless."

Of course, the literal truth of the principal's words can be called into question, and certainly might be misleading. His school resembled very much the ideals espoused by the Coalition of Essential Schools founded by Ted Sizer, who has been involved with teacher education, and was at one time dean of the Graduate Schools of Education at both Harvard and Brown. In fact, a significant body of educational research (Levin, 2003) shows that teachers use what they have learned in educational courses throughout much of their careers. However, the principal's remark expresses a perceived truth and a popular belief of some teachers and administrators that educational courses do not prepare teachers for the reality of the classroom. This disconnect might be the most acute in urban areas where the demands of new schools and diverse student bodies have not yet been fully addressed in the educational preparation process.

There are two strands of research that connect to the large topic of how new teachers get the ideas they bring into teaching. The first is that teachers have an "apprenticeship of observation" (Lortie, 1975), or "implicit institutional biographies" (Britzman, 1986). Simply put, this is the idea that teachers have spent a long time as students, and, as students, they were watching what teachers do and thus have an archetypical or stereotypical notion (Sugrue, 1997) of teaching with the teacher standing at the front of the room "lecturing" (Webber & Mitchell, 1996). When they start teaching, this strong understanding of what teachers are "supposed to do" might eclipse what was learned in schools of education.

A second strand of research (Levin, 2003) suggests that if powerful learning occurred in teacher education courses, then this learning might not get discarded but will be developed throughout teachers' careers, particularly after the first traumatic year of teaching. Still, it is not uncommon to find a perceived discontinuity across the priorities of teacher educators, education students, and new teachers. Beginning teachers frequently want hands-on, "how-to" techniques for controlling a class and delivering a lesson. On the other hand, teacher educators frequently want new teachers to take a reflective step back from their practices and analyze their reasons for doing what they do. The idea is that this type of habitual self-reflection and analytical posture toward teaching will be more useful in the long run than a recipe for successful teaching (which does not exist). Nevertheless, all the talk about "best practices" within schools of education can seem like an impractical luxury in the face of the pressures of increased accountability in the schools. The voices that follow speak to these issues and come from first-year middle school teachers.

Tyler is having trouble making connections across the worlds of teacher education and the demands of the school curriculum. In his mind, his pressing daily needs as a teacher overshadow the potential utility of educational coursework:

> *Teaching and being an education student—these are two different worlds. And sometimes I wonder why I am taking the classes I am taking because they don't apply to anything I am doing [in my teaching]. For instance in a methods course, we learned good stuff, but it wasn't applicable to what I was teaching. It was high-level stuff that my kids wouldn't get. And I took a graduate course [focusing on 19th- and 20th-century immigration] which has nothing to do with what I am teaching, early American History.... I am consumed with, "What is going to help me now. I need help now." And that was my mindset. [My educational coursework] didn't help me in the "now" and it didn't help me relieving some of the stress of teaching and planning.*

Thinking up good lessons, day in and day out, is one of the hardest things teachers do, even if the scope and sequence of subject matter is mandated by administrators. Fleshing out the curriculum framework into usable, substantive, and engaging lessons in two or three different classes each day is one of the most wearying aspects of new teachers' work.

A seventh-grade literacy teacher, Barbara uses the idea of "creativity" and "going wild" to present a lesson of folk tales.

> *The unit that we're doing is folk tales and origin tales which is about a god-like animal that explains an occurrence in nature. The one we read was about how the coyote stole fire, and gave fire to humans, and the other was how flamingos got their stockings, explaining how flamingos got their red legs. And some of the students, they had a week and a half to come up with their own "origin tale" and they came up with a lot of creative stuff which was really great. They enjoyed it because they were able to really just be wild with it. I said to them, "Be imaginative, be crazy."*

Barbara explains that she invented her lesson but that it also was based on the school's pacing calendar, a sort of monthly plan the school had developed for what was to be taught, when, as well as what textbooks were available to her in the school's limited book room. It seems clear that Barbara has her own "wild, crazy, creative" concept of good teaching. She explains that she is given a great deal of autonomy, and that when her teaching is restricted by the demands of an imposed curriculum, it all becomes much less enjoyable for her and her students.

> *This curriculum came from nowhere, my head. [The students] happened to be reading in their textbook and I chose to do it this way with them. You see, the administration pretty much allows us to do what we want. We get a monthly pacing calendar [listing sequence of lessons to be covered]. It's just so, so vague. It kind of scared me at first, but now I kind of like it because I get to do what I want with it, as long as you're kind of somewhat keeping it. Like September was "biographies," and October was "persuasive essays," and November was a different kind of essay, and December was more essays— we spent 3 months just on essays, and it was boring as hell. The kids, they hated them. So I would really just give them an essay assignment every Friday which would give them the weekend to work on them.*

Barbara does not accept the approach to writing recommended by the National Council of Teachers of English (NCTE), with its emphasis on process and revision. She prefers the formal structure of the traditional essay, as set out by the district's standardized tests. Although Barbara follows the school district's approach for writing essays, she also recognizes that it can become boring and formulaic:

> *I had maps all over the room about what the essay looks like, the structure, the "introduction," the "body," and the "conclusion." And they did like this, and they worked on it, and it was good for them because essays are really hard. They were surrounded by information. But essays, they're awful, really. I mean I've never enjoyed them, and I told them "I know they're awful, but you know what? Sometimes in life, you have to do things you don't like, you have to learn them, and you have to do it." And I think they like it when you're honest with them, like "I hate them, too!" I'm not going to lie to them. I don't like them, no one likes them. They like it when you speak to them on this level, you're not patronizing them.*

Perhaps after more time in the classroom, Barbara will recover more of what she learned in her English education courses (Grossman & Valencia, 1999) about writing as an organic process. The newer orientations to essay writing just might alleviate some of the problems Barbara has just described, but she does not see it that way at this moment. At this moment, Barbara is mediating the contradictions between the way writing was taught in her educational coursework, according to NCTE guidelines, and the way she is forced to teach artificial and contrived essays. So, she simply has given up her educational school orientation to the subject and adopted the district's point of view. Clearly, though, it is causing her discomfort.

Frequently new teachers simply base their classroom teaching on what is doable rather than anything they have learned in their educational coursework. The search for an orderly classroom environment is very important and just having a good lesson seems to new teachers a difficult enough goal. A good lesson is sometimes measured by how well the teacher can engage the difficult, noncooperative, or disengaged students.

All new teachers appropriate material from various sources as they shape their teaching practices: from curricular mandates, personal experience, and teacher education courses. Dealing with students on a daily basis quickly refines new teachers' understanding about what lessons work and do not work in classrooms. In this process, the kids sitting in front of the teacher each day provide the final verdict on what works. If they are reasonably busy, engaged, and learning, then the lesson and classroom management can be deemed a success. Student teachers, in particular, often disparage the utility of their education coursework because it does not necessarily translate into providing a lifeline of lessons to keep the new teacher afloat. In our experience, by the second or third year of teaching, these harsh judgments about the utility of teacher education tend to abate. What teachers come to recognize is just what they earlier chafed at: the theories of learning, lesson planning, and assessment they draw on to help them meet the ever-changing challenges of classroom practice.

Responding to the Issues

1. What do you think are the most profound influences on teachers' lessons during the first years of teaching? (a) personal experiences; (b) mandated curricula, textbooks, and the threat of high-stakes testing; (c) formal education courses; or (d) the students and school?
2. Many schools of education have only a few courses in "methods" of teaching a particular subject, if that. More coursework is done outside subject-specific teaching methods. How much—and what kind of—specific preparation do new teachers need in the teaching methods of their specific subjects or content areas?
3. If you are a teacher, think of and jot down how you came to teach the lessons you did today. What factors influenced what you did in the classroom? If you are not yet teaching, ask three teachers why they decided to do what they did in their classrooms in their two most recent lessons.
4. "Most of us know a good lesson when we see one" is a commonplace assertion. Do you agree with this assertion? List the specific factors you would look for in supporting your judgment that a lesson is "good."

REFERENCES

Britzman, D. P. (1986). Cultural myths in the making of a teacher: Biography and social structure in teacher education. *Harvard Educational Review, 56*, 442–456.

Bronfenbrenner, U. (1970). *Two worlds of childhood: US and USSR.* New York: Russell Sage Foundation.

Costigan, A. (2003, February 18). *Finding a name for what they want: A study of New York City's teaching fellows.* Presentation given at the Association of Teacher Educators Distinguished Research in Teacher Education Award, Jacksonville, FL.

Csikszentmihalyi, M., Rathunde, K., & Whalen, S. (1993). *Talented teenagers: The roots of success and failure.* New York: Cambridge University Press.

Csikszentmihalyi, M., & Schneider, B. (2000). *Becoming adult: How teenagers prepare for the world.* New York: Basic Books.

Dewey, J. (1991). *The school and society and the child and the curriculum.* Chicago: University of Chicago Press.

Grossman P., & Valencia, S. (1999, April). *Transitions into teaching: Learning to teach writing in teacher education and beyond.* Paper presented at the annual meeting of the American Educational Research Association, Montreal, Canada.

Levin, B. B. (2003). *Case studies of teacher development: An in-depth look at how thinking about pedagogy develops over time.* Mahwah, NJ: Lawrence Erlbaum Associates.

Lortie, D. (1975). *Schoolteacher: A sociological perspective.* Chicago: University of Chicago Press.

Meier, D. (1995). *The power of their ideas: Lessons for America from a small school in Harlem.* Boston: The Beacon Press.

Sugrue, C. (1997). *Complexities of teaching: Child centered perspectives.* Washington, DC: Falmer.

Webber, S., & Mitchell, C. (1996). Drawing ourselves into teaching: Studying the images that shape and distort teacher education. *Teaching and Teacher Education, 12*, 303–313.

Chapter 7

Accountability, Autonomy, and Responsibility in the Classroom

In conversations with new teachers, we have heard again and again about the problems they face due to the current climate of high-stakes testing. While testing has always been a feature of schooling, the notion of "high-stakes testing" is a recent phenomenon. Increasingly, tests are the primary, if not the sole factor, on which teachers are evaluated, and students judged ready to advance from grade to grade, and even to graduate from middle school and high school.

In New York State, the Regents examinations, once taken only by a minority of students, replaced the less difficult Regents Competency Test at the end of the 20th century as a requirement in certain key academic subjects for all students seeking a high school diploma. As we have seen, the high-stakes testing program nationwide is one strategy in an overall effort to reform American education, part of a 20-year march since publication of the *A Nation at Risk* report. It remains to be seen whether testing reforms schooling in an educationally worthwhile fashion, and whether testing is ultimately judged to be worth the price it exacts.

Some indicators of resistance to high-stakes testing can be found. For example, parents in Scarsdale, a wealthy suburb of New York, revolted against testing of fourth graders because they believed these tests actually were destructive to the excellent education their children were getting. They even went so far as to withhold their children from schools on test days. In other states, such as Massachusetts and California, students and parents have begun rebelling against these tests. New information has also surfaced about the large numbers of students who have dropped out of school from Texas to New York because they failed the tests repeatedly. As other provisions in the No Child Left Behind Act disrupt good schools from Chicago to New York, clearly more developments related to this reform agenda will play themselves out. One of the most difficult of these consequences for urban schools has been the option of allowing students to transfer out of failing schools to other schools. This option produced massively imbalanced class sizes during the fall of 2003 across New York City, with class sizes in some middle schools coming close to 50 students.

ACCOUNTABILITY IN SCHOOLS

Who is going to argue against accountability? There is no doubt that measures of accountability are essential in any system, including education. However, when and where the issue of accountability gets raised, and what mechanisms are put in place for enacting an emphasis on accountability all have their own political dimensions, hidden agendas, and unanticipated consequences. Thus, the story of the accountability initiatives of the last 20 years is a highly complex one. To lay it out with any degree of comprehensiveness would take this chapter well beyond its page limitations. Nevertheless, it is abundantly clear that the effects of new accountability measures are having a sizable role in shaping the lives of new teachers today. This is true in some places more than others, for sure, but in no place can their pressures be entirely ignored.

The backlash against certain features of the national educational reform movement by means of high-stakes testing has been building during the last decade. Books by prominent authors such as Sacks (1999), Kohn (2000), and McNeil (2000), to highlight just a few, have all documented the negative effects of high-stakes testing on teachers and students. One interesting study took place in the state of Massachusetts concerning the Massachusetts Comprehensive Assessment System, a lengthy and arduous test of English/ language arts, mathematics, and science and technology first given to 201,749 students in 1998. Wheelock, Bebell, and Haney (2000) examined drawings students made of themselves taking this test. They then talked to those students about their drawings. The researchers found that, although a small minority of pictures showed students as "diligent problem solvers" (p. 1), a larger number of drawings presented students as "anxious, angry, bored, pessimistic, or withdrawn from testing" (p. 1). This study, along with other research focused on high-stakes testing and its impact on new teachers (Costigan, 2002; Crocco, 2002), suggests the detrimental effects on both groups. Moreover, many experienced teachers express a high degree of skepticism concerning the learning outcomes of such tests.

It remains to be seen whether the regimen of high-stakes testing will need to accommodate itself to political and economic realities as many school districts struggle to make ends meet. Despite the mandate of higher standards, federal support for the new educational initiatives and demands for teacher quality has not been adequate to meet the new requirements imposed. Likewise, some schools report that certain subjects, such as social studies, have been abandoned in the press of meeting literacy targets.

The narratives show new teachers struggling with the effects of these "reforms" on their teaching. New teachers need several years to develop their teaching repertoires. When new teachers' classroom practice becomes dictated by standardized instruction, especially scripts for teaching tied to high-stakes tests, they often want to leave the profession. The dumbing down of teacher work that these new regimens often produce is undermining the very factors that induced bright new teachers to enter the field. Dealing with the pressures of testing without abandoning the profession could be a task confronting many of them in coming years. Assessing the climate around testing as part of the job search process is imperative if you wish to work in an environment philosophically compatible with your own values.

The following narratives come from new teachers located within a mile of each other in a large urban district. This district was formerly the home of many third-generation Eastern European Jewish, Irish, Italian, and Near Eastern residents. Over the last 15 years, it has become a middle-class residential and commercial area comprised of first-generation Korean, Chinese, Russian, German, Eastern European, and Middle Eastern newcomers. The neighborhood continues to exhibit the hallmarks of the thriving immigrant neighborhood it was a century ago. Beth, Sarah, Julian, and Debra are all new teachers in this neighborhood who have been interviewed multiple times about their teaching practice.

In one of her first interviews, Beth explains the challenges related to high-stakes testing that she faces:

> *The pressure is on. The test is in two and a half months, and the principal told my cooperating teacher that every day the principal wants a review in the class. "They have to know these words." And this is reiterated constantly. The principal told [my cooperating teacher]: "We spent a lot of money on getting these packets to you and giving you review sheets because the school has to spend the money on the review. The district just gives the test. In their eyes it's a message that says, "You do what you have to do to get these kids to pass the test; we pay for the test."*

Beth realizes that the type of teaching she is required to do is at odds with the more student-centered methodology presented in her education courses. She explains to her former teacher education professor:

I remember when you came in and observed. You were turned off by how we have to teach. Well, trust me; no one is as turned off from it as we are. But we are mandated to do this. And although there are certain parameters [of teaching] from which [teachers] can venture out, and make it somewhat more enjoyable, on the whole, there's only so much enjoyment that you can get out of this. So although some of the advice from you people is very ideal- istic, I don't think it's very practical when you actually are doing it. I don't think it is realistic advice, because I still have to answer to my principal. They can come in at any minute and see what you're doing. And I certainly don't want to jeopardize my job, so I feel like I have to do what I'm told.

All these new teachers share similar concerns about teaching in a world of educational reform driven by high-stakes testing. Beth continues:

It's always there; it's that lingering thing that's always on your back. I mean, it's just constant. I mean I've been so worried I talk to my family about it. I stayed up last night and wrote a three-page letter to the parents of my stu- dents. The letter said to the parents you must, must, must—must underlined, bold print—go over these with your kids. I bought every child a plastic word box and wrote their name on it, and as we speak my mother is sitting at the dining room table cutting out word [flash] cards that I've made for every sin- gle student in my class.

We have to fit it in. So, we don't have any allotment in our schedule—which is quite regimented. So we have to fit it in where we can. And I look at my kids every day, and they can't read the questions. If I could read the questions out loud, they would have no problem. So I feel the test doesn't test anything they've learned. The test only tests if they can read the questions. That's the only thing it could possibly test, because if the [state] really were interested in what they knew, they would allow me to read the questions.

Altering curriculum to focus on test preparation is only one part of Beth's frustration. She believes that high-stakes testing has actually harmed her relationship with students:

Some days I don't recognize myself. I go out into the hallway and cry. I feel the pressure that he or she is going to be judged on every little piece of paper that goes into their [student] folder … so I feel the pressure that I'm judged on it, so I judge every little thing they do … and every day I question myself …. There's always the matter of having to move on, because you have to fit ev- erything in. You start teaching and you have to decide to review. If enough kids are having trouble, you do. If it is a couple, you do the best you can with them, but it's always you have to move on. You can't stop and say, "Okay, let me explain this all one more time, let's spend another day on it," because that means 1 day less of something else that has to be fit in. And sometimes some of the stuff that I'm teaching them—I don't remember doing it at that age. I feel like these tests are crazy sometimes and I don't know what it is they're supposed to understand.

These four new teachers all shared the negative effects they were experiencing in teaching in this age of accountability:

There's a lot of pressure on read aloud and writing. Actually we're having a problem with this because we're so influenced by the testing. They're worried—that is, my principal is worried—about how their writing is constructed, rather than the content. In other words, these children write really well; however, they'll have misspelled words—they're only in the second grade. But they focus so much on misspelling, reading, and how [the writing] looks and all that, so it doesn't matter that my kids are doing advanced work. Their content is really good. Their writing and reading is above grade level; however, [the administration is] so unhappy with the student works' appearance. So there's more rewriting that's going on— rather than more writing.

They're writing things over to get it perfect, rather than writing and going on to other topics. I wouldn't emphasize rewriting so much. I'd allow for spelling errors, and the grammar errors, as long as they're not making kindergarten and first-grade errors. In that school, it's no matter what the error is—if there's an error—it's wrong ... There's a lot of time wasted on rewriting and getting it perfect, rather than writing new things and learning new things and writing about that.

It's not really that I think about the testing, it's that that seems to be the school's priority, so everything else is based around that. In my mind, it's not about the testing. In my mind this is what the school wants. But what the school wants has to do with the testing. What they want is the third- and fourth-grade testing, so in the first and second grade we have to be preparing them for that. So they're big on the writing. I have to hand in to my principal writing samples every Friday from my classroom—from each child. She looks at that. They have to be doing writing every day, and more than sentences, and paragraphs. It's really kind of odd there.

Testing can be one of the chief factors in my wanting to leave the profession. It's turned me off to teaching ... It's totally test prep. Everything's timed. First you teach each reading skill. There are about 15 reading skills. You know, cause and effect, sequence of events—all those skills. Every week there's a weekly skill. So everything you teach revolves around that

skill, to try to get it through to them ... You do it for the week, you know,
you're exercising the main skill, and you're trying to get it to them.

Like teachers, school administrators might also be ambivalent about the unintended consequences of high-stakes testing. They are in a difficult position because they, perhaps even more so than teachers, are being held accountable for the performance of students in their schools. This new teacher recognizes how important the support of an administrator can be to the work of teachers and acknowledges the way in which the new accountability systems have affected everyone working in schools:

My principal is really great. She backs you up. She constantly is showing
us things and teaching us. It's not that I blame her. I have the utmost re-
spect for her, and I think she's a very good businesswoman. It's like the
trickle-down system. She's pressed for these scores, too, so it just goes
down the line. We've even had conferences with her about this. This is
crazy—and she admits it! She is a principal who was a teacher, and she
knows the deal. So I think that these standards that are mandated have
made everybody crazy.

Teachers are not able to be free in their teaching styles because every [stu-
dent] has to be taught for the test. We started already in my classes, and
they don't have to take the test for three semesters ... And I think that that
takes away from the creativity of the class ... It's like the teacher, as well as
the student is in a straightjacket. And they are forced to teach for the test. It
always comes back to that.

In these teacher stories, each narrator reports strong negative reactions to the ways in which high-stakes testing is shaping his or her classroom practice. At this juncture, it is necessary to explore the many ramifications of this new regimen as it relates to the lives of new teachers. As we proceed, and certainly in the last chapter of this book, we need to explore what possibilities exist for creative classroom practice, given these constraints.

Responding to the Issues

1. How do the experiences of these narrators compare with your own and those of other teachers you know?
2. Teachers are decision makers who have some measure of control over what goes on in their classrooms, despite external pressures. What strategies do teachers use to follow their own values in a world of increased accountability? What are the risks for a new teacher in

trying to exercise professional judgment contrary to administrative expectations?

3. The preceding statement in Question 2 might need modification in situations in which scripted lessons are being used. In some schools, teachers must follow carefully a standard protocol indicating where their lessons should be at a given time and day. Are scripted lessons being used in your district? If so, what reactions to them have you heard?

4. Do some experienced teachers welcome a reform movement regulated by curriculum standardization and testing? How do the veteran and new teachers in your school talk about testing? Are the costs of testing different for honors students than for those having trouble passing courses in school?

5. Do an inquiry-oriented project around high-stakes testing in a school near you. Find out all the ways in which the school has been affected, or not, by high-stakes testing over the last several years. How are these changes viewed by teachers, students, administrators, parents, and the local community? Have some positive results been identified?

WHO'S TO BLAME?

Whatever the ultimate utility or detriment these reforms bring with them, it is clear that many new teachers find a curriculum of high-stakes testing to be devastating as an introduction to teaching. Many have said that mandated curriculum, scripted lessons, and the pressures to improve scores without adequate support for accomplishing this end are the chief factors driving them out of teaching. They question, as more experienced teachers do, whether they should be held accountable for the performance of their students in the ways in which the high-stakes testing regimen dictates. In other words, if students do not learn, is it always the fault of the teacher?

One new teacher, Arnie, finds that the tests have imposed stringent accountability measures on administrators as well as teachers:

> *And part of me wants to leave teaching because there are so many problems with the school system right now, especially the fact that it's basically that the top management is in disarray. Our principal is one of 50 who got fired, and I was just appalled because ... they went about everything just totally the wrong way. And it rippled out, had a horrible effect, on the school, the teachers, and eventually on the kids.*

Time and time again new teachers report similar problems and the larger issue that these changes signal a lack of trust in teachers, which results in a lack of autonomy in teaching. Frank, a New York City teaching fellow, found the oversight inflicted on him as a new teacher oppressive:

> *I was observed formally seven times, which is bordering on harassment. And I was rated satisfactory each time. But they wanted documentation that "I'm not using the program." Not using the [required curricular] program! This was in every [lesson] observation written up about my teaching. And the supervisors came in informally a good solid 25 times on top of that. They brought the district office in to watch. It was just constant, constant.... It was a huge struggle.*

Jane, a new high school teacher from the large public university's teacher education program, reports that oversight by administrative officials included telling her how to arrange her students' desks.

> *I had observers in all the time, and it was hard for me to fit in and test around constant observation. There was a school mentor coming in 3 days a week, and we also had the college supervisor coming in. And then we had the observations which had to be performed by the assistant principal. And there were several times I had the district office where they would just pop in and say, "Oh, you need to change the desks. You need to teach in certain ways, and you need to place the board here and you need to change the room around." And then they came back 2 days later to see that I did it. So rules like that really turned me off. I couldn't develop in my own way.*

Andy is considered an excellent new teacher by his colleagues and supervisors at the middle school in which he works. He devised an innovative curriculum of field trips and "ethnographic" reports by his students about their communities that gave scope for creativity but also managed to raise test scores. By his second year of teaching, Andy was considered one of the "star" teachers at his school. Still, he fears that this is not enough for the administration to trust him to teach as he thinks best.

> *This year, I don't know, my test scores came back from [the mandated tests], and my results were—well, my kids outperformed everyone else in the school. I mean significantly! Why do I think that happened? I think it is because I didn't do only what they said to do. I mean there were test preps that happened [in my class] but they happened in context of other things. And, in reading books that the kids choose, that I found ways to work into my lessons ways that would be reflected on the tests, and we did more—so much writing, and so many projects and used portfolios. And if I had done just the scripted program that they had given me, I don't think it would have been the same result. I mean the kids worked. They came in on*

Saturdays; they came in until the end [of the semester] for it ... and I took a lot of heat thought the year for not doing everything as given to me ... and now the principal has removed all of the other eighth-grade teachers, except for me, and they've all been teaching for 20 years. And she's going to give me the top honors classes, so I'm going to be set up that way for the next year. But there are some catches coming with that, like this pre-scribed curriculum which is coming. They're doing the balanced literacy format, and I don't know.

Andy finds it ironic, given the high praise for his work, that he still is not trusted:

I am now "The Favorite." Before no one listened to me at staff meetings, or paid attention to the things I was trying to do. I would really have to come in with research in hand and say, "This is why I'm doing this." And even then it still was questioning and doubting and being checked up on, and now, they want me to interview some of the people they're hiring, because they want people to have the approaches I have and want people more like me! [Yet,] some of the incredibly successful things I've done this year do not fit into their format. You know, we're doing these community service projects and creating these portfolios. They have field logs, they like write a mini thesis. And it doesn't fit into the "read aloud" format. It doesn't work like that. So many things that I do don't work like that. And, you know, I asked the principal, "Do these honor classes give me the freedom then to not have to read aloud to them, because they don't need it. They don't want it ..." And the principal said, "No! You have to read aloud, because of [sigh] the restructuring of the Regents [exams]." People are in big power plays because they have to justify why their jobs are in place ... and all I know is that the administrator who is coming in to enforce this format is going to enforce it. And [the principal] said, "Just do yourself a favor and read aloud, even if you don't think you should."

Despite his great success, both in developing a curriculum of inquiry that is beneficial to his students and raising test scores, Andy sums up his dissatisfaction in a manner too commonly heard from the new teachers we interviewed:

After a year of being resilient and doing what I wanted to do, despite the harassment, I have discovered I am very good at this. By next spring, I'm going to start sniffing around to find some other position. This is just not satisfactory.

Andrea believes the suburbs might provide a more congenial place for developing the kind of teaching practice she sees as rewarding, due to its relative freedom:

I would have liked more opportunities to make mistakes on my own, and then figure out how to solve them, or arrange my classroom in a way that would support what I was attempting to do in my lesson or in my practice.

Even experienced teachers groan under the weight of a curriculum driven by mandates and accountability measures imposed by state and federal governments. In the end, they feel their status and knowledge as teachers have been greatly undermined. In its place has emerged a system of distrust in which no one can grow—teachers, administrators, or students.

Responding to the Issues

1. To what extent has the current situation of high-stakes testing and increased accountability entered into your consideration of teaching as a profession? Do you expect to be surprised by this phenomenon when you start to teach, or have you given it prior consideration? If so, what conclusions have you come to about your attitudes about high-stakes testing and increased accountability?

2. The presentation of high-stakes testing in our research has been overwhelmingly negative. Put simply, new teachers dislike "teaching for the test" and many believe it has profoundly negative effects on their practice and their students' learning. What are your views on how to manage this brave new world of teaching so that you can create meaningful practice for yourself and high-level learning for your students?

3. The situation of testing in the schools is often at odds with the teaching practices advocated both by schools of education and professional organizations in English, social studies, mathematics, science, and other content areas. What specific assistance can schools of education or professional organizations give you to support quality teaching in a test-driven world?

4. High-stakes testing, mandated curricula, and "teacher-proof" or scripted lessons are more intensely experienced at poor, urban schools. Teachers in suburban schools often find themselves less constrained by such tests because generally their students pass these tests. Independent schools are typically exempt from these tests. What are the reasons for this? How does testing interact with race, class, language, and gender? Is this fair? What are your own views about the attractions and drawbacks of dealing with testing in urban or suburban schools?

LOST LANGUAGES: THE UNINTENDED CONSEQUENCES OF THE ACCOUNTABILITY MOVEMENT

Schools face incredible new demands related to the growing diversity of this country. The United States continues to be a destination for people from all corners of the world. In the past two centuries immigrants typically landed and stayed in large urban centers, but suburban and rural areas have become increasingly attractive places for people from Asia, South America, and the Near East. There is hardly a country in the world that does not have a community represented somewhere in the United States. In the United States, it is not just ports of call like New York and Los Angeles, but interior cities such as Columbus, Ohio, and Detroit, Michigan, where the diversity of the population has increased significantly over the last 20 years.

Given these conditions, you might think that language teaching would be a central concern of schools in this country. One of the paradoxical effects of the emphasis on literacy is that language teachers (i.e., foreign language teachers), like teachers of the arts and even teachers of social studies in many places, feel that their subject matter has been pushed to the side and is simply not seen as important to the priorities of many schools.

Along with growing immigration, and the issues of culture and diversity that schools confront, local school communities and the teachers in them are faced with a variety of educational challenges presented by non-English-speaking and limited-English-speaking students, many of whom are required to take high-stakes tests. A debate continues in the public press, as well as in schools of education, about how best to teach non- or limited-English speakers. Is instruction in the home language effective, or does it hinder learning of English? Is a bilingual approach the best, or does the bilingual classroom only confuse students? Should all instruction be in English with only assistance and enrichment given in students' home languages?

All this is compounded by the fact that a debate exists about how best to teach English even to native English speakers. Is a skills-based phonics approach best, or is whole language instruction best? Is language best learned with a workbook approach that stresses grammar and the basic elements of language, or is language best learned in the context of student-centered activities? As if the language debate were not complex enough, further complication comes from the fact that there are basically two scenarios of language teaching in schools. First, no one seems sure how best to teach math or science to nonspeakers or limited speakers of English. Second, teaching a second language to native speakers, although mandated by state departments of education, rarely is effective at producing even limited second language fluency in native English speakers. In fact, some even question the need to learn languages other than English in an increasingly English-speaking world, whereas other educators argue that each language reflects a particular way of processing the world, and that students are impoverished if they are not exposed to other languages.

Foreign language instruction is currently situated within the context of a profound ambivalence most Americans have about such learning. For instance, the United States has no official language, yet the end of the 20th century witnessed many efforts at "English only" legislation. Although these attempts have either failed, or have been largely symbolic in nature, "English only" movements have demonstrated the profound discomfort some native English speakers have with non-English speakers.

As the teaching population continues to be largely native-born and English-only-speaking Whites, many of them are unschooled in matters related to language issues—other than English—in their classrooms. Many people who do become language teachers in American high schools are nonnative speakers of English. They often feel a bit different from teachers of core subjects like math, science, English, and social studies. They might or might not be trained in English as a Second Language (ESL) work, despite the fact that they are bilingual or trilingual. Increasingly, they feel marginalized in a world where importance is defined as school subjects that get tested most regularly and where so many consequences hinge on students' scores.

The problems related to language teaching in urban high schools are complex. If a student is disruptive, then he or she is sent to the disciplinarian at the school. If the student has difficulty with English, that becomes the language teacher's problem, even if that teacher has not been prepared in ESL. The result of this ambiguous situation is that teachers of English are often asked to handle problems for which they are not fully prepared. In addition, they recognize that language learning is not valued as highly as other subjects in this country. David, a Spanish teacher in a Hispanic urban neighborhood, registers these concerns.

> One of the challenges has been trying to teach [a] foreign language in a city that doesn't appreciate or understand the importance of foreign languages. For my first 4 years as a Spanish teacher at my first school, I had no supervision or guidance. I was truly isolated from everyone because I was teaching a subject that was a minority in our school. Today I teach in a new school where foreign languages are at the same level as Math and English … As foreign language teachers we face the challenge of being "second-class citizens." As a result, we need to continue to become better every day to prove what language teaching is all about.

Many language teachers go through all of the challenges that face new teachers, such as developing teaching competence, learning to manage a classroom, and being inducted into the rhythms of school life. However, when asked about their participation in these rituals, they indicate that they feel on the fringes of these events, not fully members of the school's faculty. Nevertheless, they argue that this situation is out of sync with the demands of a globalizing world:

> *It is so important that when we think of foreign language, we also think of culture … the past, present, and future of the culture the language represents. Foreign language teachers need to teach with this understanding.*

Like David, Joanne is coming to understand that language teaching presents unique opportunities to experience different cultures. Her desire to teach comes from her having lived in another culture. She wants her own students to share the opportunity to experience another culture as lived outside the United States, even if only vicariously through learning another language. She is becoming a high school Spanish teacher through an immersion program that allows people to begin full-time teaching after an intensive summer workshop that also ultimately yields a master's program for which she does not pay a penny. Joanne wants to share her passion for language learning with others. She teaches both Spanish I and Advanced Placement Spanish, and says,

> *"I get them when they come in and when they leave."*

When asked about her approach to teaching language, she responds:

> *I go about teaching Spanish in a conservative way. In an ideal world we would all like to use the culture of teaching language approach. But I am totally taking the textbook approach where I make sure they know the verbs and they know the vocabulary. I'm taking the conservative approach because I'm scared [for my job]. I'm a new teacher and I don't want to take any risks right now, not knowing what the consequences could be because I'm responsible for 120 students [passing state exams]. Now, do I think this way is exciting? No. But, I don't feel that I would be doing my students justice if I would try to do the other approach. I would love to do it that way. I learned Spanish when I was living abroad, but I can't do it that way.*

In addition, Joanne takes a self-defined "conservative" approach because the school does not have a coherent philosophy of language learning. First, the school has separated native language speakers from non-Spanish speakers, discouraging interaction between various levels of speakers. More important, there is a laissez-faire approach to language learning. She explains, "When I came to the school, and when I entered the classroom, they didn't hand me a curriculum, they told me, 'You figure it out. Here's the textbook.'

They threw me to the wolves. They hadn't prepared me in any respect, from telling me how to do a lesson plan, to a grade book, nothing. So I took the conservative approach."

Nadine expresses her frustration with the conditions in which much language learning occurs in urban high schools, even though she teaches in a highly regarded institution:

> They're so squished in that they can't even do "total physical response." They can't get up. There are no skits. I can't have them act out anything because the desks are so put together. In learning languages, you want to act and interact.... They can't do any of that. Physically they can't feel the language. You can't do group work because there isn't any room for them to move their chairs and speak with each other. The state is really making it challenging today. Another thing is that we don't have language labs, and videos and the like. We don't have any of this. Can you imagine trying to learn a language when there's no language lab to practice? If this could happen, every student in class could participate in trying out the language—and that's all we'd do without any [direct] instruction.

> If I had it to do my way, I'd do a lot more where they are immersed, where they are listening and watching the language, and that's hard because we don't have [access to] even a TV or a VCR, tapes where they can listen to others speak [Spanish] and record themselves speaking. To me, good language instruction is being able to watch it, and hear it and speak it, and when you don't have those resources to let that happen, you can't do it. If I had my way, we'd even use the Internet—we wouldn't use a textbook. But now it's all memorization and workbooks.

Harry, another language teacher, not surprisingly found that his best success in teaching French was when he took his students to France:

> My experiences teaching languages have been quite rewarding. The challenges I find, however, are mostly getting administrative support for the language programs and trips. They often do not see the educational benefit of trips abroad, or even to a local restaurant. Yet I am very satisfied in my language teaching. It is a subject which can be very student-centered. One can also be very creative with lesson plans, and this is a class with students who are encouraged to talk and not sit silently.

> What sticks out mostly in my language teaching, for me as a language teacher, is when I took a group of seven students to live and study in France. They learned more in 3 weeks than they had learned all year. I remember one of my students remarking that she didn't know she could speak so much French.

Many difficulties exist in language teaching, not only about how to teach languages but what language instruction is ultimately supposed to accomplish. Although questions of purpose are not unique to language teachers, often they feel particularly isolated and marginalized in modern high schools where so few students actually get the opportunities to travel overseas and use the language they have been learning. The situations of language teachers are not unlike those in the arts who chronically face cuts in their programs when the local school budget does not pass. In today's climate of high-stakes testing and emphasis on literacy and numeracy at all levels, teachers in subjects such as these often feel that their work is not valued by school administrators, other teachers, and even parents.

Responding to the Issues

1. Most teachers today deal with language issues at some level. Even in math, science, and history, clear expression is pivotal for making sense of the discipline. In cases where teachers have many ESL students in their classes, language issues can be particularly challenging. What preparation are you getting for dealing skillfully with both ESL students and other language issues in your classroom? Has development of clear written and oral expression been a priority of your teacher preparation program?
2. How important is it to learn new languages? In language instruction does a "skills and drills" memorization methodology work, or is a contextualized, interactive, student-centered approach more effective? What have been your experiences with language learning? What methods are employed and how effective have they been in your language learning?

THE RIPPLE EFFECT OF HIGH-STAKES TESTING

You met George early on in the book. He is the young man with a great love of history who is uncertain whether he wants to stay in teaching or move into a doctoral program in history. In the suburban area in which he works, teachers are told that property values depend on high test scores. The pressures he faces from high-stakes tests are not the same as those faced by teachers in New York City, however, because most of his students pass the test. Pressures still exist because teacher worth is tied to student performance on these tests. Administrators see their own stars rise and fall according to how the schools in their district perform. All in all, pervasive pressures exist for focusing teaching on test preparation, even though the motivations might be different for doing so.

In George's district, as in many others throughout his suburban area, newspapers publish each school's results on the Regents exams. Realtors study the results and steer clients accordingly. George comments on the predictable results of such circumstances:

> *There are some teachers that are obsessed with the Regents. There are some teachers that reflect more of my, I mean, you know, values. I'm beginning to think that memorization is not such a bad thing. It's a skill that we all need to have in life, to memorize things. I need to memorize where I put things. The emphasis on it doesn't have to be as much as it is. And that's good. The one thing that my department chair likes and, he's a Regents sort of guy, he works for the State and he'll tell you he works for the State ... but the one thing he always tells me is that he respects me so much professionally because I don't forget where I came from as far as my graduate education is concerned. He knows about its progressive reputation and he sees that when I teach classes, and I do it through central concepts. I don't necessarily go through Regents sequences, but I try to teach kids and make it relevant. He sees that as being important. I don't know. I assume in the next 5 or 10 years I'll become more traditional in teaching. I've become more traditional in a year.*

By the "progressive reputation" of his teacher education program, George means the student-centered and diversity-sensitive approaches to curriculum and pedagogy that dominated his teacher preparation program, including inquiry-oriented methods, cooperative and group learning, role play, and simulation. These approaches contrast with traditional, teacher-centered approaches such as lecture and recitation.

Teachers often adopt lecture and recitation methods even when they recognize that students dislike such approaches because they give the impression of covering the material efficiently. Whether students actually learn more of the information being transmitted is another matter entirely. Research on effective teaching indicates that careful lesson planning, appropriate instructional materials, clear statements of lesson objectives, regular reviews of student work, and a brisk pace for lessons all contribute to student learning (Cohen, Raudenbush, & Loewenberg Ball, 2002). How many veteran teachers approximate this model of good practice is not clear, but novices like George often find that the conventional wisdom in schools concerning what works in preparing students for high-stakes tests violates these norms.

Responding to the Issues

1. What forces are at work that would move a teacher from a more progressive orientation in teaching to a more traditional one? What are the underlying assumptions behind this shift from student-centered learning, which focuses on inquiry, to a fact- and lecture-driven approach to teaching?
2. The research on cooperative learning's effectiveness shows that it improves learning, but many veterans shy away from its use. Why do you think this is true?
3. Make a list of practices and ideas about teaching and learning that you remember from your educational coursework. What seems "doable" in today's climate? What seems impossible—at least at this point in your career? What issues or practices were recommended in your educational coursework that you find appealing, but that you think are impractical? Why do you think this is so?
4. Make a list of teaching practices you have learned from teachers you consider to be effective teachers or ineffective teachers. Which practices would you try to use or to avoid. Why? How do these align with what you have learned in your educational coursework?
5. How important will it be to you to find a mentor during your first year of teaching, either one who is assigned by the school or one of your own choosing?
6. Does success in a school as a teacher depend on adopting the "party line" about teaching and schooling that dominates in that place?

ACADEMIC CONTENT INADEQUACIES

Many beginning teachers find that the content and breadth of their knowledge is not sufficient for teaching a broad array of topics at the high school level. Considerable gaps exist between what is typically studied in college and the demands of the secondary school curriculum. This is true whether the subject studied is English, science, or math. High school curricula have a form and content all their own. These all have been put in place through historical decisions made about the secondary curriculum years ago. These structures of knowledge are sustained through state learning frameworks and curriculum standards, textbook content, college achievement and aptitude tests, and increasingly high-stakes tests.

Sometimes new teachers try to use their college education as a model for their high school teaching, both in style and content. What new teachers quickly discover, however, is that college teaching, with its emphasis on lecturing, and college courses, with their emphasis on small slices of academic content, have to be overhauled for high school teaching. Lecturing generally does not work with younger students, and arguably does not work even with college students. A case could be made for giving high school students the same degree of choice in creating their curriculum as many college students get, but the educational reform movements of the last 30 years have made "electives" scarce at the high school level, especially in states like New York with high-stakes tests in content areas.

The field of social studies provides a case in point of how college curricula differ from precollegiate curricula. For starters, this field is a "created discipline" that includes such topics as world history, American history, economics, civics, and to some degree sociology, anthropology, and geography. Social studies teachers might have majored in history, political science, economics, sociology, anthropology, or a variety of interdisciplinary majors such as American studies. Similarly, a college English major may have focused on Shakespeare or the early modern novel, but not on the processes of writing, or on adolescent literature, and someone with a college degree in some aspect of math or science might not feel prepared to focus on the unique content of Sequential Math I or Earth Science.

In practice, many new teachers get assigned to world history, which in New York State consists of a 2-year set of courses, often called "From Plato to NATO." This label is not inaccurate because teachers must cover a range of ancient civilizations to start, and then move over the sequence of 2 years into the 20th century, spanning five continents, and including history and geography as they teach this daunting array of material. Like an English major having to teach reading, or a physics major having to show students how to divide fractions, crises of confidence in social studies result understandably from the unfamiliar nature of material and a sense that without deeper knowledge of subject matter, they cannot be as creative or effective as they would like in preparing their lessons.

Sarah echoes problems voiced by many new teachers:

> There were those few times when it's midnight and I still had no idea what I was going to do the next day, or I didn't like what I was doing. There were a few sleepless nights where I was terrified, because I had certain lessons and I didn't know how they would go. But, I mean, I never felt like I'm not supposed to be in teaching. I never felt that.... You know every night when I'm planning, I try to do as much reading as I can. My major in college was international relations, so I thought I would be a little bit more prepared for teaching world history, global history. But you know, what you learn at a college level is completely different from what you learn in high school. And when I went to high school in New Jersey, we didn't have world history; we had world cultures, so you studied various cultures. I don't know if

it's changed, but it was only one course. In New York State, there's a 2-year world history course. I really didn't feel academically prepared. And that's part of the reason I'm taking a world history class right now, during the summer, but I struggle a lot with the content. And I don't know if it's just every first-year teacher. I've been told by experienced teachers [that] you don't know anything [coming in], that this is where you learn it all. I don't know if I'm feeling what everyone else has felt or if I feel more inadequate. I don't know. But I definitely don't feel my academic previous experience or education has prepared me to teach this way, the way I'm supposed to teach.

Research into the lives of new teachers suggests that "academic competence" in the various content areas is, like classroom management, a major concern of their first few years in teaching. Of course, teenagers are especially adept at spotting someone who is faking it, as all these young, new teachers recognized. Even the best prepared of them ranked the content demands of their teaching as a major concern.

Some humility is in order, for sure, in facing up to the deep knowledge base required by most secondary school teaching. You should recognize that you will not know everything; nor can you be expected to, at the outset. Neither does anyone else. It is not a source of shame to share this lack of knowledge with students, within reason. Dispelling the image of the teacher as "sage on stage" and substituting a view of the teacher as a fellow inquirer might help produce better classrooms. This shift would increase student learning and student satisfaction with the very subjects that often rank low in student interest.

Each teaching specialization places different demands on beginning teachers. Teachers at the elementary and middle school levels often do not have the luxury of specializing but must develop deep knowledge in multiple domains. For all teachers and all levels kindergarten through Grade 12, unique demands exist that must be anticipated and dealt with if teaching is to be successful and satisfying. You should explore these demands with teachers at mature levels in their careers or a valued mentor. Above all, you should not feel like a failure as a teacher if it takes you several years to shore up your content knowledge. One of the exciting things about teaching is that it offers you an excuse to keep learning.

Responding to the Issues

1. Acknowledging that you will not know the answer to every question your students pose when you start teaching, how will you handle those instances?

2. How are the subjects you studied in college different from the ones you are expected to teach in school? In what ways are teachers expected to teach differently in high school than in college?
3. Have you talked to experienced teachers about their strategies for coping with this problem? What advice have they given you? How will you handle the inevitable fact that you will be asked a question for which you have no clue about the answer? How will you deal with the fact that you may be asked to teach a topic you don't know well at all?
4. In your field, how do professional development opportunities provide the ability to shore up content knowledge?
5. Dan was "excessed" as a math teacher in a vocational high school. After waiting 3 weeks for an assignment, because of the way the system operates in New York City, he was then sent to teach Advanced Placement math in one of the city's top schools. Dan feels that his students might know more than he does. What advice would you give him?

REFERENCES

Cohen, D. K., Raudenbush, S. W., & Loewenberg Ball, D. (2002, February). Resources, instruction and research. In F. Mosteller & R. Burch (Eds.), *Evidence matters: Randomized trials in education research* (pp. 80–120). Washington, DC: Brookings Institution Press.

Costigan, A. T. (2002). Teaching and the culture of high stakes testing: Listening to new teachers. *Action in Teacher Education: The Journal of the Association of Teacher Educators, 22*(5), 35–42.

Crocco, M. S. (2002). *Accountability and authenticity: Beginning teachers in social studies.* Paper presented at the annual meeting of the American Association of Colleges of Teacher Education, New York.

Kohn, A. (2000). *The case against standardized testing: Raising the scores, ruining the schools.* Portsmouth, NH: Heinemann.

McNeil, L. (2000). *Contradictions of reform: Educational costs of standardized testing.* New York: Routledge.

Sacks, P. (1999). *Standardized minds: The high price of America's testing culture and what we can do to change it.* New York: Perseus.

Wheelock, A., Bebell, D. J., & Haney, W. (2000). *What can student drawings tell us about high-stakes testing in Massachusetts.* Teachers College Record.org. Retrieved March 5, 2003, from http://www.tcrecord.org.Content.asp?/ContentID=10634

Chapter 8

Teaching Is Not Just
What Happens When You Close
the Classroom Door

As we have already discussed, during the latter part of the 19th and early part of the 20th century, the United States made a commitment to universal public education. Much of the impetus for this came from the massive waves of immigrants arriving in this country, until immigration was curtailed in the 1920s. By 1900, both private academies and public high schools enrolled only 10.2% of the population of the 14- to 17-year-old age group. In other words, 90% of American youth in 1900 chose other roads to the world of work than high school (Karier, 1986). By 1930, 51% of the population attended high school (Kliebard, 1995), and by the 1960s, not only a high school, but a college education was seen as necessary for many young people. Educational and societal changes, as we will see more fully in Part IV, have shaped education in dramatic ways over the last 100 years.

The original impetus for the growth and importance of universal schooling in this country had economic, social, and political causes. Education, as Thomas Jefferson saw clearly in the 18th century, was important in a democracy so that the electorate was well prepared to exercise the franchise. By the 19th century, as Horace Mann understood, universal public education was crucial to citizens' participation in the nation's industrializing economy. Over the course of the last two centuries, changing views on childhood and adolescence also shaped expectations for the nature and length of schooling.

The birth of modern psychology and the work of scholars such as G. Stanley Hall helped to invent "adolescence" around the turn of the 20th century. New understanding of the developmental stages and tasks involved in the maturation process all played a role in changing society's expectations for proper preparation of young people for the demands of adulthood. These new sensibilities about children's growth and development led to increased public support for state and federal legislation prohibiting child labor during the early 20th century. Optimal development of youth necessitated, according to this theory, greater investment of time in school, from kindergarten through high school (Kliebard, 1995). Today, many citizens believe that this educational development should continue through college.

The demands of schooling ever larger numbers of students nationwide brought about new views concerning the "scientific management" of schooling in the early 20th century. The emphasis was on "efficiency" (Callahan, 1962) with administrators seeing schools as factories and the daily schedule of classes as sequences of activities requiring an order that would get rid of unproductive time (Kliebard, 1995). To achieve the ends of efficiency as well as coping with the demands of increased scale, schools developed new forms of leadership: top managers (principals), midlevel managers (assistant principals), workers (teachers), and product (student performance). The "owners" of the enterprise (state and district administrators) and stockholders (politicians and the public) oversaw this hierarchical structure of management.

In a business model of schooling, raising productivity is the engine that makes the system work efficiently. However, improving teaching and learning in the United States is a costly and complicated process. Schooling is complex, intellectual work that cannot be reduced to a formulaic approach that is replicable from school to school or state to state. Sometimes it seems as if American citizens want their schools to serve as educational Wal-Marts, giant emporia of learning where a mediocre product is available at the cheapest possible price. Such an ethos of schooling will hardly raise test scores or improve learning.

However, the effort to achieve such ends in the most "efficient" manner has led to dramatic intensification within the teaching profession over the last 10 years. The emphasis today seems to be on doing more with less, or at least with no more than what was available before expectations were raised as a result of new state and federal initiatives. As we have said repeatedly, few would argue against higher standards. Nevertheless, whether high-stakes testing will, in fact, produce excellence in schooling remains a highly debatable proposition (Kohn, 2000; Sacks, 1999).

The cost in terms of teacher retention, especially in urban schools, is one that proponents of high-stakes testing seem not to have addressed.

Our research suggests that new teachers, especially the most qualified ones, chafe under a regimen that seems to demand they do more with less and that discounts their intelligence and creativity. Likewise, many new teachers actively seek to develop nurturing classrooms where they can grow in understanding of their work, students, and school. They desire to develop a personal practice that addresses the needs of all their students. However, a profound discontinuity exists these days between the conceptions and desires new teachers bring to their teaching and the accountability model promoted by many policymakers, politicians, and some educational think tanks.

Even in the best of circumstances, new teachers entering urban schools need "buffer zones" between their educational school experiences and the demands of such schools. Such transitional spaces or gradual induction experiences would include strong mentoring, reduced teaching load, and gradually expanding scope for autonomy. In addition, such induction experiences would allow for collegial conversations, regular reflection, and ample opportunity for getting support as it is needed. In such environments, new teachers could work out and negotiate a best practice, help their students learn, and develop their commitment to the profession.

New teachers regularly say that one of the biggest factors in their decision to remain in or leave the profession rests on whether the environment they work in is supportive of their practice. Unfortunately, many of the alternative teacher education programs almost immediately put new teachers into exactly the kind of schools that are most likely to drive them out of the field. Too often, urban schools in general are not the most supportive places, given the harsh realities they contend with every day. As a result, even teachers with a commitment to urban schools might find the personal costs of working in difficult, sometimes dysfunctional, and perhaps violent urban secondary schools too high.

In the following excerpts, you will encounter a range of situations reflecting the ways in which teaching goes beyond classroom experience, to the relationships forged (or not) among new teachers, their administrators, and their colleagues. One lesson to take from these stories is the importance of such relationships—for better or for worse. When such relationships work, new teachers are helped to succeed. When they do not work, the result can be an abrupt end to a teaching career.

SCHOOL RELATIONSHIPS—FOR BETTER OR WORSE

Joanne, a beginning middle school teacher in New York City, is lucky to find herself working with colleagues and administrators who help her do her best as a teacher. She acknowledges that this is not the case for most of the teachers in her school:

I have a supportive environment, both in my team and in my complex [group of buildings]. Those in my complex are very, very helpful. We work together well. I am the language arts teacher of the team, and there's a social studies, science, math teacher and we work together where we'll discuss how the children are doing academically, how they are behaviorally. There's a team meeting each week during one of our preps, but we talk about it constantly, at our preps, lunch, you name it. We're one of the few teams that are working well together. I've heard a lot of first-year teachers saying they're getting no support from their team. There are a lot of teachers who want to do their own thing, who don't want to bother with anyone. They don't really share materials or ideas. And I would find my experience much more difficult if that were the case with me.

Barbara is another new teacher, also in a middle school, who is quite clear in her view that new teacher support is essential to the decision about staying in the profession:

The new teachers who didn't get the support, and who were totally drowning, they quit.

Thom works in New York City in a school that, like many other urban schools, has a group of young and inexperienced teachers. This is good for collegiality purposes, as Thom points out. Nevertheless, such environments lack opportunities for mentoring, which can also be a critical factor in creating an environment that supports and retains young teachers:

That's another good thing about my school. It's a very young staff. You have a lot of energy, you have a lot of excitement; you have a lot of teachers willing just to put a lot into their work because they're not jaded from years and years of teaching and being in an urban system. We are also banding together because the school is new and we really haven't set up a perfect routine for the school. So everybody kind of bands together and is supportive, so things are fine in that respect, too.

Joshua, a middle school teacher, explains that the administrators at his school are not very responsive to faculty, even when it comes to disciplinary matters:

Basically you have these administrators who wash their hands of it and want you to handle everything, want you to take care of it. They don't want to hear you ask about how to handle a problem. A lot of times you feel pressured to take care of the problems yourself. But it is so important to establish that authority because basically you're independent and the assistant principals are going to get upset that they shouldn't handle the problems that you should be handling.

New teachers seek more than collegiality from the veterans in their schools. They also often desire direct mentoring from experienced teachers and administrators who are seasoned teachers. Jonathan, like George who we met in a previous chapter, finds himself in a good position because he has two support people, an experienced mentor in his school and a retired principal who serves as a consultant to his university education program and visits him frequently. Jonathan recognizes how lucky he is to have this level of support:

My first year has been so rewarding. I think two of the biggest helps have been my mentor and my consultant. The mentor is with the school district, and the consultant is from the college. My mentor is there pretty frequently, and when I am tired and need a lesson, he provides me with a lesson he used. He gives me materials that I can use in my class, materials like videotapes and stuff for motivation—like an original musket ball—little things that really make a big difference and help your lesson.

He's been almost like a father, calling me when I was sick to see if I was okay, and asking me if I went to the doctor. The consultant and the mentor were a major balance. The mentor was supportive and the consultant was supportive, but he also had a supervising background, so he would bust my chops on things, make sure I was on top of things. He would point out things in my lesson ... so I would always be prepared [for official observations] because he would point out the weak parts of my lesson before I was observed. So he was like the tough guy, bad cop, and my mentor was the good cop. And they also set up meetings with the administration so I would know where I'm at with the principal and administrators. Getting this type of support is crucial.

Levels of support in a school depend on the willingness of administrators to prioritize the development of new teachers. Administrators need to provide some vision of their role as leaders of teaching and learning, as opposed to simply management and oversight for evaluation purposes, if this support is going to work. If administrators see themselves as leaders of teaching and learning, then they are likely to offer support for these activities or find someone who will. However, if they see their role as simply making "the trains run on time," then they will be less likely to get involved in the school's academic program. Department chairs often face the same choices. In any case, administrators, like teachers, are often overburdened these days with their own pressures around high-stakes testing. They often find themselves ill equipped with time or money to support what new teachers need.

In the next case, we meet Ruth, a new teacher with two master's degrees—one in history and the other in education—and review her story at some length. Ruth was a career switcher; she had worked overseas and in the United States for about 5 years before deciding to become a teacher. Her story is emblematic of the power of administrators to shape a teacher's satisfaction with a teaching position.

Ruth began work in an academically ambitious restructured New York City high school, teaching social studies. In this school, Ruth initially believed she had found a compatible environment for enacting her own progressive teaching philosophy. Many of her fellow teachers had graduated from the same master's program in which she was enrolled at the time she was hired. In this passage, Ruth shares her reasons for entering teaching:

> I think I went into teaching because of the kids. I think I went into teaching because it just seemed to fit. You know I also saw that the major thing was that you could branch out into so many facets of the world from teaching; education was a key to open up many doors. I think that's why I went into teaching, because it was a place where I could grow.

Sadly, Ruth had a terrible first year of teaching. She felt "persecuted" by an administrator with the reputation of being difficult. She was also frustrated by the bureaucratic aspects of teaching, especially in New York City. When asked how she negotiated the work demands of her institution and the paperwork associated with her teaching, she responded:

> I have a gift and an enemy at the same time: I speak my mind. So, although I learned not to speak it [a lot of the time], when I would tell them something was too much, I'd get a nasty look in return.… The New York City Department of Education needs help. I mean there's a lot of wasted paper [and] it takes a lot of time … I thought my preps were for planning and grading, but they were spent doing a lot of paperwork and photocopying. Besides, the school politics are just horrible. Tenured teachers are treated like gold; teachers who are not favored for whatever reason were treated really badly. There were school politics in every which way, from the students, to what you're supposed to tell the administrators, to what you shouldn't tell the administrators, everything was done through the union constantly … [And] they broke the contract with me a couple of times. But when it suited the administrator, they would stick by the contract.… Then there was my principal, who started meeting [with me] once a week on Fridays, which was a horrible experience because it was usually about her yelling at me … Another new teacher and I were treated like we were worthless because we were first year, and our

*opinions were really not that important. And we had a lot to say, but it really
wasn't worth much because we were first year.*

In this case, as with other urban and suburban teachers we interviewed,
beginning professionals found the teachers' union invaluable in providing
support for new teachers. Nevertheless, Ruth's frustrations were extensive.
In her interview, she was eager to share every facet of the unjust treatment
she had received at the school:

*I was told, over and over again, all year that my students all passed the global
the year before, and if they don't all pass the American history test this year,
that there was going to be trouble. I had one student who didn't make it. And I
knew from the very beginning of the year that he would not make it, and I did
everything that I could possibly do to get him to pass. But he just doesn't get
it. So, I don't know how many times I recommended for him to have special
education, and it was always refused. It's bad, because this is a new school.
The performance of the school is judged by the performance on tests and not
by what the school is really, and because of that, the administration puts a lot
of pressure on the teachers, instead of making it no big deal—just a test, like
any other test ... As far as curriculum, there were so many times that I was really annoyed that I couldn't veer away from the curriculum and do something
more in depth. And the students wanted it more in depth. They're like, "Why
can't we spend more time on this?" And I'm like, "we're on a timetable," and
they would get really annoyed and frustrated, and I would get really annoyed
and frustrated. I think that the Regents, after grading both the global and the
American history tests this past week, is the most biased, slanted, ill-pre-
pared test. There were problems with the rubric; there were mistakes in the
rubric; there were misprints in the rubric, which, for a high-stakes test, is a di-
saster. I think that students are graded more on how they follow directions
than their ability with history.... At the same time, though, it does give a sense
of structure that without it, having taught government and economics with a
curriculum framework, having the structure there does make you go through
the curriculum at a more even pace. Because I would get stuck in one area in
economics and stay there, because I wanted to stay there, but maybe I
shouldn't have stayed there as long as I did.*

There is so much that one could talk about in these passages: Ruth's relationships with administrators, peers, and students; high-stakes testing and
its effects on curriculum; issues around evaluation and assessment; the
community of tenured and untenured teachers in a school; and learning to
get along by making personal adjustments in any work organization. Perhaps it comes as no surprise to readers that Ruth left teaching after her first
year, disillusioned with a number of dimensions of the teaching life. Still,

Ruth remained in education, having taken a job for an educational company that created curriculum materials in a country overseas in which she had lived before.

As Ruth finished up her work in New York City, she was convinced she had been driven out of teaching by a supervisor who had persecuted her. In the end, perhaps, teaching just was not for her. As we have acknowledged before, teaching is not for everyone. In Ruth's case, over time, she might come to admit that her departure from the school reflected this reality more than any other. There is no shame in the fact that teaching is not for everyone—just as accounting or office work or carpentry is not for everyone. Still, at the time we spoke with Ruth, she was clear in her conviction that the system and an overzealous, even tyrannical, supervisor had driven her out of teaching.

In this discussion of such challenges, we are not arguing that new teachers need hand holding. Nor should their stories be interpreted as whining. The problem does not lie in novices who are not tough enough to make it in the real world of work. Many of them were, like Ruth, seasoned employees who held a variety of other positions before they made their way into teaching. The complaints these new teachers registered were widely shared. Moreover, their judgments have been supported by other research into new teachers in urban areas, such as the Harvard New Teacher study cited earlier.

The new teachers who are the subjects of this book clearly see themselves as emergent professionals. They desire a balance between autonomy and support. However, they recognize that a "sink or swim" approach is not in their best interests, at least on many days during their first years of teaching. They want scope for the risk taking that leads to personal development. These are not contradictory wishes, but finding a balance between these two poles requires sophisticated leadership from their principals and department chairs.

The following brief statements from three different beginning teachers are fairly typical of the positive comments many made about their administrators:

[My] principal was very practical minded. She wasn't one of these "You must do it this way." She said, "You know what is required of you, I am not going to be looking over your shoulder."

I want enough help from administrators—like getting books and supplies— as well as having them give me ideas for teaching. I don't mind when my assistant principal comes into my class because, despite writing the lesson up, she always has good things to say.

The [curricula] I use are generally guided by the administration and the pacing calendar, but within this, I'm allowed a great deal of latitude to do

*what I want. I just think of it as the administration interviewed us so strin-
gently, that I think he feels that the people he hired can really handle it. He
trusts us.*

One teacher adds a comment about her expectations concerning her
school leadership that is especially significant to teachers in New York City
but might be shared by teachers everywhere, whatever the size of their
bureaucracy:

> *The principal is a big umbrella, protecting me from what hits the fan ... This is
> important in an insane bureaucracy such as New York City's.*

There are clear historical and social reasons why schools act and look like
they do, which are explored more fully in Part IV. Likewise, the next section
digs deeper into the reasons why teachers frequently remain isolated and
overextended with too many students struggling with a mandate to cover
the material and pass the tests—or else. Within difficult school environments, in particular, a balance of support and autonomy seems to be the key
not only to survival and growing competence, but also an essential factor in
new teachers' decisions to remain or leave the profession.

Responding to the Issues

1. What types of support do new teachers need to develop a successful
   teaching practice? What types of autonomy are necessary to grow as
   teachers? How can a balance be kept between an adequate level of
   support that is not too controlling, and a level of autonomy that allows a teacher the scope for working out his or her path without letting him or her sink or swim?
2. Over the next week, investigate one aspect of school that you have
   taken for granted: a bell schedule, grading, breakdown of subjects
   into various disciplines, the Pledge of Allegiance, the administrative structure of a school, hall passes, or any other policy that is part
   and parcel of conventional American school life. Where did these
   behaviors and conditions come from? Why do they continue? How
   do teachers and students feel about it? Could the school function
   without these condition and managerial behaviors?
3. How are students treated in schools? Are they products to be developed, or are they persons to be developed? What are five beneficial
   ways students are treated by schools, and five questionable or problematic ways schools treat students?

SCRIPTED LESSONS

Sophia is an eighth-grade literacy teacher in a poor neighborhood. In response to a question about how she was doing, she gave a common response of many new teachers that she has had "good days and frustrating days." She went on to explain her difficulties with her work as it was presently constituted.

She was told to teach two separate scripted lesson systems, which were written by national testing and textbook companies. The students' work generated in these lessons was sent weekly to the district office. Additionally, she had to supply evidence of her students' work to an administrator on a regular basis. An administrator was appointed daily to go around the school to see that teachers and students were doing the scripted lesson and that a proper "objective" was on the board and that the lesson was on track down to the minute in its relation to the master schedule. Now, Sophia is a highly articulate and intelligent young woman who entered teaching from a successful business career. She was well aware of the difficulty in teaching in a poor, urban area, and, as she commented, "I knew what I was getting into." That does not mean that she enjoys what she is doing.

Sophia's story is distressing, and there are no easy solutions to her problems. As with an increasing number of teachers, she was simply forced to follow scripted lessons. Although Sophia's situation is an extreme one, it is symptomatic of teaching in an era of increased accountability. All teachers face administrative demands to teach a certain way, and to "cover" a certain amount of material in a certain time. In Sophia's case, a schoolwide standardized test identified eighth graders who were reading at a second- or third-grade level. These were formed into a class, and were given to Sophia. She explains:

> I teach several reading intervention programs which stress small picture books with easy content and high interest, picture books for middle schoolers, really. One program involves "graphic organizers." Another focuses on employing certain strategies such as "modeling, predicting, clarifying, questioning, and summarizing." All this involves "consumables," but they don't pay you to have all of the required material. The kids don't have workbooks to write in. You have to photocopy the one workbook they bought—every day. You have to provide all this extra material yourself.

When asked how the young people responded to the program, Sophia explains,

> The kids hate the program ... They think that they're being treated like babies. Each small book is a 5-day lesson, and I keep it to 3 days because it goes exceptionally slowly. I mean the text they have to do is second- or third-grade

level. They can't do it, but they just don't like to be asked to be doing that—they see other classes work on the wall, and they see that other classes are reading 1984 and they are reading Sally Opens a Pet Store.

Obviously this is stressful. Sophia reflects on how this has affected her teaching life.

What's frustrating for me is that I think I became a teacher because I think I have interesting ways to help education happen. But when you're given these scripted books—Well! I'm checked up on constantly and have to turn in evidence of student work … because they want to make sure I'm using the program. With the other classes, I'm not checked up on as often, but I do have to turn in from 3 weeks to a month of writing samples. It's incredibly time-consuming. And I don't think that it's necessarily helping them progress. The school's concerned. And I don't know why they pretend that they're not about teaching for the test. They say that education is about "Education," but that is not the case. Every meeting we have is about improving the reading scores … every promotion meeting is about their scores. It's not about "Are they becoming literate students to function in a literate world?" The program focuses on "What color is Jack's hair?" You know they start to ask, "On page fifty-six, paragraph two, why does Jack say this, and what does it mean, and how is the character changing?"

Sophia compares this artificial approach to other, more engaging approaches to reading:

What I want to have is a book club. I don't think you need these programs to achieve the goal of getting them to join a literacy club. One thing is that this is fake literature. Literature created for going into the manual for the test. They're not reading novels, but "constructed short stories." With a focus and a purpose abundantly clear from the beginning. You know, "In this story there is this"—clearly constructed for a purpose.

I guess test taking is a skill because they have to do it a million times in their lives. But is that what is important about being a literate person in the world? Are they learning about their world? Are they participating and communicating with other people in any sort of effective way? In prescripted methods, teaching them how to "search for detail in paragraph three," is that what literate people do in the world? All of the enjoyment is gone. I don't enjoy teaching it, they don't enjoy reading it, we all hate talking about it, but we have to do it.

I don't want to teach for the test. I get [administrators telling me], "You know you want to be an eighth grade teacher with your own room. Then, you will turn these in by the next week." It's so heavy handed there, I don't know what to do. I have all these great ideas, these great things. And the kids love them—doing projects. And I'm not allowed to do them at all.

This mandated curriculum, which is painfully at odds with her developing sense of good teaching practice, has affected Sophia's desire to be a teacher. She spoke of a curriculum she had developed:

I had no ideas of all of this coming. When I started this year, I started this project, called "The Culture of Excellence." It's a form of cultural literacy where they had to pick a field of "school, community, classroom, or self," and had to find a way to improve it. And then they came up with their own projects. They write up their own plans, [and] came up with their own proposals. They keep their own field logs ... And the kids love it. They come in every day begging me, "Today do we get to do it?" And I'm like "No, today we get a scripted lesson."

They're writing a mini thesis now, but they don't have time to do this. They love it. They absolutely love it. We did literature circles last year, when we were reading the book Night *by Eli Wiesel, and oh they loved it. Loved it. Ate it up. Came in every day in the morning before class to make sure that literature circles were happening. They love real things. They hate test prep and scripted lessons, and I'm with them.*

Scripted lessons have had an enormous impact on Sophia's job satisfaction,

I feel like I came into teaching because I have something to offer. And I don't know where I am in my own classroom. I don't see myself there most of the time. And it's horrible. The things that I do that I love get wedged out—like this "Culture of Excellence" program is beautiful, but I have to scrape for time to do it. And it's not fair. The attention and effort that it should get should be twice as much as it is.

When I first started teaching, I worried about how to handle the students. But it's never been the students. My frustration is never the students. I love the students. I want to help the students. They're good. They're smart. They just are not where "they" want them to be. They are very connected to me. The students are never why I would not want to teach anymore. And that's the saddest thing you've ever heard. The reason you don't want to teach anymore is not the students. It has nothing to do with teaching. Isn't that absurd?

Besides Sophia's distress at being forced to teach in a way she finds contrary to her own understanding of good practice, she sees negative effects on her students' views about schooling,

I mean they have to pass the test. It's a reality. Is it particularly important or im-pressive to me? No. To everyone else? Yes. In my school my students under-stand that you don't get promoted if you get a "one" on your reading and math test. It doesn't matter what your grades are—at all. If you failed every single class and got "twos" on reading and math, you are promoted. And the kids know that they don't have to pass the class, and they don't have to go to sum-mer school, and they don't even have to pass the test. They just have to pass the test with a "two" at the end of summer school to be promoted. I don't know what to do. I don't feel that I'm doing well by my group of students right now. In the end, it's the kids who lose out. It's a pain in the butt for me, sure. But I don't want to leave teaching and know that Jose will never learn how to do this, that he'll be taking scripted lessons for the rest of his career. I feel so bad for them.

It is frankly saddening that highly creative, intelligent, and nurturing new teachers are placed in such situations. An education professor at-tempted to help Sophia resolve her problems with scripted lessons. The professor suggested she go to another school where administrators would be more supportive of the insights and creativity of its teachers. Sophia quickly pointed out, "You have to wonder why you should have the need to subvert it?" Of course, Sophia is right. As distressing as her story is, it re-flects a number of pervasive, troubling issues in schools today, especially those found in urban areas where teachers' judgments have been overrid-den by programs designed to help students but having the unintended con-sequence of obstructing the very qualities of teaching that most bright, creative, ambitious individuals are attracted to in the first place.

Responding to the Issues

1. Why does the situation of scripted lessons exist in our schools? What are the underlying assumptions about issues of teacher au-tonomy, trust, and skill implicit in such arrangements?
2. Sophia's situation can be interpreted as a form of mental servitude— strong words, for sure. Yet, are not all middle and high school teach-ers in some way forced to think, act, teach, and learn in ways that are counter to their gut feelings, what they know about teaching, or to their development? Isn't Sophia an extreme manifestation of the sit-uation in which all teachers find themselves? To what extent are most teachers required to teach against their instincts? Why doesn't teacher judgment count for more in schools today?
3. What advice would you give Sophia to solve what clearly has be-come an intolerable situation? How would you attempt to assist this highly talented and creative teacher to remain in the profession?

4. Scripted lessons and increased accountability are more prevalent in failing schools in poor and urban areas. Are students in such schools in need of more structured curriculum than those in suburban areas? What evidence exists for your point of view on this matter?

5. How could Sophia, along with other teachers, parents, and students, go about building values that would support different approaches to curriculum and skill improvement among students? In other words, are there alternative approaches to the problem of low literacy levels that might achieve better results in Sophia's school?

FINDING ROOM FOR DECISION MAKING

In affluent suburban districts, most students pass the high-stakes tests. Nevertheless, even in some suburban districts, parents' protests have erupted over the degree to which tests steer curriculum. Some New York City teachers and schools have also protested mandatory Regents tests, especially the small schools that were forced to give up graduation by portfolios and join in giving Regents exams to their students.

A prominent negative effect of testing, especially in urban areas, has been to increase the number of students dropping out of high school (Haney, 2000). In schools in urban areas, dropout rates are already quite high. Another concern that has recently received attention from educational researchers is the possibility that such forms of accountability might drive high-quality teachers out of schools with low test scores (Mintrop, 2003). This is precisely the point of Sophia's story.

We met Claire in an earlier chapter. Claire teaches at a small school in New York City. She wears many hats and works long hours teaching social studies and running a technology team of students. She is bright, hardworking, and dedicated. Claire has serious concerns about the effects of high-stakes testing on her students. One of the ways she is coping with the pressures of high-stakes testing is by negotiating a more rewarding and sound teaching practice that does not undermine her need to teach in an intellectual way nor undermine her students' need to pass the Regents tests. In other words, she has adopted an inquiry stance to teaching in the form of a research project she conducted at her school.

The whole movement [toward standardized testing] is very destructive of innovation ... I don't know what's going to happen politically with this whole push for standardized tests, but the more I'm teaching the more I become against high-stakes tests. I did this research project this year where there were teams of two people [student teacher and cooperating teacher] at each school doing the research. One of those teachers is leaving; she's in the middle school and her leaving is directly tied to the standardized tests. I just think that, because of the pressure that's been put on her, the ways she's had to change her curriculum, that she's thoroughly dissatisfied with what testing has done ... so I think that whatever happens politically is going to have a big impact.

In this case, we have a beginning teacher clearly anguished by the prospect of damaging effects of high-stakes testing on her students. Raising standards and focusing on accountability measures can have paradoxical results, as McNeil (2000) and others have shown. If one of the effects of these tests is to drive good teachers out of teaching or out of failing, urban schools, then how will standards ever be raised for all students?

Despite these pressures, new teachers like Claire eventually do begin to moderate the demands of testing and regain some autonomy in teaching. David speaks of "tweaking" the official curriculum:

Almost every time I was teaching, there was someone standing in the back of the room watching my teaching, because I had, you know, one of the "showcase rooms" and I was one of the teachers [about] whom the principal said, "Go to his room. He knows how to teach a lesson, and he's usually got the kids working." So they left me to do my thing. As for the new curriculum: I never [physically] received it! [Laughs.] Because we started hearing about Balanced Literacy and I said, "I was taught about it [in university courses]." As for scripted programs, I basically looked at it and changed it to base it on my own instincts. Because I thought that the kids should be reading every day and they should be writing every day, and the scripted programs didn't make that happen, so I made it happen. And they were comfortable with that. They saw results.... So I did a lot with music and dancing, and acting. Because I believe that they need to be out of their seats, and I got praised for things like teaching them to write musicals and plays and do drama ... but that wasn't in the scripted program.

Josephine, an English teacher, has reflected over her second year in teaching about what she considers good teaching and how this contrasts with mandated curricula driven by tests:

What I think should be going on in the English classroom does not involve daily test preparation programs. Is that what literacy is? You know, if I had to give a kid five things to take away from being in my class, it wouldn't be this ... I feel that [the mandated curriculum] is missing out on everything that makes me excited about reading and writing and everything you went into the profession for.

Despite the pressures, Josephine's reflection brought her the understanding that more space for autonomy could be found than what she first thought existed:

> You know, last year we did Romeo and Juliet, and I chose that play myself. We did an interpretation activity. I did things like that, and did they love it. Suddenly they were taking home Shakespeare. I only assigned one scene to interpret. Then, they ended up doing three other scenes. They elected to do it. They loved it. They presented it to another school. And that's learning to me. And the nonsense of going over "inference" for the thousandth time, and completing test packets for the district office, while this woman comes into my class to see that I've written the daily standard on the board. That seems so not the point of what we should be doing. I feel I come in with all of these wonderful fresh new ideas … but I don't get to do them that much.

Again and again, as these interviews suggest, new teachers came back to the tests. With a monotonous regularity, we would begin discussing another topic such as innovative approaches to teaching literacy, and they would return to the constraints imposed by testing. If the topic of testing is becoming oppressive at this stage of the book, then you get a sense of how new teachers are experiencing this phenomenon in their classrooms.

Given this reality, it might seem paradoxical to include a story here about one teacher's decision to spend more time on test preparation, even though her students were doing well with their scores. Yael, an immigrant who wanted to teach middle school so she could teach American history in a creative fashion, had an interesting perspective on how she would change her curricular focus in response to the new eighth-grade social studies test:

> The way they told us about the [new eighth-grade social studies] test was that it's to measure us as teachers … so if you have a lot of kids failing, they're going to take a closer look at you [as a teacher].… But it's actually a pretty easy test … it's my first year, and I didn't want to teach to a test. I wanted to do whatever I wanted to do … but every single thing I did was on [the test] … The whole last part of the test was posters of World War II and then an essay about World War II. One of my lessons [included] World War II posters all over the room, and [students] had to write observations and conclusions.… It was just the funniest thing that the same stuff I did ended up being on the test.

Clearly, Yael felt gratified by the symmetry between what she taught and what her students needed to know to succeed on the test. In the end, her students did very well. Interestingly, when asked whether she would just continue to do what she had done this year, her response suggested the insidious effect of testing, even on those whose students do well on tests. Listen to the ways in which she retreats from her first statement about the effects of testing on her curriculum as she develops her comments about testing:

> *After having seen it, I don't think it's going to touch my curriculum at all, just because I felt my own instinct about what I think is important was good enough and I really don't see myself really changing anything. I probably see myself focusing more time on some things that I was afraid to do before because of the pressures. But I'll probably focus more on testing skills, because that's really what I did to prepare them with it ... with the bottom classes, I did a lot of testing and strategies. That's all I did with them for the last 2 weeks: "What do you do when you get to this kind of passage? How do you work with a map?" And that's all. I didn't give tests all year. Instead of focusing on just 2 weeks of that, I would do mini-lessons on that throughout the year because it's good for them; the reality is that they have to take tests.*

Evaluation and assessment are critical issues in creating fairness and responsibility in a classroom. This section raises concerns about the scope for teacher decision making in schools dominated by scripted lessons and high-stakes testing pressures. As Karen Zumwalt lays out in more detail in the concluding chapter of this book, finding room for curricular decision making in such environments is essential to sustaining interest in a profession that intelligent people find attractive largely due to its intellectual aspects and knowledge demands. As the following questions get at, reflecting on what space exists in your teaching for curricular decision making is an important part of your teacher preparation process.

Responding to the Issues

1. How important is professional autonomy and decision making to you as a new teacher or future teacher? Do you feel you have an understanding of the testing and accountability issues "out there"? How might these issues influence your choice of which level of students to teach?
2. Beginning teachers sometimes find mandated teaching practices appealing because they give direction to the confusing realities in the complex world of teaching. Is that your perspective at this moment?
3. In one sense, mandated curricula are an attempt at a remedy for weak teaching found in a minority of certified teachers. As you have entered the teaching profession with high ideals and the desire to be a successful and effective teacher, to what extent do you think you will be able to "outperform" the minimum requirements and guidelines that will continue to be imposed on teachers?

4. What is your developing understanding of the curriculum and its assessment in your field? In what ways will your personal practice in these areas outperform what is demanded by mandated standardized practices in curriculum and assessment? What do you know about the qualification requirements for special education teachers and how these might impact your situation as a classroom teacher?

THE PARENT TRAP

A potentially stressful aspect of beginning teachers' lives is parental pressure. Over the last 10 years, many schools have made new efforts to involve parents and families in educational decision making. Parents now play new roles on school committees and involve themselves more than ever in decisions at the local level. Teachers encounter parents most commonly when they call with news about their children or in the context of formal parent–teacher nights. New teachers often ask how to deal with potentially difficult conversations with parents. Although some teachers call with good news about a child, the negative news conversation is still the most common form of interaction with parents.

In many schools today, efforts are being made to engage parents more regularly in the educational process of their children and to focus on how parents can help produce good results, rather than merely intercede when a problem occurs. These efforts take different forms depending on the culture of the region and expectations of teachers by school districts. Where teachers work with the children of immigrants, bringing parents into the picture can be particularly challenging. Susan, a teacher introduced at the beginning of the book, who teaches in Chinatown in New York City, mentions a number of factors complicating her interactions with parents:

> *Well, the parents don't speak English, any of them ... so it's impossible for them to call and yell at me, because I wouldn't understand what they were saying. But it's also hard because you want to contact a parent about any kind of issue at all, and you can't. You have to have a translator. And we had one woman who was sort of like a secretary; she did lots and lots of different things for the school ... and she spoke fluent Chinese. But you couldn't always expect that she would translate for you. You'd have to get an older sibling or someone like that to translate for you, but you would never trust that what they were saying was true, for sure ... And we had parent–teacher conferences. But this also shows the culture of the school. Parent–teacher conferences were on Sunday because those were the only times that the parents could make it in. And that, again, was a choice*

*among the teachers to give up their Sundays to do that: three or four times
a year, all day, Sunday.*

Neva is a Pakistani American woman, like Susan, with a master's degree and teacher certification in social studies from an elite private university. Neva worked in a very different environment from Susan's—an
affluent, almost exclusively White, setting. She complains about the role
of parents in her school in the following passage. She found the parents
in this community to be intrusive rather than appropriately supportive
of their children:

*The parents just drove me nuts. They really drove me nuts. They drove me
almost home on certain days. I felt, I can't stay here anymore. The lack of
diversity [in the school population] and the parents were both really difficult problems for me ... The parents were very demanding. They tried to
push you around and you really had to set up your limits in the beginning.
But then I'd get parent complaints on almost anything. Like, "Oh my
child—you didn't accept my child's late homework." "Well, no, because I
don't accept late homework." Or, "You told my child to be quiet, and my
child feels like you're picking on him." "Well, yes, because they're constantly talking in class" ... Or I'd call home and say, "It's been 3 weeks and
your child has not made up this test." We have a clear homework policy, or
makeup policy of 5 days, but you can never do that because if you give that
child a zero, you will have a parent calling and harassing you.... There's a
lot of grade grubbing, a lot of giving in to parent demands. If you fail a
child, a parent can call you and make you unfail the child. I never anticipated it. I had no idea how to deal with it, and it was really discouraging
and disheartening. I don't know how teachers do it. By the end, I really had
a phobia about getting messages, where I would walk to my box and if I
saw a message there, I would just freak.*

Sarah, another suburban teacher, acknowledges that parents could be
difficult in her district but she also notes that most of them are quite helpful:

*I was warned from the very beginning by my department head, especially
for first-year teachers, new teachers, for some parents, "They just smell
blood," he told me, to quote him. And they will go all out after you. Overall,
though, generally, most of the parents are very supportive when you call
them or send them progress reports, they're very concerned, very interested. There's not much blaming on the teacher, that kind of stuff. Most of
the parents are very concerned about their kids, how they're doing. They
want them to do well and support the teacher. Then you have those exceptions, where ... they'll call you every week, e-mail you every week: "What*

*work is he missing?" "Why didn't he do well on this test?" "Why is your test
so hard?" "Why do you ask those types of questions?" "Why aren't you preparing the kids for the Regents by now?" All kinds of things like that.*

In these situations, new teachers typically look to administrators for support. Sometimes, administrators will need to investigate a complaint, which
does not necessarily mean that they do not support a teacher, just that professional responsibility requires looking into the matter and appeasing the
parent to some degree. Undoubtedly, new teachers are vulnerable in ways
that veterans are not. Finding an ally in a good administrator is very helpful
in negotiating difficult situations.

Bernard, a White man, was teaching in an urban vocational high school
with roughly half the students from Puerto Rico or the Dominican Republic
and half who were African American. Here, he discusses a situation that
presents problems not easily solved:

> *So there I was teaching my class and in came this White kid. I got him settled
> in his seat and I thought, "Maybe this kid doesn't fit here?" and I thought
> about all the trouble I could get into—like being called a racist—because of
> this White kid, who I later learned was from the Czech Republic and who just
> arrived about a week ago. Well, I looked into the situation and a vocational
> school in Germany, Poland, or Eastern Europe and the like is completely dif-
> ferent than here. I mean, in Germany a vocational course of study means you
> work with Mercedes Benz, or something like that, and get a lifetime union
> job. There vocational education is as valued as an academic one. Our poor
> vocational school was decrepit, and falling apart, and I just thought that this
> might not be the right place for this brand new immigrant.*

Bernard explained that he was not a racist. He did not think that the
Czech student needed a better school than his Hispanic or African American students. He simply felt that it might be hard for the young man because he was so different from the other students. At the very least, he
thought he should talk to the parents. "After all," Bernard reported, "when
we get a kid who is gay, or being harassed, or needs special help, we talk with
him and sometimes we send him to a school which has a program or which is
safer than ours." Bernard continues:

> *And so I spoke with the AP [Assistant Principal] and the guidance counselor
> and some others [teachers] and it turned out that a teacher had a Czech girl-
> friend and could speak in that language. So, we brought the parents in and
> showed them the school and talked about our programs. The parents de-
> cided to keep the kid in the school, and the kid agreed.*

The story had a happy ending because the student did quite well in the vocational school, graduating with honors. Equally important, he made friends with students who were different from him and he shared his own culture with these urban kids. Although this is a unique case, Bernard's handling of the situation suggests some good tactics for dealing with students. It is part of every teacher's duty to maintain good communication with parents about not only their child's successes and failures, but also about how that child is fitting in with the educational environments of the classroom. Bernard faced a potentially difficult situation well by not going it alone, by involving other teachers, administrators, parents, and perhaps most important, the student in the process right from the outset.

Should any question exist about how to handle situations you encounter as a new teacher, you are advised to get advice from a supervisor before moving ahead with any action. This is particularly important if your response might be difficult or even controversial for students and parents. Learning what situations provoke such responses is a product of time and experience. In the meantime, do not be afraid to ask!

Responding to the Issues

1. Some parents view getting a child dressed and ready for school as parent involvement. Others check in about school every night around the dinner table. How has parent involvement been defined in your personal and professional experience? How did the quality and level of parental involvement assist or inhibit the students' learning?
2. What is the culture of parent–teacher relations in your school or a school you have observed? How intensive and extensive are the lines of communication between administration, parent, teacher, and child? What are the healthy aspects of the lines of communication, and where are the problems?
3. Urban teachers in poor communities frequently complain of a lack of parental involvement in their child's schooling. Suburban teachers and those from wealthy communities sometimes complain of hostile or difficult patterns of involvement with privileged, demanding, or threatening attitudes on the part of parents. In both poor and rich communities, what are some rules, or patterns of communication, that can assist proper lines of communication among administrators, parents, teachers, and students?
4. Can you separate a nagging parent from his or her child? In other words, how will you ensure that you will not visit the "sins" of the parents on their offspring? How will you be sure to treat students fairly even if their parents become a nuisance?

5. What are some essential rules, or do's and don'ts that can assist new teachers in conversing with parents in a nonjudgmental, positive, and nonthreatening way? How should teachers interact with parents on informal occasions, in phone conversations bringing bad or good news about the student, or in formal parent–teacher conference settings? Do schools have protocols concerning these matters?

Many students no longer come from the traditional family with father and mother living together. A student's parents might be divorced, separated, absent, single, lesbian, or gay; or the student might be living with a guardian or relative. More than one teacher has reported to us over the years that the child was living in a homeless shelter. How comfortable are you in dealing with students from nontraditional families or living situations? What are the regulations and guidelines in your school for discussing a student with someone who is not the birth parent or legal guardian? What preparation for dealing with drug and alcohol abuse is provided by your teacher education program?

REFERENCES

Callahan, R. (1962). *Education and the cult of efficiency*. Chicago: University of Chicago Press.

Haney, W. (2000). The Texas miracle in education. *Education Policy Analysis Archives, 8*(41). Retrieved May 10, 2003, from http://epaa.asu.edu/epaa/v8n42.html

Karier, C. J. (1986). *The individual, society and education. A history of American educational ideas* (2nd ed.). Chicago: University of Chicago Press.

Kliebard, H. M. (1995). *The struggle for the American curriculum: 1893–1958* (2nd ed.). New York: Routledge.

Kohn, A. (2001). *The case against standardized testing: Raising the scores, ruining the schools*. Portsmouth, NH: Heinemann.

McNeil, L. (2000). *Contradictions of reform: Educational costs of standardized testing*. New York: Routledge.

Mintrop, H. (2003, January 15). The limits of sanctions in low-performing schools: A study of Maryland and Kentucky schools on probation. *Education Policy Analysis Archives, 11*(3). Retrieved May 10, 2003, from http://epaa.asu.edu/epaa/v11n3.html

Sacks, P. (1999). *Standardized minds: The high price of America's testing culture and what we can do to change it*. Cambridge, MA: Perseus Books.

Chapter 9

The Global Village
of the Classroom

Diversity is an increasingly important fact of life in the United States, and the effects of a new mix of population—linguistically, culturally, religiously, and economically—quickly made themselves felt in the classroom. It is hard to overstate the importance of this issue. In the residential borough of New York City in which many of the new teachers profiled in this book received their teacher preparation, more than 50 different languages are spoken. Several schools are located in the immediate vicinity of this college, along with several large public housing projects, an Orthodox Jewish community, a wealthy enclave of expensive homes, and a Chinese neighborhood that is quickly becoming predominantly Korean, as well as areas settled decades ago by Irish, Italian, and German families.

Moving slightly further out from the college are other neighborhoods that are Jamaican, Hispanic, Indian, and Pakistani. Yet metropolitan areas are not the only places of diversity today. Across the country, immigrants are choosing to bypass big cities entirely and settle in smaller ones or in suburban enclaves such as Morris County, New Jersey—a distance of over 40 miles outside New York City—where a growing Central American population has developed over the last 10 years. Another example comes from Lewiston, Maine, which recognizes the following population groups among its residents: Armenian, Chinese, Franco-American, Greek, Hispanic, Irish, Lithuanian, Somali, and Togolese. Michigan and Wisconsin have become centers of immigration for the Hmong people, and southern states such as Tennessee, Virginia, and Georgia have become destinations for people from Fujian, a coastal province in southeastern China (Lee, 2003). California and Texas, as everyone knows, are states with a large population that came from Mexico and Central America originally. Less well known, perhaps, are the thousands of Vietnamese families that reside there today. The largest Muslim population found in any city in the United States is Detroit. The list goes on and on.

Difference comes in many forms: race, ethnicity, socioeconomic class, national origin, age, gender and sexuality, religion, and language group, to name just a few social markers by which people define themselves and others. In the United States today, few would deny that learning to get along with others is a key challenge for civic education. Attention to diversity should be an essential part of an educational system that prepares young people for citizenship in this country (Marri, 2003). As new teachers encounter this diversity, they often experience their own transformation as teachers and human beings ever more fully.

Although the teachers profiled in this book are not the first to teach in urban schools, in some senses they are urban pioneers. Given all the conditions we have described, urban schooling today is frontier turf. In entering this terrain and engaging with new communities, the new teacher changes: "She makes a new version of herself. She makes herself comprehensible to others in a new sphere. She is, if she engages fully in this process, transformed" (Cook-Sather, 2001, p. 18).

The typical candidate for teacher education in the United States and Canada is a White, Anglo-Saxon, lower- or middle-class female who has grown up in a suburban or rural area. She is monolingual in English, has traveled very little beyond a 100-mile radius of her home, and has attended a local college or university close to her home. She hopes to teach average, middle-class children in a community similar to the one in which she grew up (Wideen, Mayer-Smith, & Moon, 1998).

There is certainly nothing wrong with being White, middle class, female and suburban, but the fact remains that many teachers feel unprepared, uncomfortable, and afraid in taking on a classroom that includes adolescents with backgrounds very different from their own. The question remains, then, of how new teachers can create classrooms that celebrate diversity and enhance democracy, despite these conditions.

In becoming a new teacher, it is important for you to uncover the ways in which you define your own identity, and critically assess your own level of comfort in dealing with people with backgrounds different from your own. Numerous books, such as Delpit's (1995) *Other People's Children*, Tatum's (1997) *Why Are All the Black Kids Sitting Together in the Cafeteria?*, Banks' (2002) *An Introduction to Multicultural Education*, and Ladson-Billings' (1999) *The Dreamkeepers*, and many other useful books, can offer assistance in learning how to teach to the global village that will most likely be your classroom.

CROSSING CULTURAL DIVIDES

Time and time again, the new teachers we have spoken to have told us that they felt unprepared to deal with students from so many different backgrounds. Furthermore, they noted that neither their own backgrounds, nor their education courses, nor the policies and programs of the schools they were in thoroughly helped them develop a coherent approach to dealing with diverse students.

As Paley's (1979) book, *White Teacher*, recounts so well, many urban teachers today represent the only White face in a classroom. In almost all classrooms across the United States these days, sensitive issues arise around difference. Nancy is a teacher in a suburban New Jersey district who felt different from her students. In this case, the difference had to do with class, rather than race and religion. Nancy came from a solid middle-class background and her students were upper middle class. Cultural divides come in all sorts of forms, going well beyond the racial ones made famous by Paley's book.

In the last chapter, we met Neva who felt out of place as a Muslim teacher in a suburban school district where 95% of the students are Jewish. Often, she found herself put on the spot to explain the "Muslim" point of view about geopolitics. Part of her educational work was teaching students at this high school that because the cultural range of Muslims around the world is so vast, no one point of view exists on most matters. Today, religion can manifest itself as a particularly fractious form of diversity in schools; dissatisfaction by some parents with what is perceived as the "secular" culture of schools has resulted in unprecedented growth in home schooling in many communities. These are important issues in education today and will only grow more important over the coming decades.

Dorothy, a new teacher working in a school not far from her college of teacher education in New York City, got right to this point:

> My school is about 40% Indian-Pakistani, 20% Guyanan and West Indian, and 30% African American. There are very few Whites. It's a struggle to know how to reach out to all these groups, to engage with them.

Tyler, another student from this teacher education program, contrasts the school in New York City where he was beginning his career with his own upbringing in Iowa:

> There's an incredible diversity here compared to where I grew up in Iowa! So I'm just overwhelmed with the cultures—and the students have the most amazing pride for their nations. And they're so aware of their culture, and where they came from, and what they're all about, even though they might have been born in the United States. They seem to identify more closely with

their parents' countries or where they might have come from than anything in the United States … [I've got] mostly Dominican, Puerto Rican, Guyanese— those are the three main ethnicities.

We have met Steve before. Here, he notes that not only do his students differ from his own background, but also from each other:

It's really odd how the Jamaican and Haitian students are different from my African American students. Those from the islands are here to make it in this country. They don't have the history of oppression in this country that African Americans do. The immigrants value education; the African Americans tend to distrust the [educational] system.

In her book, *The Dreamkeepers*, Ladson-Billings (1997) recommended that one way for teachers to become knowledgeable about students is to be members of the communities where their students live. In this way, teachers develop a deep understanding and respect for their students' lives. Years ago, this was the norm. Today, this arrangement is probably less common. Issues related to diversity permeate schools today. Whether you work in an urban or suburban district, you will not be able to steer clear of the demands presented by diverse students and their families.

Although most new teachers struggle with aspects of diversity in their classrooms, most of them told us they do value diversity. New teachers told us that they were not racist, that they were not anti-immigrant, nor biased against any other group. Yet, the picture is more complex than these statements would suggest, in at least two significant ways.

First, it is sometimes the case that new teachers hear other teachers making a statement such as, "I teach math. I don't care if my students are Black, White, male, female, or 1 week here in this county. Math is math regardless of who you are, and fractions get divided the same way for everybody, regardless of background." The same argument is made by teachers whether they are teaching Shakespeare, physical education, or economics. What these teachers mean is that they have a neutral stance toward their students, or so they believe.

The best thing that can be said about this approach is that it might be a sincere attempt to level the playing field for students from diverse backgrounds. Of course the playing field is never level, and such neutrality might ignore the fact that affluent White students come to school much better prepared for traditional academics than people of color, poor, or non-English-speaking students.

The second point to be made here is that, protestations to the contrary, almost all teachers are biased. At first, this seems a harsh or unfair statement. After all no one reading this book would readily admit to being racist, sexist, anti-immigrant, or homophobic, we suspect. Yet, research suggests that all of us are culture-bearers tinged with ethnocentric responses to difference, even in our classrooms. We do not really need research to understand why this is so.

A little common sense lets us understand that humans tend to associate with people who are like them. An unfortunate corollary is that teachers tend to want to teach students who come from the same backgrounds as they do. Given what we know about teachers today and the American population, this poses a problem because classrooms of the future will be predominantly non-White and teachers for the foreseeable future will, in large proportion, be White.

One problem with the pretense of the "I don't see Black or White, just kids" posture is that it ignores differences that sometimes make a difference in the classroom. Research has shown, time and time again, that who students are, where they come from, and where they "live"—physically, mentally, ethically, and emotionally—matters a great deal. Females have a different experience of the classroom than males; urban African American males might hold values that are at odds with the schools they attend; and various immigrant groups hold different expectations for schooling.

The starting point for effective teaching and learning is always the student. Not only should teachers attempt to "teach the students you have, not the ones you want," but they must also acknowledge that students do not come to them as blank slates, but as human beings who live culturally rooted lives with a great deal of knowledge about certain things. Recognizing these cultural backgrounds and the "funds of knowledge" your students bring to the classroom will result in better learning experiences for all your students.

Responding to the Issues

1. Sometimes schools are characterized as "communities." Is this a realistic appraisal of the relationships to be found in a work environment? How do teachers respect their own privacy and space if they live in the communities in which they work?
2. Why do you think educational theorists believe pedagogy that is culturally relevant is more effective? Or should curriculum and pedagogy be "color blind"?
3. There is strong evidence that people associate with people like themselves—and any visit to a school cafeteria will attest to this. Visit the lunchroom or other public spaces of your school where people assemble. What does this tell you about the types of groups students identify with? Does the same go for the way teachers form

groups in the teacher's room? Can and should this human tendency be addressed in the classroom?

4. What particular training or education would assist new teachers in being prepared for dealing with diverse groups of students in the classroom?

5. As our communities have become more diverse, do schools play an even more critical role today than they did 100 years ago in doing citizenship education that promotes intergroup harmony?

DIVERSITY FINDS THE TEACHER

Sharon, a mother of two and new teacher in New York City, tells a story that shows something of the complex cultural interactions found in today's classrooms:

I had an interesting thing happen the other day. This very religious Spanish kid came up to me and said, "Ms. Johnson, Mitrazi drew a swastika on her arm! She might bomb us, or something!" And I went up to the student and there was this swastika on her arm. And then she shows me there's this swastika she's also drawing in her notebook. Now Mitrazi is not from this country and can not really read, and I mentioned to her mother that she should probably be in sixth grade [rather than seventh], and the mother said that would be fine with her. But the school decided to keep her in the seventh grade. And she's the quietest child in the class, and she has no friends. And I've tried to fix her up with some kids, and that didn't pan out, because no one really wanted to work with her. And I asked Mizzi, "Why did you draw that?" And she sort of shrugged her shoulders, and she said "It's a tattoo." Well, then I called her mother that night, and her mother didn't really seem to know what a swastika was ... So then I did some research, and I talked to the guidance counselor, and I came in and drew a happy face, a confederate flag, and a swastika on the board, and I asked the kids to respond to the different symbols. And I said, "Does anybody recognize the swastika as a Hindu symbol?" And Mizzi raised her hand. And it was interesting. And the other students said, "No, Ms. Johnson, it's bad, it's bad!" She told me it's the "god symbol," and when the arms are going in the other directions, it's a Native American symbol.

Obviously, this was a teachable moment for Sue who took the time to make telephone calls, do research, and check with colleagues about a potentially troublesome situation. She also taught a mini-lesson on symbols, their meanings, and their potential for misunderstanding. Yet, the fact remains that Mizzi remains isolated, and the school has been unresponsive to both the teacher's and the parents' wishes that the student be put in a lower grade because of language difficulties. This story also highlights the particularly difficult situation around religious differences in schools today.

None of this is necessarily new today, although the degree and complexity of the backgrounds students bring into classrooms has certainly changed. Marybeth tells two stories that happened to her in one day:

When we were talking about slavery, I learned that almost two thirds of one of my classes had [worked] in sugar cane fields. I mean, I mentioned the triangle trade—you know rum, molasses, slaves—and one kid told of leaving [the United States] to help his grandmother do work over vacation in the cane fields. Other kids talked about how your hands got all sliced up picking cane. And that was just fascinating. A lot of them are from the Caribbean.

And another time we were doing memoirs. I read this memoir about somebody from the Peace Corps who had watched this African man dig a fish pond with a shovel, and this boy said, "Oh I helped my father dig a hole like that." He's from Guyana.

Despite often feeling inadequate to the task of responding to such comments, most new teachers are greatly interested in their students' backgrounds. Don explains:

I take absolute advantage of their heritage. I try to connect those emotions that they have with their home country and connect it somehow with the lesson so they can remember those emotions and recollect the lesson. For instance, we were talking most recently about the Salem witch trials. So we were talking just abut the Puritan beliefs and how they wanted to create a society that was completely Puritan. But the students didn't understand a lot of this because they didn't understand the Puritan beliefs and why they wanted this isolation.

So I brought in information about how all of our cultures in our contemporary neighborhoods are isolated. And they began to understand from their own experience how societies, even in the mix of diversity, can be totally insular. They began to connect with that. And they see that in the city itself, by all the different neighboroods, [that this] backs up the need to be together and create a common culture ... Well, we talked about the idea of "utopia" and how everyone has a different understanding of what utopia is—so they can connect that idea with their pride from where they come from.

Of course, you have to have a lot of trust and rapport with the students so that they don't go running to their parents and the administration. This is not something that I would choose to do at the beginning of the year, but this was recently when that relationship was developed.

Cross-cultural issues do not involve just the students who come from outside the United States, of course. Problems exist across the many cultural divides within this country as well. Every school has a student culture or a range of student cultures. Teaching in a poor, urban neighborhood, across from public housing projects, Janine tells the story of a young man who was reluctant to write an autobiography because he, like many students, came from a single-parent family.

I learned this because he had done an autobiography, and he came to me and said, "You know, do I have to talk about my father?" And I said, "No, of course not, if you don't want to"—and a lot of them don't know their parents. And I told him you don't have to mention him at all, and he told me that his father was in jail and he didn't want everyone to know. And he's like [sighing,] "Okay, thanks." They need to feel like they can approach you and talk to you about things, about students who are bothering them, and problems at home.

Many divides characterize schools today: gender, race, class, religion, politics, and sexuality. Helping students negotiate these divides and creating classroom communities where all students can learn is an important, albeit difficult, responsibility of new teachers. Recognizing how each of you is situated with regard to these dimensions of difference is helpful in dealing with students who might be very differently situated from you.

Responding to the Issues

1. Everyone steps in various "circles" of ethnicity, language, class, religion, gender, sexual orientation, geography, and economics. What circles are you standing in at this moment? How have these circles defined who you are, as well as the substance and style of your teaching? Circles have circumferences, or boundaries, in other words. How have these defined you as well?
2. Are there any forms of diversity that make you uncomfortable or even angry? Are there types of people, or groups of people, that have negative connotations for you? What past experiences led you to these thoughts and feelings? How can you overcome them so that you create a classroom where all types of diversity are welcomed?
3. Pick an ethnic, religious, cultural, or linguistic group, such as "Irish American." List all the information you know about the group. Did

you find that you had rich knowledge? Or, did you find that your knowledge base was stereotypical and limited? What further information do you need to know about this group to interact with its members? Where would you go to get this information? Is it possible to go beyond information to experience? How could you facilitate face-to-face encounters that would expand your knowledge base about different groups?

4. What formal preparation in diversity has your teacher preparation provided? Has this been helpful in shaping a sense of good practice?

CLASS IN THE CLASSROOM

Diversity issues include differences in socioeconomic class as well as race, religion, ethnicity, and the like. In our experience, Americans sometimes seem to be even less comfortable talking about class than they are about race and sexuality. As Leo, a White male teacher from a wealthy suburb, pointed out about his students from a Puerto Rican and Dominican urban neighborhood, "My students know a great deal about living in Washington Heights. I have to admit, I know nothing about living in Washington Heights. I have no clue about my students' lives. As one of my students told me, 'If you can't even tell me the difference between a green plantain and a yellow one, how are you going to teach anything else?' "

Claire had a similar problem, which she recounts here:

I think I dealt with a lot of issues this year just being from such a different background than so many students, being middle class, White, not growing up in the city, and growing up in the Midwest. So I think that was something I worked through all year. Once I had kids in my classes, I think they were fine. But because our school is so small, we are always dealing with all the kids, not just ones we have in class. And I always could sense that my early interactions with kids were based on the fact that I was so different from them and until I sort of earned their trust or their respect that was definitely an issue. Another issue we have as a school is that we're not as diverse as they even were last year. We only have 12 to 14 teachers, depending on how you count. Last year, we lost two teachers of color, which is a big number when you're only talking about 12 people. Both of them were replaced with two White teachers. So, not intentionally, it's not like that was an intentional decision, but that's something I think we're all very aware of is that our staff is becoming much more, we're just not as diverse as they even were last year and as we wish that we were.

Norbert, a teacher in a private school that contains students who are from families at the upper end of the income ladder, relates a story of a troubled young man he knew there:

Well, this student, Joe, was always getting into trouble. I couldn't do anything with him, and no other teacher could. He would not do anything, he was insolent. His father was a lawyer and his mother was some kind of [medical] specialist. Most weekends they went away to their second home and left him there [home]—with a charge card and a sports car. Can you imagine how much trouble a kid can get into with a charge card and a sports car on the weekend! No wonder he won't listen to his teachers.

Each person's worldview, if you will, is shaped by his or her own background. Some backgrounds open students up to the world of differences; others close down this process. In Nancy's global studies class, these issues are tackled head on:

In comparative world studies, one of the main things we really try to teach [are] these concepts of ethnocentrism and cultural relativism and seeing things from someone else's perspective. And that's really difficult with some of these kids. I mean I don't think some of them have made it out of their hometown! They come to the mall and that's as far as they've gotten. And you start talking about the way things are in the rest of the world and some of them literally don't believe you. They honestly can't conceive that people live that way, how can you sleep on the ground because "Everyone sleeps on a bed," you know. These are their attitudes. But by the second part of the class on human rights and global security, they commented that they were really more interested in what happens in the world and concerned about these issues and able to see things from a different perspective. And that is great. If they really don't remember the information part, that's not important to me. Maybe it should be, but just changing the way they think about these issues was definitely encouraging.

Some new teachers in affluent suburbs report a certain disdain for teachers found among parents and students in the schools. These teachers report that some of these families view schooling and teachers as commodities that can be manipulated by those with power and money in the community. Teachers clearly do not make large salaries. In days gone by, in many communities, teachers were respected professionals, the solid citizens of their communities. This was certainly the case in many African American communities of the early 20th century. It is still the case in many immigrant communities.

The status differences between teachers and the students in a wealthy district might tinge their relationships with parents and the community at large. This is not always the case and it is not helpful to generalize this point too broadly. In any case, class differences between students in your classrooms and between you and your students and their parents might be an issue you confront when you begin teaching. Most likely, you will need to consider this issue when you begin your own job search.

Responding to the Issues

1. The term *cultural capital* refers to the fact that certain people have more access to the dominant culture (money, power, social standing) and thus an advantage over those without similar skills and knowledge. Consider your own cultural capital. How will this affect your teaching of students who come from backgrounds with more, or less, cultural capital?
2. Think about a time you have experienced feeling different, "other," marginalized, or silenced in school. Can you tell a story about when some aspect of your self was respected, celebrated, ignored, or disrespected? What does this tell you about such experiences in the classroom?

SORTING STUDENTS IN MODERN HIGH SCHOOLS

In this section, we turn our attention to the ways in which students get divided up in modern high schools. Some of this, but not all, relates to what is known as *tracking*, or ability grouping. We discuss tracking within the context of a chapter on the "global village of the classroom" because prominent research (Oakes, 1985) on this subject has revealed the degree to which tracking in schools correlates with racial, ethnic, and language factors. However, this is certainly not the only way in which students get sorted in high school. Language differences as well as gender and sexuality can also shape school choice today.

Intellectual and even behavioral differences—perceived or real—play a large role in sorting students into classes and in classroom dynamics generally. In the past, many school districts had academic, business, and vocational tracks for students. Until quite recently, many also had special, alternative schools for disruptive or "delinquent" students. Various laws over the latter half of the last century have reflected the apparent desire on the part of educators in this country to make schools more homogeneous in their composition. Recently, however, movements away from setting schools up with homogeneous classes have gained momentum as part of a detracking movement. This movement has demonstrated the degree to which race and class have correlated with placement in low tracks and alternative programs. Some educators feel this violates equitable approaches to schooling all students (Oakes, 1985). Nevertheless, other educators feel that some degree of tracking students produces better education for all.

A religion major as an undergraduate, Martin had taken a job in a highly regarded large high school with more than 4,000 students. In shaping a student body of such size, the school district required that students apply to the school. Each grade level at the school would be comprised of a mix of academic abilities. Such attempts at managed enrollment are often found in urban districts. Such recruitment strategies bring a more heterogeneous mix of students from varied backgrounds into a school. In Martin's school, the structural goal was that 16% of students were to be above grade level, 16% percent below grade level, and 68% on grade level in reading and writing. Ten percent were to be classified as needing special education services. In terms of the selection process, 50% of the students were chosen by the school and 50% by the educational district. In the end, about one in three students was accepted at the school.

The heterogeneity of this student mix posed challenges for Martin. Overall, however, Martin was having a positive experience because his school gave him ample support in figuring out how to meet the needs of the range of skills in his classes:

> I knew that [the school] would have high standards and tell you exactly how to meet them ... The observation reports you get are really helpful. I became much better from the beginning to the end [of the year]. When I look at myself from the fourth cycle, compared to the first cycle, it was like night and day. I was observed nine times during the year. Six is the number required, and most of us were observed seven, eight, nine times. Once I got to know students in the school and sort of know who they were and what interests they had, and what worked and what didn't for the school, then you get into a kind of groove. Then, it was great because you have a rapport with them, even though you only have them for one cycle, which is 8 weeks long or 9 weeks long, you sort of get to know them and you can adapt the lessons to what you know is going to succeed. Once I had been able to do that, it was great. They could have debates, and discussions, [in which] they could respond to each other, simulations, you know it was fantastic. The last cycle—there were two classes I would have paid to keep.

Martin's enthusiasm for his work was evident here, as well as his sense of growth as a teacher over the course of his first year. Getting accustomed to being observed is an important dimension of the untenured teacher's life.

Nine observations a year, as we have seen, rankles some new teachers and conveys to them a lack of trust. It did not seem to bother Martin that much. In fact, the frequency might have been helpful in acclimating him to the experience of having an observer in his classroom.

He makes a point of saying, as well, that the observational reports were helpful to his practice. It might sometimes be difficult to accomplish, but if new teachers can view the supervision process as an opportunity for reflective consideration of their practice, as an opportunity to grow and develop through feedback offered by a seasoned professional, then this evaluative process can be truly useful. Along with his own growth and development, Martin's interview also reflects his understanding of the built-in cycles of change in the school year for students, especially ninth-grade students new to the school's rhythms, rituals, and expectations for performance:

> *I would come in each day [of the first cycle] and I felt I had a decent lesson plan [but] it's the hardest cycle to teach ... because you have kids that are new to the school, who aren't used to the ways of the school. They don't have the skills that they need, so a lot of what you're doing is building skills that they need to succeed in the next cycle ... They're just out of junior high school, like, "Why don't you just tell me the answers? Why don't you just write notes on the board and we'll copy them down, we'll memorize them, you give us a test." And, plus, the discipline, I wasn't as good at classroom management. But that's the way it was first cycle ... The third cycle was kind of disappointing. I had three below grade level classes, one self-contained [special education] class, and one inclusion [special education with grade level] class. That cycle was kind of frustrating just because the students aren't interested, or they don't have the skills to understand it. The classes are a mix of kids who just aren't good students, who have had terrible preparation, who come from a poor background. A lot of them are very smart, but are recent immigrants and don't know the language well enough and so they can't communicate what they knew, or they can't understand. They do have the skill to understand it in their native language, but not in English.*

Next, we hear from Jay. At the heart of Jay's statement is concern for the constant difficulty teachers face in covering the curriculum for classes with a wide range of academic abilities. Jay also conveys his uncertainties related to labeling students as "special education" students:

> *I really can't tell the difference between my classroom, and a self-contained [special education] classroom, except that they have four, five, or six students, and I have close to 30 that might show up at any day. Forgetting about the two mainstreamed [special education] kids, I have two or three who are on level [of reading and writing] pretty good. I can see them going to a good*

college. The rest need some real help, and about five can't write, are functionally illiterate. The thing is I don't know what to do. And the administration isn't helping. They don't know what to do. So I plug along. The good students get it, the rest struggle and a few are always totally lost.

A homeless, depressed, abused, or bullied student might not be stupid at all, but he or she might be labeled so by the educational system. Many issues surround the situation of special education in schools today—far too numerous to engage here. Because all teachers face "inclusion" classes today with a broad mix of students, with or without the help of an aide in the classroom, this is obviously an area in which new teachers might need abundant additional help.

Responding to the Issues

1. How diverse, in terms of ability level, are the schools in which you will do your student teaching? How diverse in terms of culture and language background are the communities in which these schools are located? Make a list of the different "diversities" you find in local schools.

2. What kinds of experiences of heterogeneous and homogeneous classrooms have you had as a student? As a teacher? Have you developed an educational philosophy that addresses this issue? How much will this issue be an important consideration in your job search?

3. To what do you attribute intellectual differences: innate ability, background, physical health, home culture, local community, or other factors? Do you believe that some students will always be able to perform better on tests, or in your classroom, or in school in general? If so, why?

4. What strategies will you use to try to bring about success for all students? What do you know or believe about teaching ESL students? About students with learning disabilities? What supports exist for teachers that provide help in dealing with inclusion of these types of students?

5. Do you believe in mixing students of perceived different abilities in your classroom? Or would you rather teach a group that has been labeled in some form as advanced, average, or remedial? On what evidence do you base your opinion about grouping students homogeneously or heterogeneously, or for preferring one type of student over others?

GIRL (AND BOY) TALK

The educational research community has also paid attention to gender differences in schools over the last 30 years (e.g., Koch & Irby, 2002; Sadker & Sadker, 1993). According to one study (Brown, 1999) few teacher education programs provide systematic attention to issues of gender. Increasingly, in places where gender does get attention, teacher educators acknowledge that talking about gender is not just talking about girls. In fact, a spate of books have appeared on the market in recent years registering concerns about the growth and development of boys in our culture (Garbarino, 2000; Medzian, 2002).

Nancy was pleased that she had an opportunity to get to know her female students outside of class:

I think that certain students would pick me out. They'd come to me after school, mostly girls—all the girls. You know, the quieter girls, usually. One of my main concerns [in teaching] is dealing with these young women in my classes. It's the kind of school where the girls are getting nose jobs. They go to tanning salons, and they go with their mothers to get their noses done, and that's kind of the culture. So, one of my goals was to get them to think about alternative ways of looking at themselves. So, I did a lot of surveys in my classes, asking the kids, "How has your thinking changed? What was interesting to you [in this class]?" I really wanted to know what their thinking processes were. In the class that I co-taught with the English teacher, we had them for the whole year, which was great, because we really could see some of the girls changing. Girls who would not even talk in class came out of their shells, almost became leaders in the class. And even as they still go shopping and do whatever it is that they do, but they understand that they could do something on their own, and be important in the classroom.

Another teacher, Katrina, who worked in a suburban middle school north of New York City, brought women's history into her teaching through use of what has been called the *hidden curriculum* of the classroom. This term refers to all the messages schools send students outside the formal curriculum. A graduate of a prestigious woman's college, Katrina believed strongly in the need to infuse gender into her teaching. She decorated classroom space with quotes from Martin Luther King to Sandra Day O'Connor and pictures from around the world. She was shocked at how little women's history her students knew:

One day, I walked in with a women's history poster and somebody said, "What's that?" It's basically a list from January 1st to December 31st, with dif-

ferent women in history and when they were born. So all the students were coming up and seeing when they were born, and one student turned to me and he said, "You know, you have all this stuff about women's history." And I said, "Why do you say that?" He says, "Well, you have Rosie the Riveter over there, and you've got a picture of this one over here, and quotes from women over there, and another picture of this one over here. It's all over!" So, I said, "Really, well, let's go around the room and count how many images of men in history there are." And certainly, the men were far outnumbered. So I said, "Scott, do you feel bad?" He's like, "Yeah." So I said, "Now you know how women have felt for the last 2,000 years!" And he said very reflectively, "Oh."

Like other idealistic novices schooled to teach with an eye toward social justice (Darling-Hammond, French, & Garcia-Lopez, 2002), these young teachers are interested in more than simply transmitting a knowledge base to their students. Their hopes lie in using education as a means of empowerment for their students, many of whom have been disadvantaged by race, class, ethnicity, and gender from gaining the same foothold in the middle class that these beginning teachers claim as a birthright.

Many teacher educators also believe that teachers who are role models for their students can be important. While an undergraduate, Clarissa, a young Black woman, had a teaching experience in a school with many impoverished African American students. Her students were amazed at how much education she already had as a 20-year-old woman. They were also amazed that she did not have children yet and that she wanted to make teaching her career. Here, Clarissa talks about the differences between her own background and that of her students. In particular, she comments about the gender "pull" of the girls in her classroom:

I wasn't raised in an urban environment and so I have my own expectations of what a 12-year-old girl should be doing, and what she should be thinking about and everything. So that definitely, definitely concerned me.... With my girls, there was just a natural connection. There were some girls that I was able to just have, at least in my mind, useful conversations about being a strong female. I would tell some of my girls all the time that there's so much going on in their minds that's so important and they need to be able to cultivate that as well as their fashion sense and stuff.... Over the year, I learned a tremendous amount about myself, as a person, as a human being. And I learned a lot about the way that I work with people, and I interact with people, because the students saw all my true colors this year, and I saw theirs. And I learned so much about my own strength and weaknesses. I just gained a lot about my expectations about education and about society, about racism, about classism. Just all those things kind of impressed [themselves] upon me this year.

Nancy was concerned about the limiting and even destructive gender messages the girls in her affluent suburban school were getting. Her female students seemed more concerned with enhancing their appearance than with participating at a high level in their classes. She hoped that by including women's history in her curriculum she could provide alternative models of female achievement. She also tackled issues of sexuality in her classroom:

I kind of expected to have some resistance from male students about how much I talked about women. And I don't think that they really even figured out that, you know, I only talk to them about women sometimes, and we did a lot with women, especially in U.S. history. In comparative world studies, I did a whole unit on women's rights. But I think that the kids were really receptive to that. And the girls who were really interested in it kept it going. I had some interesting comments from some of the male students when we did women's rights, such as, "This is really terrible. I would never want that to happen to my mother or my sister." And you know, that they could even identify with that was good. Dealing with issues of sexuality was a lot harder. They recently established a club in our school. It's called PULSE, but I can't remember what it stands for. Basically, it's a support group for gay and lesbian students. And you know they make it very clear that you don't have to be gay or lesbian to attend meetings. It's about support. Some of the kids are very open about it and will talk about it and really kind of carry [the topic of sexuality] for you. We actually had a student who did a presentation on the gay rights movement and she was just fabulous. It was probably a half an hour or 40 minutes long when it only had to be 15, but she brought in movie clips and she had so much information and was so matter-of-fact about it that I think the kids just had to accept what she was saying.

Responding to the Issues

1. What will be your attitude toward teaching female students? What approaches, if any, will you use to deal with the unique concerns of female students? How will you allow them a voice in the classroom and not silence their concerns?
2. Do you believe that there are differences in learning styles, abilities, or interests between male and female students? If so, can you put a name on these differences? Or, are you inclined to treat both sexes as the same and equal in your class?
3. What do you think of the strategy of surveying students in your classroom to find out what is on their mind? How will you offer students a class evaluation instrument for expressing their opinion about how you have done as their teacher?

4. Why do you think many teachers are afraid of gender, sexual orientation, or ethnic issues in their classrooms? What are the dangers of opening up such a conversation? How can you create a classroom that embraces differences, allows different voices, and is safe for all students? What would be the parameters, boundaries, or rules that you would set up so that students can be safe revealing themselves and their feelings?

MOVING TOWARD A CURRICULUM OF PEACE

Violence surfaced repeatedly as a theme in the narratives of these new teachers. Even those working in so-called "good" schools expressed distress about the forms of verbal or physical violence they witnessed there: inappropriate or threatening language, fighting, and various forms of aggression and harassment, both against other students and against teachers. We start out by exploring the general problem of violence in schools. Then, we take up the more particular problem of violence as it impacts one highly vulnerable group—lesbian, gay, bisexual, and transgendered (LGBT) students.

Only recently has violence in schooling become such an enormous concern for teachers, school administrators, researchers, students, and the public. This is because the levels of violence have escalated so markedly, as evidenced by the tragedy at Columbine, among other places. However, the antibias and antiviolence conversations have been inadequate so far, and schools continue to be places of verbal and physical violence. Furthermore, violence, once thought of as an urban phenomenon, has become a prominent issue in suburban and rural schools as well, inside and outside of class, in team sports and in various hazing rituals. Where guidelines have been established by school districts, these are often selectively enforced, leaving students and teachers feeling helpless in the face of verbal and physical violence.

Almost all the new teachers interviewed over the last few years reported that violence was a concern for their students and their colleagues. They were surprised by the levels and extent of violence in their schools and they felt unprepared, either personally, or through their education courses, to deal with the culture of violence they encountered. The following excerpts from a variety of new teachers speak for themselves about the problems of violence in schools today:

- *Our school is very overcrowded and we have so many physical incidents and fights that the union actually came in the first week and declared that the school's enrollment be "capped" and that more security be brought in.*

- *We've had three teachers quit in the past 2 weeks because they were assaulted—and one of them was sexually assaulted, and the other two—men—were physically assaulted. All of the APs [assistant principals] were out at one time or another because they were assaulted, or knocked down. One of them had a broken ankle. It's every challenge you can imagine.*
- *Even though things are going very well, I've never been in an environment where the kids are so hostile. They're extremely violent. And no matter how good the administration is in setting rules and regulation, fights happen constantly, and it comes to the point where some of the teachers are afraid of what is going to happen.*
- *I even had a fight in my classroom. We can't do anything about it. We're not allowed to touch the kids. We can't get in the middle of the kids ... All we can do is go down the list of phone numbers and try to call someone So it's a matter of just hoping and praying that the kids respect you enough to listen to you and stop when you say "Stop."*
- *This fight was actually two best friends and one comment came out, "I can beat you up." And the other one's, like "No, you can't." And then all of a sudden the anger builds and they just went at it in class. It's stupid stuff. I mean most of it is based on rumors, and I have a lot of kids that are always getting into fights because of "She said this," and "He said that," and "Blah, blah, blah." And when you try to back up that fighting is not the answer, they go, "Well, my dad tells me that if someone says something bad about you, you need to fight them." And so we have these parents telling them at home something different than the school is trying to tell them. It's been hard in that respect and you just have to hope that the students respect you enough when you tell them to stop fighting.*
- *When I hear the "N" word used by African American students, I don't know how to respond. Don't they have the right to use it?*
- *Oh my God, I've heard stories about other schools, and their administration. They don't report incidents—incidents like sexual harassment—because they don't want to have the school look bad. They ignore violence in the classroom.*

Violence is an acute problem for gay and lesbian students (Jennings, 2003). The following slur is one that too commonly echoes around the hallways of schools these days. The "response" by teachers is also all too common:

I must hear the word "faggot" 20 times a day in my school, but I don't know what to do. If I challenge the student, they only launch into some homophobic tirade. The teachers—and I—ignore these outbursts.

One in 10 students is gay or lesbian (Besner & Spungin, 1995). Issues of sexual orientation and of socioeconomic class tend to be among the taboo topics teachers avoid addressing overtly in classrooms. Recently New York City expanded a small alternative school with a few gay and lesbian students into a comprehensive high school for gay and lesbian students, the Harvey Milk School. A public debate in the media ensued about whether such an institution was beneficial, or even healthy in "segregating" LGBT students. Opinions about the school seemed independent of political persuasion or sexual orientation. On the opening day of the new school, sadly enough, students were greeted with protestors who came from other states, carrying posters saying, "God Hates Fags" and "Queers Deserve to Die."

Research about LGBT students indicates that these marginalized students are particularly at risk for violence from other students (Besner & Spungin, 1995). Unfortunately, teachers and administrators might actually make the situation worse through neglect (Crocco, 2002). The LGBT community's experience of verbal harassment and physical violence is a symptom of a larger problem of violence in school communities particularly— but not only—in the United States. Human Rights Watch (HRW; www.hrw.org), the American Civil Liberties Union (ACLU; www.aclu.org), and the National Gay and Lesbian Task Force (NGLTF; www.ngltf.org), among other groups, all report the harassment and violence LGBT students face across all school districts.

A number of recent studies reveal disturbing statistics. A typical high school student hears antigay slurs as often as 25 times a day. When these slurs occur, only 3% of faculty members speak out against their use. Nineteen percent of gay and lesbian students have also suffered physical attacks in school, and 13% skip school at least once a month due to problems with harassment Twenty-six percent drop out of school altogether due to these problems (Stein, 1999). A study of 14 cities reveals that 80% of gay, lesbian, and bisexual youth have experienced verbal abuse, 44% have had threats made against them, 33% report having objects thrown at them; and 30% report being chased (Checkley, 2001).

Schools, unfortunately, seem to be breeding grounds for sexism (American Association of University Women, 1993, 1999) and homophobia. In many places, "the lack of involvement by administrators and faculty made the homophobia and abuse more pervasive and intense" (Crocco, 2002, p. 225). Many teachers seem uncomfortable working with LGBT students in their classrooms and with LGBT teachers in their schools. Overall, there seems to be a level of hostility and a negative atmosphere in most schools toward LGBT students (Schwartz, 1994).

Schools can be violent places for all students, and there are signs of increased violence against teachers as well. Given the situation of violence in all sorts of schools today, both urban and suburban, rich and poor, is it not part of teachers' jobs to create a culture of democracy, negotiation, conflict resolution, and antibias education—a peace curriculum, if you will—as an essential part of our practice?

Responding to the Issues

1. Write down or share a story where you suffered verbal or physical harassment in school or outside of school. What happened? What was the cause for it? What resources did you have? What did you do about it? What could you have done about it? What support did you receive? If you are uncomfortable sharing a personal story, record or share one you have witnessed.

2. Go online to the ACLU, HRW, and NGLTF sites listed previously. What concerns does the material there highlight about school violence? How does the increasing information on school violence compare with your experiences of school violence at the schools you have attended?

3. What, if any, responsibility do teachers have to create a curriculum of peace? Is this only the responsibility of the administration, deans, counselors, or those trained in conflict mediation? Or, do teachers have a responsibility to teach antiviolence and antibias as a regular part of their instruction? Have you ever been in a school where peace was actively promoted?

4. Over the next week, visit your school's hallways, cafeterias, libraries, and classrooms. Make a list of the types of violence you encounter or see. Is your school peaceful, cooperative, and a healthy place? Or, is it a place that contains a culture of violence?

5. Ask teachers about their views of LGBT youth, or Asian, African American, or any other minority group. What do they tell you about these groups? Do teachers tell you what is politically correct, or do they reveal their true feelings about different groups of students? Locate a known trouble maker in your school. See if you can interview that person. Why does he or she act out? How does he or she feel about the school?

6. What will you do the next time you hear "faggot" or another slur in your school? What antiviolence measures are in place in local schools? What are the disciplinary policies for handling infractions of school rules? How effective, do you feel, are these procedures for dealing with troublesome students? Is there a conflict resolution program in place?

REFERENCES

American Association of University Women. (1999). *Gender gaps: Where schools still fail our children*. New York: Marlowe.

American Association of University Women. (1993). *Hostile hallways: The AAUW survey on sexual harassment in America's schools*. Washington, DC: Author.

Banks, J. (2002). *An introduction to multicultural education*. Boston: Allyn & Bacon.

Besner, H. F., & Spungin, C. I. (1995). *Gay and lesbian students: Understanding their needs*. Washington, DC: Taylor & Francis.

Brown, S. (1999). *Gender in teacher education*. Unpublished report prepared for the Marymount Institute for the Education of Women and Girls, Tarrytown, NY.

Checkley, K. (2001). A persistent intolerance. *ASCD's Education Update, 43*(2), 5.

Cook-Sather, A. (2001). Translating themselves. Becoming a teacher through text and talk. In C. M. Clark (Ed.), *Talking shop* (pp. 16–39). New York. Teachers College Press.

Crocco, M. S. (2002). Homophobic hallways: Is anyone listening? *Theory and Research in Social Education, 30*(1), 217–233.

Darling-Hammond, L., French, J., & Garcia-Lopez, S. P. (2002). *Learning to teach for social justice*. New York: Teachers College Press.

Delpit, L. (1995). *Other people's children: Cultural conflict in the classroom*. New York: New Press.

Garbarino, J. (2000). *Lost boys: Why our sons turn violent and how we can save them*. New York: Anchor Books.

Jennings, K. (2003). Harassed students need schools' support. *AACTE Briefs, 24*(12), 1, 4.

Koch, J., & Irby, B. (2002). *Defining and redefining gender equity in education*. Greenwich, CT: Information Age.

Ladson-Billings, G. (1997). *The dreamkeepers: Successful teachers of African American children*. San Francisco: Jossey-Bass.

Lee, J. (2003, January 4). For immigrant family, no easy journeys. *The New York Times*, B1.

Marri, A. (2003). Multicultural democracy: Towards a better democracy. *Intercultural Education, 14*(3), 263–277.

Medzian, M. (2002). *Boys will be boys: Breaking the link between masculinity and violence*. New York: Lantern Books.

Oakes, J. (1985). *Keeping track: How schools structure inequality*. New Haven, CT: Yale University Press.

Paley, V. (1979). *White teacher*. Cambridge, MA: Harvard University Press.

Sadker, M., & Sadker, D. (1993). *Failing at fairness: How American schools cheat girls*. New York: Charles Scribner.

Schwartz, W. (1994). Improving the school experience for gay, lesbian, and bisexual students. *Eric Digest, 101*. (Eric Clearinghouse for Urban Education, No. EDO-UD-94-7)

Stein, N. (1999). *Classrooms and courtrooms: Facing sexual harassment in K-12 schools*. Wellesley, MA: Center for Research on Women.

Tatum, B. (1997). *"Why are all the Black kids sitting together in the cafeteria?" and other conversations about the development of racial identity*. New York: Basic Books.

Wideen, M., Mayer-Smith, J., & Moon, B. (1998, Summer). A critical analysis of the research on learning to teach: Making the case for an ecological perspective on inquiry. *Review of Educational Research, 68*(2), 130–178.

Going Further
and Checking It Out

Americans are very fond of the heroic individual myth: the strong man—or woman—who makes a difference. In this sense, many new teachers conceive of themselves as pioneers. They consciously "take on" a profession that they know will be complex, difficult, and generally unrewarded by society, either with money or status. Their stories are often heroic, although they generally go unheralded by the public. Teachers do make a difference in many people's lives, for good or ill. Rarely, however, do they gain fame or fortune because of their positive impact.

In crediting teachers with such possibilities for making a difference, it would be a mistake to see their actions as solo performances. Although teaching can be isolating, communities and relationships are central to the work. Connecting to those communities—of students, colleagues, parents, and administrators—is the hallmark of successful teacher work. However, it takes time and effort to learn to get along, just as it does to learn subject matter and pedagogical strategies.

One of the chief challenges in today's school environments is the diversity found there. As stimulating as diversity can be, negotiating difference can be a tricky business. The new teachers to whom we talked seem well aware of the difficulties difference can bring into their classrooms. These new teachers recognize that their vocational choice involves addressing difference, building relationships, working with other novices and veterans who are their own parents' ages, and communicating effectively with students' parents.

For the most part, the new teachers with whom we talked recognized the problems of racism, sexism, and homophobia permeating their school environments. They are struggling with how to treat all students fairly, questioning whether this means treating everyone the same or acknowledging difference openly. They know that abuse, harassment, and physical violence can make schools unsafe for themselves and their students.

191

Teachers sometimes think that when they close the door, they are on their own. As they mature in their work, they come to understand how many factors influence their classrooms. Some of these are external factors, such as state and federal mandates, school culture, administrative oversight, and the cultures of students and communities. Other influences complicating classroom practice are internal ones. New teachers' own school and life experiences, the nature of their educational preparation program, the views they bring into the classroom about different students, and the values and goals they have on entering the profession all strongly influence and channel what they believe possible in classrooms.

Take time to reflect on the factors shaping contemporary classroom practice in your community. Use the following exercises to explore these factors systematically so that you enter your own classroom with a comprehensive understanding of the factors influencing what is going on there.

1. Analyze the racial and gender demographic profile of your community's schools: elementary, middle, and high schools. Look at both the teachers and the administrators. Note where the men are found—in which subject areas and at which levels? Compare the racial profile of these schools to that of your community. What conclusions can you draw from this analysis?

2. Review the publications of Gloria Ladson-Billings. Ladson-Billings is known for her work in culturally relevant pedagogy. Take a look at her books, and see what she believes essential to crossing the divide of race in teaching today.

3. In groups, distribute from three to five pieces of paper to each participant. On each slip of paper write one particular "circle" in which you are standing. "Circles" can be anything: Democrat, musician, student teacher, unemployed, White, sports fiend, anything. Do not put your name on the paper. Put all the slips of paper in a hat, shake them up, and have every person retrieve at random five slips of paper. Going around the room, listen carefully to all the self-defined circles people are standing in. What does this say about the cultural capital in this group? How empowered or disempowered is it as a group? How can teachers bring the rich and varied understandings of self in community into the classroom?

4. The chapters in Part III have focused on many issues that affect what goes on in the classroom, both for teachers and for learners: how lessons are created, where lessons are created, and for whom lessons are created. Write a personal statement of your philosophy on lessons, accountability, or students. What are your emerging ideas about setting up the best classroom you can? What do you think will hinder you from fulfilling your expectations? Is there any

way you can keep your personal philosophy and allow it to develop so that you maintain a personal best practice in teaching—one that you see as gratifying for yourself and beneficial for your students?

5. Choosing lesson creation, accountability, or diversity as themes, go out and ask teachers in your school—or a school you are observing—what they think and how they feel about these themes. Once you have interviewed several teachers, can you see any themes or strands in their thoughts and feelings about these topics? Is there any consensus at your school on these matters? Furthermore, to what extent do you agree with what you have found out about your colleagues or the teachers you have talked to?

6. Repeat #5 with students or a group of students—you can ask individually or as a group. What are the students' concerns and beliefs? How do they differ from teachers?

7. This book has advocated an approach to contemporary teaching that calls for a high level of teacher autonomy so that new teachers can grow into their teaching practice, one that is critical of high-stakes testing and increased accountability, and one that celebrates diversity. Do you agree with these positions? Why or why not?

Part IV

NEW TEACHERS
AS DECISION MAKERS

INTRODUCTION

One of the central problems in discussing schooling is that in an era of universal, public education in this country, schools are so familiar that teachers, students, parents, and the general public all take the apparatus of education for granted. What education is, and should be, is simply an expected and common part of our culture. By spending thousands of hours in school, almost everyone becomes an "expert" on education. Tests, 42-minute class periods, bells, homework, hall passes, Carnegie units, and all the minutiae of education are simply considered the natural elements of education. It is hard to imagine that schooling could be any different from what it is today and what it has been in all the collective biographies of America's many citizens. Whether in casual conversation or heated political debate, individuals who would never speak authoritatively about how best to remove an appendix, prepare taxes, or install a new electrical grid in their neighborhoods rarely hesitate to register an opinion about how education should be handled.

Generally, what people want for education, and especially for their children, sounds very much like the schooling with which they are most familiar, that is, the education of their own youth, often nostalgically recaptured through blurred memories of childhood and adolescence. Across racial, economic, and geographical boundaries, many Americans share traditional conceptions of what schools should be—welcoming, neighborhood places where children spend time in cafeterias, playgrounds, and classrooms, sitting in rows with a teacher guiding learning from the front of the room.

195

Whether people have attended public, private, or parochial schools, most Americans have had a similar experience of school, leading to a collective conception of the very ordinariness of schooling. Schools just seem an organic part of contemporary American culture. Indeed, given the long history of public education in this country, this reality is hardly surprising.

Nevertheless, the tradition of public education in this country masks the fact that schools are created cultures, grounded in communal needs within the context of a democracy and social, political, and economic decisions about how best to address those needs. Like other cultural institutions such as the armed forces, hospitals, prisons, the Internal Revenue Service, or shopping malls, to name a few, schools are culturally created institutions. One of the key tasks of embarking on a career in teaching is recognizing the press of these factors on school climate in a particular regional or local area. Although many teacher education textbooks address these topics in an effort to provide teacher education students with an understanding of the historic and philosophical foundations of teaching, few examine the ways in which such features impinge on the daily life of new teachers, especially as lived within specific geographic contexts.

Part IV examines a number of factors shaping the political, social, and financial picture of schooling in the United States, as experienced by new teachers. The vignettes offered here show that the struggles those new teachers face are closely linked to very specific historical, legal, and cultural forces. New teachers might not consider the impact of school financing, public law, or suburbanization on the daily lessons they deliver in math, English, or social studies; however, when one listens to the voices of new teachers, the role these large social forces play seems never far behind what happens, or what seems possible, when teachers enter their schools.

Chapter 10

The Past Is Never Past

Cultural rituals, categorization of certain types of students into stock characters with attendant expectations for their roles in school and possibilities in life, and rules and regulations for making schools efficient institutions all form part of the social and cultural fabric of schooling in this country. Were we to compare schooling in the United States with that in other countries, the portrait that emerged would undoubtedly reveal some highly idiosyncratic features demonstrating the imprint of culture and historical tradition on the institution of public schooling in this country. We have already discussed how schools became like factories early in the 20th century. In this chapter, we look at other public policies related to schooling, many of them also possessing deep historical roots.

We have already explored the degree to which teaching is an autobiographical act. In this chapter, we explore the ways in which teaching is also a political, social, and historical activity that intersects with autobiography to influence new teachers' attitudes and choices. Public policies of all sorts have enormous impact on the life of the teacher. Schools have many features in common, but over the last 50 years the imprint of demographic changes in this country related to the manner in which schools get funded have set up two major types of schools: the city school and the suburban school.

It is important to point out that not all city schools are troubled schools and not all suburban schools are excellent schools. Still, public perception often stereotypes these two categories in this fashion. More and more Americans have fled cities in the last 50 years, as we discuss in more detail later. They have moved out of cities for reasons that often have a great deal to do with race. Cities became places where more people of color resided. Suburbs tended to be White, although this has changed somewhat in the last

197

20 years. As we have noted, a high percentage of all teachers are White. This fact often plays a large role in their decisions about where to teach.

In a nutshell, many teachers choose to teach in schools that feel familiar to them, where they feel comfortable. If they are reflective about their choice, they recognize the consequences of a whole host of public policies on this decision-making process. Nevertheless, this does not necessarily change their viewpoint about where they want to teach. Let us examine some of the historical forces at work in the national context that have had an enormous impact on schooling today. These are key, hidden factors rarely acknowledged in the everyday rhythms of schooling, yet important nonetheless.

JUDICIAL AND LEGISLATIVE INFLUENCES ON SCHOOLING

Consider, for a moment, two examples of major judicial and legislative influences on schools today. These two examples demonstrate vividly the enormous impact of the legal sector on schooling. Moreover, such examples could be multiplied countless times, as numerous controversial issues related to education such as school prayer, search and seizure of students' lockers, censorship of school newspapers, teachers' rights to organize into unions and to strike, and students' and teachers' rights to speak out during times of war have all found their way into the legal and judicial decision-making process during recent years. Here, we highlight only two celebrated examples that suggest the many ways in which law and politics have shaped schooling over the last half-century.

In 1954, the Supreme Court rendered their decision in what many people believe to be the most important case of the 20th century, *Brown v. Board of Education*. Up until this time, all schools in the southern part of the United States and many in the northern half were legally segregated by race. In this decision, the Supreme Court justices ordered the desegregation of schools "with all deliberate speed." This decision created complex results over subsequent decades, results that have literally changed the face of schooling in the United States (Lagemann & Miller, 1996; Patterson, 2001). This decision, itself related to a set of social, political, and even geopolitical factors (Dudziak, 2000), worked in tandem with other issues around race in shaping modern America dramatically (Lemann, 1991; Massey & Denton, 1993; Sugrue, 1996).

Two landmark pieces of federal legislation, Public Law 94-142 (1975) and the Individuals with Disabilities Education Act (IDEA, 1991), have both transformed special education in this country in highly significant ways. Up until 1975, the courts and lawmakers had promulgated a number of principles with regards to providing nondiscriminatory and appropriate education for disabled students. The principles enunciated through these measures included the notion that handicapped or disabled students have a fundamental right to special services and education in the "least restrictive environment." This provision requires that students be shielded from inappropriate segregation from their peers. Today we talk about the "inclusion" of students with disabilities in "mainstream" schools and classrooms. IDEA extended the provisions of Public Law 94-142 to ensure that students with autism or severe brain injuries be included in the provision for adequate education for all disabled learners between the ages of 3 and 21. Schools today struggle to fulfill the financial and personnel requirements associated with fully meeting the demands mandated by these pieces of legislation.

With passage of the No Child Left Behind Act, the federal government entered into schooling at an unprecedented level. Definitions of highly qualified teachers, the impact of high-stakes testing, and the press of literacy and numeracy goals are all shaping schools in dramatic ways these days. Together with the two legal interventions presented here, it is clear that large historical and cultural forces affect schooling in this country. All these forces have played a large role in defining change in public education over the last 50 years.

Moreover, in a democracy, it is to be expected that legislation such as these laws would prompt schools to respond to changes in the nature of society. In addition, other factors, such as population shifts, immigration patterns workforce factors, and methods of funding schools, have also contributed to shaping schooling in this country, as we would expect.

Studying the history of education is often a required component of teacher education programs. If you have not studied this history, we would encourage you to delve into the books cited here on your own. This history provides important insights about the major social and legal changes that help explain why schools look and act like they do today. A brief review of some of this history will build on what has been presented in preceding chapters and provide a context for the issues discussed in this chapter.

The history of urban education is an important part of the overall history of education in this country. Schools took their modern form during the early 20th century with modifications throughout the century (Cremin, 1964; Tyack, 1974). Urbanization, immigration, and industrialization, as we have seen, all shaped the means and ends of public education during the early part of the century. City councils, centralized school administrations, and educational leaders introduced kindergarten, junior high school, and high school. These innovations had tangible consequences for teachers, just as more recent historical developments shape contemporary teaching (Rousmaniere, 1997).

Between the two World Wars, an increasingly large number of young people stayed in school through Grade 12, and the high school experience became the norm for the majority of Americans (Angus & Mirel, 1999; Franklin, 2000; Kliebard, 1995). Despite uniformities, high school experiences have varied to some degree by geographic location based on how critical decisions regarding school financing, districting, and administration were made. Large schools in cities, with some exceptions, came to be seen as dysfunctional institutions in the second half of the 20th century with considerable student alienation, high dropout rates, gangs, and violence. In short, these places were "blackboard jungles," to borrow the name of the 1955 movie about one all-male urban high school.

Even though certain scholars label today's era a postmodern and postindustrial age, as we have seen, an industrial approach still pervades school organization and administration. Big high schools remain the norm, despite the progress of the small school movement in many big cities. The "grammar of schooling" (Tyack & Cuban, 1995) introduced during the early 20th century continues to ground many people's expectations concerning what schools should look like, be, and do. Versions of school that deviate from these expectations are highly suspect for many citizens of this country (Tyack & Cuban, 1995). Attempts at reforms have rarely succeeded in changing the fundamental structures of schooling. Such reforms have often led, according to some scholars, to unintended and negative consequences, even when they have been widely heralded efforts at improving schooling (Ravitch, 2000).

A key demographic shift that has occurred in this country over the last 50 years has been suburbanization. The movement out of cities has had enormous consequences for schooling. Cities have changed from thriving centers of industrial production at the beginning of the 20th century to struggling, if not poor and depressed, downtown centers surrounded by increasingly wealthy suburbs at the end of that century. Cities were once key places for manufacturing and finance. The jobs available in cities were a mix of blue-collar and white-collar occupations. This changed as the nation's economy shifted many of its manufacturing functions out of cities, to rural parts of the South and West, and increasingly overseas.

During the first part of the 20th century, many people who owned businesses or worked downtown actually lived in cities rather than just commuting in and out of them as they do today. The culture of cities, characterized by residential, often ethnically delimited neighborhoods, with men and women who lived in some proximity to their workplaces, meant that individuals with different incomes and racial and ethnic backgrounds lived closer to one another than they often do today.

Over the course of the 20th century, the transportation patterns linking neighborhoods in cities together and cities to outlying areas changed. The growth in mass transportation provided commuters with a number of new options for going from home to work and back again—first, by train, subway and trolley, but later, by bus and car as well. As the transportation options improved and commuting time was reduced, many members of the so-called middle classes, such as clerks in banks, workers in government and the legal professions, as well as managerial staff at factories, large downtown department stores, and small family-owned businesses, moved out of cities into the suburbs that were, at first, simply incorporated into city boundaries.

With the advent of the automobile and a national highway system after World War II, suburbs began an expansion and reshaping of metropolitan areas that very much continues today (Cohen, 2003; Jackson, 1985) . Around most big cities today are suburbs that have grown into sprawling and decentralized regions with malls, town centers, and housing developments dotting the landscape. The arteries dissecting these regions are the roads and highways connecting inhabitants to their jobs. Most urban downtown areas have been abandoned by a considerable proportion of their populations over the last 30 years, providing, at most, places for weekday work life and weekend entertainment. The connections between these regions are negotiated in large measure by the automobile. In the last 20 years, suburbs that are close to major cities have also become the homes of the poor, immigrants, and minorities as well as the middle and upper middle classes who first moved there (Teaford, 1979).

By the 1980s and 1990s, certain cities witnessed the return of young urban professionals who reclaimed some of these previously abandoned areas. Newly gentrified neighborhoods now stand in many places in contrast to large areas of poor neighborhoods. Many within this young professional class choose to send their children to private schools or to select magnet public schools, which do not share the problems of understaffed and underfunded neighborhood public schools. However, access to expensive private schools is, of course, limited largely by income and there are not enough high-quality magnet schools to meet demand in most cities.

Increasingly around the globe, citizens live in "metropolitan societies," comprised of such residential arrangements (Jones, 1990; Kasinitz, 1995). More and more, these metropolitan cities reflect the hallmarks of the processes of globalization and internationalization of their populations (Sassen, 2001). By the 1990s almost half the population lived in the suburbs of a metropolitan area and roughly 30% lived in the center city (Putnam, 2001). By 1996 only 20% of the population of America lived outside such metropolitan areas.

The patterns of wealth distribution that have followed demographic shifts over the last 50 years have produced high degrees of variability in funding of schools across this country, both among states and within states. Contrary to almost every other leading postindustrial nation, schools in the United States are funded locally, not nationally. Because school budgets rely largely on local funds, when cities became impoverished, so too did their schools (Glickstein, 1995).

American schools exist politically and financially in more than 16,000 districts that bear the primary responsibility for funding their own schools (Verstegen, 2002). Federal support, although growing, is still not the key component of school funding in the United States as it is in other counties. Moreover, school funding in the United States depends primarily on property taxes, which vary dramatically by location. Schools in different districts, even in the same state, could have dramatic differences in spending levels. Property values shift markedly by neighborhood, city, and region of country.

Long-standing practices by realtors, mortgage lenders, and White homeowners have contributed to patterns of residential segregation by neighborhood. Differences in property values, a by-product of residential segregation, strongly influence available funding for education. As housing has remained highly segregated throughout the United States, the racial composition and economic character of schools have reflected these patterns, despite the stated intent of *Brown v. Board of Education* back in 1954 to integrate the nation's schools.

THE TYRANNY OF THE LOCAL

Many citizens from outside the United States are surprised to learn that it has no national system of education. Schools are local, yet they have a national mission: that of preparing citizens for a democracy. In keeping with this philosophy, most Americans believe that people should be educated to the best of their abilities, and that merit, not birth, should determine one's role in society. Education is seen by many Americans as the great equalizer in our democracy, providing each student with an opportunity to achieve in life, regardless of his or her race, religion, or class.

Most Americans also believe that opportunities exist in American society for social mobility and that education provides an important means to social advancement (Johnson & Immerwahr, 1994). However, it is important to keep in mind that endorsing equality of opportunity is not the same as believing in equality of outcome. Citizens of this country, generally speaking, seem more comfortable with the former than the latter. In either case, schools have a long tradition of being seen as the conduits of opportunity for individuals from poorer origins on to a better life.

Many new teachers bring an oversimplified view of these distinctions to their teacher preparation process. They equate suburban schools with good schools and urban schools with troubled schools. Although it is true that schools in wealthy districts tend to have better buildings, more certified teachers, and greater funding, excellent schools and successful and happy teachers can be found in urban areas. Meier's (1995) experiment in the 1980s in creating a successful small school in East Harlem, as well as numerous schools associated in cities with the Coalition of Essential Schools and other urban school reform movements reflect urban exemplars of excellence.

Finding teachers who will be open to understanding the complexities of teaching, schooling, and learning environments in cities today will demand recruiting teachers from all backgrounds, many of whom will have grown up outside cities, might not themselves be from minority cultures, nor have gone to school with students different from themselves. Knowing something about the historic and social conditions that have shaped schooling in this country will empower all new teachers to do their job in a more critical and informed fashion.

WHERE SHOULD I TEACH?

Teachers tend to want to teach in "good schools," a term often used as a proxy phrase for White, suburban schools. With the teacher shortage, teacher education students and new teachers have many options concerning the schools in which they choose to teach. Attracting highly qualified teachers to urban schools and retaining them in those schools, as we have seen, poses an enormous challenge (Crocco, 2002; Ingersoll, 1996; Ingersoll & Rossi, 1995). However, providing and retaining good teachers in both urban and suburban schools across this country is essential to providing an equitable education for all American children.

Although schools and districts vary widely in financial support and academic culture in the United States today, a profound agreement among teachers, parents, and students, across all racial, social, and economic boundaries, exists concerning what schools should look like (Johnson, Farkas, & Bers, 1997). However, in many poor neighborhoods and districts, making this image a reality is very difficult due to severe financial limitations.

Students, parents, and teachers in this country all believe that schooling is the gateway to economic success, financial stability, and social advancement. Even students who are failing school and show no signs of academic success readily state their lofty aspirations for a career. They register their understanding that education is the key to the American dream, even though for many children mired in poverty, education long ago lost its meaning as a ticket out of their bleak situations (Kozol, 1992).

Despite many Americans' faith in the value of education, historians find a profoundly anti-intellectual grain running through the culture (Hofstadter, 1963). Put another way, Americans tend to value learning for what it does, rather than what it is. Worse yet, for many Americans, especially those who live in communities where education is not valued, learning is a chore, painful, and unconnected to short-term, tangible rewards.

It is sad to say that many American students at the middle and secondary school levels do not exhibit any aesthetic, emotional, or intellectual engagement with poetry, history, science, or any school subject (Johnson et al., 1997). Many teachers admit that their students find schooling difficult, boring, and even meaningless. Unfortunately, even more teachers find this fact unsurprising, a reaction that reveals the cultural assumptions Americans bring to their understanding of the place of intellectual work in youth development.

Given high levels of teacher turnover in many schools today, prospective teachers might actually have choices about where they will teach. They need to negotiate these choices informed by an understanding of how social, cultural, political, and economic factors shape those choices. Moreover, they need to be mindful of how new forms of teacher and student accountability, especially high-stakes tests, can interact with the force of history to shape these options and the work cultures of schools in particular ways.

The narrative variety found in this chapter reflects the range of teaching conditions found within the New York metropolitan area. Some teachers work in a milieu driven by high-stakes testing, due to the drive to assure that their schools are deemed "excellent" or by the threat of being labeled "failing schools." Others teach in schools that do not attract strict scrutiny by administrators, politicians, and state regulating bodies because of their long-time tradition of "excellence." Several voices here come from those who have made a deliberate choice to teach in "failing schools." Frequently, the new teachers reveal in their narratives that they only have a limited knowledge of the ways in which the schools in which they work have been shaped by historical and economic factors. In fact, teachers in so-called "good high schools" (Lightfoot, 1983), or in suburban districts might "awfulize"—to borrow a word from a new teacher—the situation in urban schools. Basically, these suburban teachers are "othering" schools in places that, by definition, they find alien to their own experiences of schooling.

Overall, it is important to acknowledge that most schools in this country struggle with issues around funding, have some degree of difficulty in attracting and retaining excellent teachers, and are working with an increasingly diverse student body—with issues of differences including a range of abilities and disabilities, family situations, scholastic aptitude, language background, class, race, gender, and love of learning. The ways in which we define, assess, and respond to these diverse aspects of the human condition are shaped as much by history and culture as they are by finances and individual choice. New teachers will make many choices as they navigate the bureaucratic maze of their profession in the beginning of their teaching careers. Being fully armed with knowledge of the many factors playing a role in shaping those choices is essential to making an informed decision consonant with their own values, desires, and goals in teaching.

Appreciating the Possibilities of Urban Teaching

Many small urban schools have been shaped with an ethos of commitment to school, students, and community. In earlier chapters, we met Claire, who sought out work in a small urban school for just this reason. Charlie is another teacher who has made a choice to teach in the city. He is pleased with his decision and intends to stay the course. Note that he finds urban teaching provides independence for teachers, a view at odds with what we have heard from numerous other urban teachers, but one that must be acknowledged:

> As I find myself teaching global studies for the third time, there is a sense of pride. Yes, pride. Pride in having the opportunity to teach this subject in the city. Students in the city tend to be extremely diverse, as opposed to some schools in the suburbs. There are more obstacles when it comes to teaching in the city, but the system is so big that it allows a teacher to be independent.
>
> Teaching in a suburban school would not provide this opportunity since the students would assume that history be taught only in a perspective that ensures they [White people] are seen in a positive manner. It would be an insult to mention that there were other great cultural events taking place, say, for example, in Africa or even in the Americas at the same time.
>
> The fact that there are many obstacles—such as a lack of vital resources—can surely make it difficult to stay in the school. However, one learns to adjust and overcome these problems. At the moment, in my school we have five overhead projectors—however, not one has a working light bulb. It turns out that I have to spend money out of my own pocket. When I was done using the projector, I would take the light bulb and save it.
>
> It is our assumption that when teaching in the suburbs, there is no limit on resources that a teacher may need. Within a week, a teacher is able to obtain what they desire.... Hence there is a sense of pride to teaching in the city since I am able to accomplish most of my goals with students, especially considering the conditions that I find myself [in].

Charlie's comments suggest the point made earlier that urban teachers tend to think the grass grows greener in the suburbs. It might, or it might not. Clearly, he has found that his school provides space for him to work independently, something he clearly values.

Desperately Seeking Support

One new teacher making career decisions based on assumptions about urban and suburban schools is Joseph. Joseph is a talented young musician who entered into teaching through the NYCTF Program, which has provided him with financial aid and certification in teaching music in urban schools. Added to his love of music was his concern, which began as an undergraduate, about issues of social justice. He entered teaching with the desire to use his profession to offer pleasure and opportunity to young urban kids through the medium of music.

Because of a variety of autobiographical attachments to the city, Joseph chose to teach in a city school. Given his background, he thought he knew what he could expect. Joseph started his program well aware of the fact that city schools tend to be underfunded, and that some schools in poor urban neighborhoods are hard to staff or labeled as "failing schools." Joseph also knew that music and art had seen their funding cut repeatedly in city schools due to budget crises over the last 20 years.

Because of the special program in which Joseph received certification, he has made a 2-year commitment to city schools. At the time of the interview, he had decided that as soon as he fulfilled this commitment, he was leaving city schools.

Joseph complains that he gets little support from his school district and school administration for his work as an arts teacher. He does not have his own classroom and carries a large teaching load of students. Joseph has become disaffected with teaching. A large part of the problem is the fact that he is teaching a "special subject" and must divide his time between two schools to have a full-time job.

Issues of isolation and the intergenerational mix of teachers are present in many schools, whatever their geographic location. Still, Joseph seems to believe that by moving from an urban to a suburban school, he might be able to salvage his brief career as a music and art teacher:

> I feel nonexistent in my two schools. In one school, I'm teaching in a corridor, and my administration has done nothing to improve the situation. Likewise, my fellow teachers are also unhelpful. Most don't even know my name. I feel intrusive if I try to converse with them. They are very "clicky." Worse, they are all quite different from me. I'm young and male. They are mostly middle-aged and female. The music curriculum is terrible. There isn't one. And there's no money to improve it. It takes funds to form a successful band, but as it is, I see my students once a week, their instruments are often in disrepair, and they have difficulty retaining lessons on a weekly basis. My well-being is at stake. I'm exhausted and stressed out, angered and hurt at the end of every day. The children have no reinforcement at home, and teachers have no administrative discipline to rely on when our in-class methods fail. I cannot find happiness when I work in a failing system.

> I was placed at my school 1 day before the opening day. I only have one other fellow to share my thoughts with. The program completely neglects the arts,

which is still unacceptable. I'm in two elementary schools, Kingside and Coleman, [each in a different poor neighborhood]. Were I to continue teaching, I would leave them both. Kingside has no space. I'm currently playing [music] in a stairwell and cafeteria storage room. In both schools, I know of no teacher who likes or respects the district office. The office seems to seek not to improve teaching, but to simply cover its tail by finding inadequacies with the teachers. Of course, they ignore me because they don't appear to care about the music program. I suppose their neglect is positive, since it seems anything they touch just gets worse.... Support has been nil. My needs [such as] legitimate space to teach and the proper allocation of funds to maintain a band program have not been met. I have more instruments that do not work than those that do.

I practiced music since early childhood, and specialized in trumpet and composition in college. Then, I expanded my interests to social justice. I thought teaching would be a great venue to improve society. I had family in the city, so I thought teaching there would be ideal. I figured I could enact change in a very concrete way by teaching young minds. But the change has been minimal, and I believe I can improve the world better elsewhere. This job is exceptionally difficult. I'm not cut out for it.

Joseph's words are distressing. Perhaps he is right and he simply is not "cut out" for teaching. Even if this is the case, Joseph has registered some of the same concerns that other new teachers express about teaching in poor, urban schools. It is important to be realistic about what urban teaching demands and how these problems might reflect societal disregard for providing an adequate education for the poorest children in this country.

Joseph has unfortunately not been able to access a support network that would assist his survival in this urban school. Perhaps Joseph simply has not tried hard enough to find one or to establish such a support network himself. He obviously feels something of an outsider in his school—by dint of age and gender. Were he to move to a suburban school and remain in teaching, he would be well advised to find one school in which he could work full-time and with a generational mix that he found compatible with his needs.

Joseph might not be able to handle this school, in which case the problem could lie with him. Or, perhaps, the school is really as dysfunctional as Joseph claims. A mythology exists in teaching that strong individuals learn to teach in troubled settings by dint of some interior force, personal expertise, or will. This approach obscures the fact that some schools are simply unhealthy places, with a school culture that is disconnected to any shared vision among teachers, administrators, students, and local community. Whether Joseph's school could be characterized as unhealthy is unclear at this point. Perhaps the greatest irony in this story is that Joseph is part of a teacher preparation program designed as a "quick fix" to the problems of urban schooling that sends resourceful, talented individuals, with minimal educational preparation, to teach in troubled schools. It seems clear that Joseph's 2-year commitment will be the end of his time in urban schools—at least for now.

Rich and Poor Schools

A slightly different case can be found in the following story. Richard did not plan to teach in the city but he gradually came to recognize that this option would provide him with a unique experience, despite the obstacles and lack of funding he knew he would encounter there:

> The job in [a poor neighborhood] gave me my first real taste of the teaching experience. I was not a certified teacher, but it did not matter; most of the other teachers were not certified either. I learned much about a real inner-city school and its problems. The school I work at has a shortage of everything—books, supplies, security, etc. The school I work at is so short on everything that teachers must chip in from their own pockets to keep the copy machine going in our department. This year, half of the teachers are new and not many plan on staying. I have spoken with many, and they tell me the same problems: the students have no discipline, poor reading skills, poor motivation, and no respect for the teachers or the school. Most of them tell me they plan to seek work in the suburbs. Those teachers who have previously worked at my school and now work in the suburbs tell me stories of their problems. However, when I ask "Do they compare to my school?" they laugh and say that their schools are not that bad.

Richard has also made some judgments about his students' family backgrounds that contrast with his image of students from suburban schools:

> I imagine students who come from complete families as opposed to where I work. [At] the school that I work at, the students mostly come from broken homes. The students at my school have fewer chances at opportunities than suburban school students. Researchers say the teacher is the most important element in the classroom. However, it is my opinion that it is the family that makes a difference. Two parents are needed to give their attention to the student, not one. Two parents can give more money to the child. These inner-city students suffer not only from having one parent, but also from the fact the youth culture puts pressure on youth to spend tremendous amounts of money on things they do not need. Many of my students work at an age I never worked, and I teach 10th graders.

If I could do it over, perhaps I might [do] like my mentor and start off in the wealthier suburbs. However, this is the path I chose. I have learned to deal with inner-city students. I try all the time to encourage learning of the past. I try to connect it to their lives. It is difficult, especially knowing the statistics show many will never go to college. Thus, for many students in my school they are happy when they just barely pass.

I am often asked whether I will stay. I always say, "Yes." I am fairly well known. The small number of students I have inspired to learn global history on their own puts a smile on my face. I recently learned from a Jamaican girl, formerly my student, that she will soon go to Germany and experience history outside of New York City. What really burns me is the fact there are schools in the same state I live in that receive more money for supplies and a greater salary for the staff only because they are located outside of New York City.

Like Richard, Stephanie has had positive reactions to her urban teaching experience. In fact, she believes that urban teaching holds unanticipated benefits. She believes that urban schools provide a stronger sense of community, a freedom in teaching, and a deeper relationship with students than can be found elsewhere. Despite the problems that exist in these schools, which have been well documented in these pages, urban schools offer many teachers something they cannot find in other school settings. As we have attempted to argue throughout this book, new pressures on urban schools as a result of high-stakes testing have placed new burdens on those teaching there. This is not an argument for avoiding teaching in these schools, but a call for thinking creatively about how best to address new realities, through reflection, collegial support, and hard work.

Stephanie's comments reveal her own set of preconceptions about the world of suburban schools. Perhaps this suggests that the grass might not always be greener in other settings, just that an individual's own situation might not allow for an accurate assessment of other people's realities.

First, I am needed here. I don't think I would be needed so much in a wealthy school. Here, the teachers pull together—it's not a 7-hour job only. And then, I know the pressures in the suburbs, how you have to be politically correct, go to the right church, say the right things, because some of your students are the children of the mayor or the school board. Here, none of that matters; it's just you and the students.

Hitting Bottom

Greg is a new teacher whose story is an extreme case of the problems found in some urban schools. Greg is leaving his urban school for the suburbs, despite feeling conflicted about his decision. In the wealthiest country in the world, it should be a national scandal that such a school exists.

There was nothing wrong with the kids, nothing like that. It was the school, the administration, the other teachers. The place was a zoo. There were broken windows, the men's room had 3 inches of water on the floor, and the stairwells smelled like piss because they were used as urinals. No one cared. No wonder the kids didn't care. New teachers called the school "The Sewer" and we were called the "Sewer Rats." The place was filthy. They even still heated it by coal! You never saw the principal, and the teachers were just about as downhearted a group as you ever saw. My classroom was a revolving door. I got five new kids in my class the day before Christmas recess! Kids disappeared from my rosters never to return. Kids were gone for 3 weeks at a time and reappeared. I even worked in the attendance office, calling [the students'] homes. I could never get through. I taught kids who lived with three different relatives on different nights of the week. More than one of my students was homeless. I am sorry for leaving and for letting the students down. They needed someone who cared, but I just don't have it in me—not with no support from anyone and a school that did not care.

This long section has presented a variety of stories related to the question of "Where should I teach?" Choosing the first job thoughtfully is one of the most crucial decisions you will make in your career. As we have seen in this chapter and in early ones, this decision can have major consequences. Sometimes, a bad school drives a young teacher out of teaching entirely. Making the right decision means getting beyond stereotypes about schools and students and researching the options carefully.

Responding to the Issues

1. Make a list of your current understanding of the following four categories of schools (a) urban, (b) suburban, (c) "good schools," and (d) "troubled schools." What characteristics do the different categories have in common? Do "good" schools share their characteristics with "suburban" schools? How much does this list reflect stereotypes or the reality out there in metropolitan areas today?
2. What judgments or preconceptions can you find in the narratives presented in this section? Do these match your own?
3. How could Greg's story have turned out differently?
4. What set of factors will be most important in your own decision about where to teach? Why are these most important? Are there any factors that you feel are relatively unimportant in this decision?

THE CONSEQUENCES OF SCHOOL SEGREGATION

The definitions of segregated and integrated schools were clearer in the years before the 1954 *Brown v. Board of Education* case. Before *Brown*, segregated meant entirely separate. No White students attended Black schools; no Black students attended White schools. A single Black student was enough to "integrate" an entire school. As history has shown, one middle-aged Black woman sitting on a bus, a handful of African Americans sitting at a Woolworth's counter, or one Black student enrolled at a state university were perceived as dire threats to an entire social order. The Jim Crow regime of legal segregation prevented Blacks and Whites from attending the same schools, eating in the same restaurants, or staying at the same hotels. In most northern states, where segregation was not codified by law, social norms kept racial mixing to a minimum.

Today, such clear-cut dichotomies have largely disappeared. Racial categories have become more complicated over the last 50 years, especially as people from Latino backgrounds enter the third and fourth generations and overtake African Americans as the largest minority group in this country. As we have also seen, Asians from a large number of countries have come to numerous regions, where they have been touted as the model minority, a label many of them find problematic (Woo, 1999).

Schools remain largely, if more loosely, reflective of segregated residential patterns around race, ethnicity, and class. Sometimes rigid residential arrangements, especially those demarcating the boundaries between city and suburb, set the poor off from middle-class citizens. As a result, schools remain segregated places, none more so than in the northeastern part of the United States.

In comparing the levels of segregation in schools, politicians and policymakers typically talk about how many White students have exposure to Black or Latino students in their schools, and vice versa. However, although a White student might attend a school that is composed of over 90% Black and Latino students, and although he or she will have a high exposure rate, it does not necessarily follow that the White student actually interacts with students from different backgrounds.

Ethnographic research into a high school in a highly diverse region of this country with a wide variety of immigrant groups indicates that schools can be spaces that sort their students into highly constricted physical and academic spaces that admit of little mixing between races, ethnicities, genders, and classes (Olsen, 1998). Thus, levels of so-called exposure to people of different backgrounds might do very little in and of itself to engender communication, understanding, or empathy. As West (1994) so aptly put it, race matters in our society. So, too, in education, where race, ethnicity, and class all play a large role in shaping educational experience.

Nan is a young African American teacher who grew up in a poor Black urban neighborhood in a large metropolitan area. A graduate of public schools, Nan was known as a very good student, and through the help of several scholarships, was able to attend a historically Black college in the South. Nan explains, "I know it may seem corny, but I do want to give back to the community. I mean I made it. So can many others [African Americans]." Nan is teaching in a specialized high school in a poor, urban, and predominantly African American area. She is quick to point out that the situation in her school, which is roughly 90% African American and 10% Hispanic, is, in itself, a product of racism.

> *You know, years ago this was a White middle-class neighborhood. And then [in the 1950s and 1960s] when the Blacks moved in, Whites began fleeing it. Back then, this was considered one of the finest schools in the system, but now it's been totally trashed. Clermont High, which is not 10 blocks from here, has remained White, and I can't help thinking that this was a decision they made years ago—to "sacrifice" Central [High] to the neighborhood, which is poorer and Blacker ... and to send kids from outside the neighborhood—the White and Asian kids—to Clermont.*

> *And Clermont gets an [entrance] exam, a barrier, and only the "smart" kids get to go there. It is almost as if there are no smart kids here at Clermont. Students who are Asian and White come from all over the city to be at Central, but Clermont is strictly a "zone" [neighborhood] school ... You only have to visit each school to see the difference. The teachers have agreed to work a longer day—had to get permission from the union—at Clermont, and they get paid extra for it, all because they think that their school is more of a college prep than this one. Well, we are college prep, but when that's not the focus of the school, or when teachers and students perceive it to be second class, well, then there isn't much hope. If this situation [of two schools and two populations] is not racist, it comes awfully close.*

Nan has very clear ideas about her own vocation:

> *I know why I'm here. I chose to be here. I chose to be a teacher when I didn't have to after college. They were recruiting bright young African American women from where I graduated. I feel, being "of color," that I can understand where these kids are coming from. I came from where they are now. The other teachers, however, aren't that concerned with looking at educating the African Americans. They talk like all students are equal, that math is math, and English is English, regardless of your background. Many teachers here are well intentioned, but I know that this school was not the first choice for many of them. Why wouldn't they want to teach at another school*

*where the kids choose to be, rather than here, where kids are sent? The
older teachers just landed here sometime in their careers and are waiting
out retirement. As good as some of the younger teachers are, and a few of
the older ones, I just am not sure that they are committed to teach the children of this neighborhood.*

Yet, Nan also notices that she is viewed primarily as a teacher, rather
than a teacher of color. She is someone, though, who brings a unique perspective to the classroom.

*An incident happened the other day. There was a fight, and we broke it up. I
got one of the fighters, Shawn, and I decided to talk to him. I asked him what
he was doing, how the fight reflected on him, and we got to talking about his
future. He didn't respond to me, really. At one point he said, "You don't
know what you [are] talking about." I said, "What?" He said, "You don't understand where we [the students] are coming from, all the problems in [the
neighborhood] Clearview." I told him, "Shawn, I grew up in the South Side; I
know exactly what's going down here." He told me, "No you really don't."
No matter how I tried to explain that I share a background with him, he really
didn't believe it.*

Nan's words suggest the many boundaries that can interfere with teachers' ability to connect to their students: age, gender, race, class, and many
others as well. However, Nan is working hard to use her background to give
back to her community some of the educational opportunity that has
shaped her life thus far. She plans on staying in teaching for a few more
years and then moving to another helping profession, probably counseling.
As she needs more coursework to reach the maximum salary for school employees, she is thinking of getting a master's degree in counseling. Yet, she
is clear that the problems in areas such as Clearview are not with her students, but with a racism that is institutionalized and systematized to such a
degree that it is often invisible to observers. In other words, the segregation
of schooling has become one of the commonplace features that few people
make any note of anymore in this country. Despite these insights, Nan is de-
termined to make a difference:

*You know, whether I'm a counselor or a teacher really doesn't matter. The city
made decisions years ago to make this neighborhood Black and to keep it
poor. The city maintains racism. The good schools are White, and the bad
schools are Black. There are exceptions, of course, but the trend is that the
bad schools, the failing schools, are all in poor Black neighborhoods. The
same goes for Puerto Ricans, Dominicans, and other new immigrants, but
they come to the city to make it, to become Americans. They don't have the*

history. Even the Haitians and the Jamaicans whom I've taught don't under-
stand the systematic racism and downtrodding of African Americans. They
believe in the [American] dream. But it still is systematic segregation—how
many years after Brown? All you have to do is to look at where I teach and look
at the good public schools, where they are and who goes there.

Years ago, teaching was a well-respected profession that provided middle-class respectability, especially for African Americans and Irish, Jewish, and Italian immigrants in urban areas. Today, numerous other opportunities within business, industry, and the professions exist for well-educated members of these groups. Teaching does not hold the same attraction as it once did for women because other occupations have opened up to them. Nor has there been much success in attracting men into teaching, especially at the elementary level.

Cynthia, a middle school literacy teacher, appreciates her African American and Dominican students but has learned some lessons between her first and second years in teaching:

I love my kids. That's why I'm here. It is the relationship that I have with them
and them with me. I find them funny, they make me laugh, and it's good
laughter. They grow and they do outrageous things, and I get to see that.
That's the most rewarding part of teaching, if you ask me.

At the beginning [of my teaching], they were just running around the room; I
didn't have control. And I remember thinking, "Well, this isn't helping me out,
but it certainly is not fair for them either." One conversation made it clear to
me exactly. It was our first open school night in October of my first year. I re-
ally didn't have my records in order, or know what I was doing—I got very little
help from the administration and was on my own. And one mother came in
and talked to me about Trina. I told her that I liked Trina, but that she wouldn't
listen to me and wouldn't do her work—and I went on like that to the mother.
Then she said to me, "Well, Trina behaves for me at home," and she looked at
Trina who was there, "or she knows what she'll get, right Trina?" And Trina
nodded, wide-eyed. And the mother told me that I've got to be strict with Trina
and the other children.

Of course, the mother was right. If I didn't come down on the children, get
them in order, what good was I doing? So I've become a drill sergeant, not a
mean one, not all the time, but I am clear with my expectations. The kids don't
get out of their seat without permission; they don't even breathe without ask-
ing me. I think this is what the kids want and the families of these kids want.
Many come from hard situations at home, and more than one parent, or sib-
ling, or family member has said to me, "I can't do anything with my child, can
you help?" I have found that in most cases I can.

Cynthia reflects on how her understanding of her students and their needs contrasts with what she took from her academic coursework in college. In some respects, Cynthia has learned lessons that Delpit (1995) wrote extensively about in trying to address the misunderstandings that can arise when White, middle-class teachers work with "other people's children."

> *All of this progressive stuff we learn in college is fine, but it assumes something that the kids don't have. I can't put a name on it, but "Johnny, let's put the book away?" This doesn't work as well as "Class, put your books away... now! You, too, Johnny!"*

Many new teachers never choose to open themselves up to the possibilities of work in schools that might stretch their comfort zone a bit. Some who teach in poor urban schools note that it is neither the students nor the neighborhood community that make certain schools unattractive, but rather the neglected conditions of schools with few resources, poor administrators, and too many unlicensed or inexperienced teachers. Often these circumstances come together in schools in poor, typically urban, Black communities. However, it is not the color of the students in these schools that produces the problems; it is the lack of resources.

Responding to the Issues

1. Visit the public spaces of a local school, such as hallways, cafeteria, or offices. To what extent do you notice implicit signs of integration or segregation of different groups? Who is talking to whom? How do they talk to different people? What "hierarchies of discourse" are in place? Which type of student seems to have power in this setting? Ask students to write about the different groups they notice in their school. Do they feel that there is any segregation operating in how the school functions?
2. How do administrators, teachers, parents, or students identify themselves? Do they reflect the culture of the local neighborhood community?

REFERENCES

Angus, D., & Mirel, J. (1999). *The failed promise of the American high school, 1890–1995.* New York: Teachers College Press.

Cohen, L. (2003). *A consumer's republic.* Cambridge, MA: Harvard University Press.

Cremin, L. (1964). *The transformation of the school: Progressivism in American education, 1876–1957*. New York: Vintage Books.

Crocco, M. S. (2002, February). *Accountability and authenticity: Beginning teachers in the social studies*. Paper presented at the meeting of the American Association of Colleges of Teacher Education, New York.

Delpit, L. (1995). *Other people's children: Cultural conflict in the classroom*. New York: New Press.

Dudziak, M. (2000). *Cold war civil rights: Race and the image of American democracy*. Princeton, NJ: Princeton University Press.

Franklin, B. (2000). *Curriculum & consequences: Herbert M. Kliebard and the promise of schooling*. New York: Teachers College Press.

Glickstein, H. (1995). Inequalities in educational financing. *Teachers College Record, 96*, 722–728.

Hofstadter, R. (1963). *Anti-intellectualism in American life*. New York: Vintage.

Ingersoll, R. (1996, August). *Teacher quality and inequality*. Paper presented at the Annual Meeting of the American Statistical Association, Chicago.

Ingersoll, R., & Rossi, R. (1995). *Which types of schools have the highest teacher turnover?* [Issue brief]. Washington, DC: American Institute for Research.

Jackson, K. (1985). *Crabgrass frontier*. New York: Oxford University Press.

Johnson, J., Farkas, S., & Bers, A. (1997). *Getting by: What American teenagers really think about schools: A report from Public Agenda*. New York: Public Agenda.

Johnson, J., & Immerwahr, J. (1994). *First things first: What Americans expect from the public schools*. New York: Public Agenda.

Jones, E. (1990). *Metropolis*. New York: Oxford University Press.

Kasinitz, P. (1995). *Metropolis: Center and symbol of our times*. New York: New York University Press.

Kliebard, H. (1995). *The struggle for the American curriculum, 1893–1958* (2nd ed.). New York: Routledge.

Kozol, J. (1992). *Savage inequalities*. New York: Perennial.

Lagemann, E. C., & Miller, L. M. (1996). *Brown v. Board of Education: The challenge for today's schools*. New York: Teachers College Press.

Lemann, N. (1991). *The promised land: The great Black migration and how it changed America*. New York: Knopf.

Lightfoot, S. L. (1983). *The good high school: Portraits of character and culture*. New York: Basic Books.

Massey, D., & Denton, N. (1993). *American apartheid: Segregation and the making of the underclass*. Cambridge, MA: Harvard University Press.

Meier, D. (1995). *The power of their ideas: Lessons for America from a small school in Harlem*. Boston: Beacon Press.

Olsen, L. (1998). *Made in America: Immigrant students in our public schools*. New York: New Press.

Patterson, J. T. (2001). *Brown v. Board of Education: A civil rights milestone and its troubled legacy*. New York: Oxford University Press.

Putnam, R. (2001). *Bowling alone*. New York: Simon & Schuster.

Ravitch, D. (2000). *Left back: A century of failed school reform*. New York: Simon & Schuster.

Rousmaniere, K. (1997). *City teachers: Teaching and school reform in historical perspective.* New York: Teachers College Press.

Sassen, S. (2001). *The global city: New York, London, and Tokyo.* Princeton, NJ: Princeton University Press.

Sugrue, T. (1996). *The origins of the urban crisis: Race and inequality in postwar Detroit.* Princeton, NJ: Princeton University Press.

Teaford, J. (1979). *City and suburb.* Baltimore: Johns Hopkins University Press.

Tyack, D. (1974). *The one best system: A history of American urban education.* Cambridge, MA: Harvard University Press.

Tyack, D., & Cuban, L. (1995). *Tinkering toward Utopia: A century of public school reform.* Cambridge, MA: Harvard University Press.

Verstegen, D. A. (2002). Financing the new adequacy: Towards new models of state education finance systems that support standards based reform. *Journal of Education Finance, 27,* 749–782.

West, C. (1994). *Race matters.* New York: Vintage.

Woo, K. (1999). *"Double happiness," double jeopardy: Exploring ways in which ethnicity, gender, and high school influence the social construction of identity in Chinese American girls.* Unpublished doctoral dissertation, Teachers College, Columbia University.

Chapter 11

Teaching as a Political Act

Students enrolled in courses at one large public university are usually surprised when they are told that the stated mission of the school of education is to reform the local educational situation. Frequently, new teachers look at the educational system as monolithic and unchangeable, and see themselves as relatively powerless practitioners, people who have much to learn to achieve even basic competence in teaching. This reaction is an understandable response to the myriad competencies teacher education students recognize they need to acquire to make a successful transition into teaching.

Undoubtedly, gaining basic knowledge and skills, learning to manage a class, finding and keeping a job, and developing good relationships with students and colleagues are, of necessity, the main concerns of new teachers. There simply is neither time nor energy to think of larger issues, like reforming schools. In fact, many experienced teachers might chafe at the notion that reforming a huge, bureaucratic school system should be part of their work responsibility. Along these lines, in some school districts, new teachers might feel that they have to remain silent, accept the status quo, and hope to effect small changes at best in their own classrooms.

This is not necessarily cowardice on new teachers' parts. Even in school districts with a strong union presence, teachers who are critical or outspoken can find themselves in difficult predicaments when they speak their minds in a manner that threatens the administration of their school.

Teaching is always a political, social, and relational act. Politics has to do with the exercise of power in an institution or a society. Politics also concerns the enactment of values. As we have seen, schools exist in this country in large measure to enact democratic values and to create citizens who will support democratic ends. Many educational theorists (e.g., Apple, 2000)

219

would add that schools also exist in this country to reproduce the social order, underscoring the role schools play in developing students' capacity for contributing to the economic system.

Although this perspective holds some validity, it is not to say that no possibilities exist in schools for interrupting the press of these forces on students, teachers, and classrooms. Teachers can and do serve as gatekeepers on many fronts, most obviously in terms of curriculum and instruction (Thornton, 1991). However, they can also make their influence felt in countless other ways. As we have seen, they can serve as role models; and they build community or not. They develop aesthetic appreciation or knowledge of other cultures, perhaps where none existed before. Many teachers, as we have seen already in this book, bring high ideals into the profession, both for themselves and their students, even if these ideals sometimes get lost in the hectic rush of the first few years of teaching (Costigan, 2003).

Undoubtedly, some will scoff at this vision of teaching but it is, nevertheless, a pervasive and widely shared understanding of the work. It is clear from our research that many young people today enter the field because they do want to change the world, or a small piece of it, and because they want to make a difference in the lives of students.

Given these realities, it is not taking too high a moral tone to say that teachers have a duty to engage in educational reform, both for the betterment of the lives of children and for the betterment of the profession. The type of reform, the scope of the engagement, and the level of commitment all have much to do with who a particular teacher is, what her or his vision of education is, and, of course, the nature of the teacher's particular teaching situation. Too many unhealthy schools exist today, many of them in urban settings. In some cases, a teacher has a responsibility, for his or her own physical and mental well-being, to leave that position and find another that will nurture and develop the teacher's abilities. A burned-out teacher is of no use to anyone. In other cases, however, a teacher has a responsibility to fight the good fight in a school, working to improve what can be improved there.

Engaging in educational reform requires a balancing act, especially for new teachers. Put simply, reformers of all kinds have made it clear that much is wrong with the educational system in the United States today. Recent research has affirmed what all experienced teachers know full well: Teachers are the basic and most important element in changing the educational landscape today. In the next section, you will read an exceptionally long narrative of one teacher's efforts to become an agent of change. Although it is not a happy story, it does provide special insights into what taking on this role can mean. Also, because it deals with a veteran teacher, it provides a cautionary tale for new teachers.

TEACHERS AS AGENTS OF CHANGE

School cultures change over time. This is something that might not be obvious to a new teacher of 1, 2, or 5 years' experience in a particular school. Yet beginning teachers—and experienced teachers for that matter—tend not to take into account the effects of these large social and historical forces on their daily practice. Getting students to pass their state exams, preparing a good lesson on the circulatory system, or even attending curriculum meetings and turning in grades on time are all forces that compress a teacher's vision to a set of concerns that can result in a microview of the teaching profession. Teachers seldom can afford to take the time to look around at the cultural shifts happening around them. Nor can they get the distance to analyze from a comprehensive standpoint the increasing complexities of their daily teaching lives, even when those pressures are symptomatic of widespread shifts in the culture extending far beyond teaching into many other segments of the workforce (Hargreaves, 1993).

Given the difficulties of diagnosing problems beyond one's own school, much less developing solutions to those problems in a comprehensive way, it seems appropriate to think of reform in terms of the microlevel. Despite the broad societal forces that impinge on teachers, possibilities do exist for effecting change at the local level. Moreover, perhaps reform efforts are best directed at the smaller elements that comprise the school day. Collectively, teachers might be able to lengthen instructional periods, add advisement programs for students or mentoring, coordinate curriculum in an interdisciplinary fashion, or begin a new extracurricular offering. These are all examples of how teachers can make changes in their own and their students' educational lives.

At some level, teachers know that they cannot change the world, and that reform, if it is to come, will come in small increments. School reform movements have tended to focus on the pedagogical, administrative, or policy questions in education without taking up their larger social implications (Lagemann, 2000). In other words, school reforms are conceived of as occurring within school walls and within the context of the elements of traditional schooling. Educational reformers tend not to situate school reforms within the context of the student's family or community.

In addition, teachers might also be partly responsible for maintaining the status quo. Some new teachers certainly do want to reform schools. The problem on the microlevel has to do with making changes within an old and very strong set of academic traditions, as well as having less and less control over the contextual demands shaping schooling on the macrolevel, such as increased accountability for students and teachers and intensification of the demands associated with the working lives of educational professionals.

Taking on the task of school change is not necessarily a project for a beginning teacher. It can be tough work, especially where the scale of the project is large. The following narrative represents a punctuation point within the larger set of stories drawn from beginning teachers that are contained in this book. The vignette featured in this section examines the efforts of a group of teachers to effect comprehensive school change in a city school. It is sobering reading, indeed.

Tom shares his experiences in coming from a rundown neighborhood school in a poor urban neighborhood to a magnet school where the focus was on business. This magnet school had lost its old student population due to suburban migration. Tom and a group of interested teachers worked hard, as you will see, to keep their school from deteriorating as the culture of the neighborhood changed. Tom's story brings up the fact that a school is a culture that is intersected by a neighborhood community, a community of teachers, an administrative culture, and a unique history of that school, among other factors. Yet, it remains unclear what makes a school successful. Added to the factors of what creates a school culture is the fact that schools change over time. Tom's story reveals how he and some well-intentioned teachers attempted school reform with mixed results.

About 10 years ago, I was appointed as a fully licensed teacher at Lower West Side High School, one of the city's "themed" public high schools. I chose to be appointed at the school because I saw it as an improvement from the [neighborhood] school in which I had been teaching, a large and physically dilapidated school in a poor neighborhood, a school which I thought showed little promise of improving academically, particularly given the administration, which seemed only to be paper pushers and not concerned with turning things around.

The original school I started out at was typical in cities. Lower West Side High [the new school] at least physically was better. The floors were swept, the walls were free of graffiti, most windows were intact, and the stairwells were not garbage dumps. Besides the physical aspects, the school seemed to be under control, and gangs did not seem to be wandering the halls at will. The staff seemed to be dedicated and the assistant principal who interviewed me had been very active in trying to hire young concerned teachers who seemed genuinely to like the students—a far cry from the aging and dispirited faculty I had found at my first school.

I am telling this story because at Lower West Side I first became familiar with an intellectual discontinuity I saw between educators' willingness to engage students and their inability to do so. While teachers and administrators showed great concern about the students, they could only conceive of teaching these students the way they had themselves been taught. In other words, the teachers and administrators believed that they had the students' best interests at heart by teaching them math and science the way they had been taught—by lecturing and tests. They were not concerned with where the students were coming from, with their life stories. They seemed to believe that their good intentions, coupled with a nurturing "passing down" of the skills and data of their disciplines, would be enough to help the students learn better and to achieve the American dream of education and social mobility.

My awareness of an inherent discontinuity, however, was slow. Indeed, at first, Lower West Side seemed a good choice and I was happy there as a beginning teacher. The school was "solid" and traditional, and the school had a reputation for serving several generations of Italian- and Irish-American students who lived in the neighborhood, giving them a solid vocational training, and preparing for college those students who wished to go there. The school had a culture: For decades it had recruited from local Catholic junior high schools and actually had a Newmann (Catholic) Club that met on the first Friday of the month at a local church. As the neighborhood became gentrified with a wealthy population who sent their students to private schools, and as the middle-class Italians left for the suburbs, Lower West Side's students now came from several poor African American and Hispanic neighborhoods. Yet, the teachers there thought that they could serve these new groups of students, as well as they had served the former Italian and Irish generations. But there was a difference that I didn't realize for a long time. The old third-generation Italians and Irish sent their kids to the school so that "something could be made of them." They often sent their less than academically inclined [children] to our school—the "brighter kids" went to St Joseph's, the local Catholic school. When they got rid of automotive repair and electrical installation for business and accounting, I am not sure anyone made the jump that this would serve the new Spanish and Black kids. Not that they couldn't learn this stuff. In fact their parents sent them to Lower West Side because it was better than their neighborhood schools. But there was no connection. Automotive repair served a need. I am not sure if business and accounting, separated from the lives of students in their neighborhoods, ever created a connection between the school, the students, and their families. The old school served several generations of a working-class community. The new group just went to Lower West Side.

My aspirations seemed to fit well with the school's culture. Although this was no longer primarily a neighborhood school, there was a selection process for students to enter. This selection process, however, was not highly selective, and the students were, as measured by test scores, only marginally better than a typical neighborhood school in a poor section of the city. There was no parents' organization, and no involvement from the students' home

*communities. The students often had to travel a considerable distance out-
side of their neighborhoods to come to Lower West Side, and I enjoyed
teaching New York City kids under better circumstances than at a dilapidated
and disorganized neighborhood school. However, the center did not hold.
The school's culture of a caring atmosphere, a traditional education, a
"hands-on" practical vocational orientation, all supported by generations of
a predominantly local community, no longer worked. The school came under
enormous stresses.*

*Over a period of some 8 years I became disillusioned. The students were not
learning. In fact, test scores were falling dramatically year by year. The
school became the last choice of students who wanted to attend a specialized school. At one point we were rated worst in the state on one standardized exam—as adjusted for family income! Amazing that it got that bad!*

*The faculty became dispirited. An old but satisfactorily maintained building
became dirty and depressing. Students wandered the halls, violent incidents
became prevalent, and attendance rates dropped dramatically. There were
many reasons for this—one being that many of the hands-on trades such as
electrical installation and automotive repair had been eliminated for political
reasons. But I believe that one of the essential reasons for the decay of the
culture of the school was the inability of the faculty to reflect on the educational strategy used. Caring teachers who could entertain the students
enough to develop skills and impart information—as measured by test
scores—was a given. No teacher knew of any student-centered alternative in
their philosophy. In retrospect, it was as if the receding community involvement and the evaporating school culture had left the academic focus on
skills and information high and dry.*

*Nevertheless, the faculty, in good faith, attempted to improve the school.
When the principal of some 40 years retired, a group of us teachers saw our
opportunity to take some control of the school. But Mr. Bernard, a former
fighter pilot, had begun his student teaching at Lower West Side and had,
through a series of promotions, become principal. He was a strict disciplinarian and ruled as a strong authority figure who did not value teacher, staff, parent, or student input.*

*We teachers, however, felt we wanted a more nurturing school. Things
needed to change. We formed a restructuring committee and made big
plans to reshape the school, to give it a new name and a new orientation to attract a diverse population of students from around the city. Still at no time did
we question the norm of subject disciplines, classrooms, 45-minute periods,
bells, and the fact that the students had to be measured by performance on
multiple-choice and essay tests. The textbook and workbook were the educational norm. We simply did not question that this approach was not work-*

ing for the kids who were now literally bussed into the school—not to mention the fact that we never saw the need to become involved with the students' home communities, or to take their needs and experiences as the starting point for school reform.

Despite our best intentions, our plans came to nothing. Over 10 years the school actually decayed from a marginally satisfactory school to one of the worst in the city. Lower West Side High's test scores—for what test scores are worth—are today 20 to 30% lower than the city average, and the newspaper published that our English examination passing rates, as adjusted for family income, are the worst in the state.

Part of the reason for this failure was a lack of creative initiative on the part of the administration; part was a system that essentially is a bureaucracy which rewards conformity instead of creativity; and, part was that we were not involved in any larger groups such as the Coalition of Essential Schools or the charter school movement. We were clueless, "thinking on our feet," and reinventing the wheel.

Still, part of the responsibility for the school's ultimate failure remained with the teachers and administrators who daily were on the front line, interacting with students. We simply were unprepared for and unfamiliar with a student-centered approach and we had no knowledge that there existed an educational philosophy which was concerned with the voice of the students, or multicultural issues. If carpentry and automotive repair were now unpopular and to be replaced, we had nothing except a traditional, transmissive, "talk and chalk" education to offer the students, so that they eventually "make it" in American society. The students were unimpressed.

The English and language departments, for instance, contained young, interested mostly White teachers who had come to the city from the suburbs, and even from other parts of the country, and we had not a few very concerned African Americans from the city teaching there. The teachers all came from good colleges, with good academic backgrounds, including a few Ivy Leaguers. Ultimately, the institutional educational biography of our department may or may not have been significant, but it reflects the commitment on the part of some administrators to change the nature of the school by actively seeking qualified teachers. At no time did most of the teachers question that classroom, bells, subject disciplines, 43-minute periods and assessment by testing were not the best way to reach students who did not negotiate well the boundaries of home communities, peer cultures, and school.

Eventually, Tom left Lower West Side High, disillusioned with the ability of well-intentioned teachers to make a change, even though a variety of different efforts were attempted. Tom exercised his right according to the union contract and spent his last year teaching at a "good" school in the city, one that had a diverse population of students, a newly created magnet school. After 3 years, he left high school teaching to complete his doctoral studies.

A whole host of struggles, challenges, and possibilities exist within this lengthy story. The best intentions of teachers, even so highly motivated a group as this one, sometimes are not sufficient to overcome the grammar of schooling and the way in which such rules shut down opportunities for students "unimpressed," as Tom put it, with what these highly educated and earnest teachers had to offer. Perhaps had these teachers known something of the work of Banks (2001), Nieto (1999), and Howard (1999), the story might have had a different ending.

Responding to the Issues

1. If you were a teacher at Lower West Side High, what specific strategies would you implement for reforming the school to meet the needs of a new population of students?
2. It is hard to reform a school "from within" without accessing the power structures of a large school system. What could Tom, and his fellow teachers, have done to access power systems to support change in the school?
3. Tom assumes that it is the lack of community involvement, or lack of connection between parents and students and the new business curriculum and the school, that caused reforms to be inadequate. Are these the primary factors for successful schools? Additionally, is Tom correct in assuming that the traditional pedagogy of the teachers is at fault for not better reaching the students?

RECOGNIZING OPPORTUNITIES AND ACTING ON THEM

The voices that follow come from new teachers in their second year of teaching. By the second year, new teachers become more attuned to ways in which they can find a teaching practice that is personally gratifying and beneficial for students. Nevertheless, many new teachers censor their vision of the possibilities for educational reform in their working environments. Although this might sound contradictory to the preceding example, sometimes teachers attribute too much power to the weight of the administration, their colleagues' approbation, and parental or public pressure. The "but they won't let me" argument becomes a strong inner voice that regulates and inhibits teachers' sense of what can be done to effect change, at least in their classrooms if not in their schools. Unfortunately, too often, new teachers in the contemporary climate of accountability adopt such a posture. The pressures are real; the possibilities for decision making in this environment are less clear.

One of the most productive paths out of this sense of defeatism or fatalism about contemporary teaching is through teacher networks. Groups of like-minded teachers are certainly more powerful than single teachers acting alone. Teachers everywhere come together regularly to commiserate about their difficulties and to share strategies for coping with the first few years of teaching. What new teachers need to recognize is that they can also come together to make the curriculum more inclusive of all students' histories or more responsive to all students' stories, for example. Teachers can come together around issues of writing across the curriculum or around giving a face to social justice issues in the school. The publications and online resources of the Educators for Social Responsibility, Teaching Tolerance, Seeking Educational Equity and Diversity, and the Rethinking Schools organization can provide helpful materials for doing this.

In this next story, Melanie speaks about working in a difficult school, and how she was "saved" by a group that met informally for drinks after the school day:

> *[My school] definitely was a culture of complaint. And I think a lot of schools have that culture of complaint, and the morale at the school's really low. But the teachers … It's a good environment in terms of us all connecting and we always do, you know. I had drinks last night with people from work who meet on Fridays. And there was kind of a group of young, single teachers … I mean the older teachers were great [too], and everything—and they helped us out, but they had to go home to their families.*

> *So there was definitely a group of six or seven of us. My mentor teacher, Miguel, is 26, and he's been teaching for 3 years and has been at the school for 3 years. And Kim was an English teacher there, and she'd also come in at the same time as him, and she's 27. So it's nice to have young people who were experienced to help me. And they were great. So I think that's one of the reasons, you know, that kept me, one of the main things that kept me sane. Probably, the main thing.*

Like Melanie, Steven was hired at an extremely large school located in a poor neighborhood. There were 47 teachers in his English department. He was hired, along with eight other new teachers, to replace uncertified teachers fired by the department chair. The chair wanted teachers who were more dedicated to the school. Steven relates how they began a regular "Thank God, It's Friday" group for mutual support:

> *Every Friday we'd have a TGIF get together, all the new teachers and a few of the experienced ones who were relatively new. A few of us would bring a bottle*

of wine, and maybe some chips and we'd meet in Nancy's office—who had her own office and a couch because she was the writing coordinator. It was great. We talked about teaching, about English, about what we'd read. And we'd share about the students, who was giving us trouble, and how to better relate to them. And we'd talk about teaching ideas. I don't mean it was only education talk, because we really got to know each other as friends. School let out at 2:45 and sometimes, I'd be walking out the door at 6 p.m. or so.

As we have seen, having a support group and asking for or seeking out a self-selected mentor can be helpful in making the adjustment to teaching and a school. Experienced teachers have a great deal of wisdom from practice that can assist the new teacher in making sense of his or her own work (Gallucci, 2003). Sometimes, support can come from unexpected places.

Marla is filling in as a long-term substitute in an affluent suburban school. She is very well aware of the pressure in this district from demanding parents, a situation that is often the case in middle-class and affluent suburban school districts. Here is a case, however, where parental pressure might have worked to Marla's advantage, had she been in a position to capitalize on it; that is, if she were not a long-term substitute but a regularly hired new teacher. She tells a story here her initiative in forming a lunch club focused on learning with her students. What is disturbing in this story is the resistance she received from other teachers:

You know after school, many of my students have extracurricular activities—you know they all have sports, piano lessons, all those things. So once a week or so I would give up my lunch and have them come during my lunch to my classroom. And we'd all eat together and I'd give them extra help. And the administration actually didn't like that because then it reflects poorly on other teachers. Then the parents are calling up, thinking it's a great idea but asking why the other teachers can't do that, too.

So, in a way, I thought I was helping the kids. I thought I was doing a good thing, and the administrative assistant of my building came in and told me I've got to stop doing that. Because it's basically making the other teachers look bad, and it's making me look like we really don't need our lunch hour.

They "strongly suggested" that I give it up [the lunch group], and being a brand new teacher, I really can't go against what they say, you know. So I had to stop doing it, and it was an inconvenience to me because I had to tell the students, "You know I can't do this anymore." I tried to tell my students, "You know, I'm here a half hour before homeroom every morning, if you guys can get here early," because a lot of these kids have clubs and baseball practice, or all these activities.

Marla now has a more informed understanding of the unforeseen consequences of trying to effect change in a school:

The other teachers don't try, can't try, to improve things, make things better. They just go with the tide, they don't, you know, because they're afraid to rock the boat. They're afraid to make anyone mad, any of the administrators. I mean there was this teacher, in the building ... and she's trying to help kids with the assessment that's coming up next week. And she is talking about having workshops. So she was trying to change things for the better. As some of the kids who were weaker in her class, she suggested that they should be put in to her workshop, because they're never going to pass the assessment, you know. And then, she was trying to change it for the better, and of course, the parents said, "My child doesn't need a workshop!" It's like you're insulting the parents when you're just trying to help the child. And some of these parents just take it as a personal issue.... I mean, the tenured teachers can say a lot more, but the untenured teachers, none of them want to speak up, none of them want to change anything. They just go by what they are supposed to go by, and they play by the rules of the district. That's it.

Perhaps having a union representative that Marla could turn to might have helped her out. At the national level, professional teacher organizations can also play a role in reform efforts. Their standards suggest norms which can be used as leverage for improving what happens in a school or district. Each discipline has a national organization, such as NCTE, the National Council for the Social Studies (NCSS), or the National Council for Teaching Mathematics (NCTM), and typically regional subgroups as well. Some, such as the National Writing Project, also have local affiliates. One teacher confirms the positive impact of such groups in effecting change:

I made a lot of changes in my classroom, but when I got involved with the writing group, I realized that I was bargaining [with the school administration] from a position of strength. There was an instructor who visited the school, and a group of interested teachers met once every 2 weeks for a presentation and to discuss new techniques. The instructor even invited the principal into my class to see a new lesson on free-writing and composition. That made a difference. He could see that this free-writing worked, that it could eventually lead to better essay writing.

In another positive case of change, an administrator was so impressed with Joanne's efforts that she was invited to become a change agent at the school:

When I arrived there, I met with the principal and invited her into my classroom. She takes an active part in the school; she wanders the halls every day, peeking in. She did this in my class frequently. Often she saw the class sitting in groups, and not [at desks] in rows. Or, she saw group work, and projects and the like. One day before winter break, she got me in the hall and said, "I really like what you're doing. I like the circle stuff. It seems like the students really are engaged and doing some great stuff." And she asked me to speak to the faculty about this at the next faculty conference with some other teachers who were doing some innovative stuff.

Responding to the Issues

1. Both autonomy and support seem essential to helping new teachers negotiate their own teaching practice and learn from other new and experienced teachers. What type of a support system or discussion group would work best in the schools in which you have observed, student taught, or worked thus far?
2. List three reforms that could be implemented this semester in your school. These reforms could be within the context of your own teaching, in the structure of your department, or throughout the school. How could you go about presenting this reform to other teachers, students, parents, or the school's administrative team so as to minimize the resistance from any of these groups?
3. Schools tend to be conservative places, with strong traditions. What is the best procedure to inform administrators and other teachers about your ideas for changing the status quo?

MAKING DECISIONS ABOUT THE TEACHING LIFE

As we discussed in the previous chapter, many new teachers have choices about where they want to take their first job. At first glance, the choices seem straightforward. Some might argue that it is simply easier and more satisfying to teach in well-funded schools with sufficient resources, in clean, well-kept buildings in tree-lined neighborhoods, or with students who are socialized to achieve academically. However, as we noted in the previous chapter, these dichotomies between suburban and urban settings are not as clear cut as it seems. Likewise, satisfaction in one's work does not necessarily correlate with one or the other type of school as directly as you might believe.

We return here to the subject of making choices as a beginning teacher because we believe that urban teaching offers more satisfactions, despite the intensification of work in these schools over the last 20 years, than might be apparent. We also believe it is important to the future of our democratic society that all children, rich and poor, get a good education. Good education begins with good teachers. This is not to say that teaching in suburban, well-funded schools is not a legitimate choice. However, because we know that many of you will make that choice, we are trying to offer you another option to consider. Although urban school systems are embattled, promising signs of reform have occurred in large systems such as Chicago and New York. One thing that will surely help these reforms gather steam is an influx of young and dedicated teachers.

The new teachers whose voices are captured here were all in the final semester of their undergraduate teacher education program. They were involved in sending out resumés, going on job interviews, and wrapping up their student teaching assignments. The question of where they would take their first job loomed large. As students at a university on the boundary between a large urban area and a set of suburban communities, they had heard the constant refrains about city and suburban schools over a period of many years. Most of these students were themselves the third- and fourth-generation children of individuals who had left the ethnic enclaves of the city for life in the suburbs. In their college coursework, these students had encountered many other students with diverse backgrounds. Likewise, they had an opportunity to visit both types of schools as part of their teacher education coursework.

Anita speaks forthrightly about her plans for securing a teaching position. Like many beginning teachers, she wants a position in a place that she finds familiar:

> I would rather teach in the suburbs. I am born and raised in Nassau County, Long Island. That is where I went to elementary school and high school. It is my belief that I can relate and would be able to teach better in the suburbs. This was a main reason why I decided to do my student teaching in a school from my high school district. There are also other reasons why I want a job in the suburbs. One reason is pay. Yes, money. I am not in teaching to get rich but I do like money. Why not get paid better for something I love doing? Second, suburbs have more resources for the most part. I have heard horror stories about the city schools. I know these stories do not apply to all city schools, but there must be a reason why teachers leave the city to go into the suburbs, not the other way around.

Sam also believes that similarities in social and economic background produce shared values within a community. These shared values, in turn, create a culture of expectations that helps schools to function smoothly.

> I started my teaching career with a student teaching experience in the suburbs. I taught seventh-grade American history at one school, and global history at another. Both of these locations were suburban schools with no more

than 1,000 students in the entire district. The areas would be considered middle class. I walked into the classroom with a pretty good idea about what to expect because I went to a [similar] suburban school. The students seemed to be similar versions of the same kids that I went to school with— roughly the same problems and backgrounds.

I found the educational environment that the schools provided was excellent. Teachers and administrators seemed all to be working toward the common goal of providing the best education possible to their students. There was also an obvious interest exhibited by the parents of the children. If there was ever a problem with a student, there was never any trouble getting in contact with parents and they were more than willing to work with the teachers and administrators to solve the problem.

Overall, it was a very comfortable environment for everyone involved in the school district. Due to this experience in the suburban schools … I decided to apply for teaching jobs in the suburban schools, but got no offers.

Like many new teachers in metropolitan areas, Sam realized that he had to start teaching in an urban school due to the more competitive nature of securing a job in the most highly regarded suburban districts, especially for new teachers. At first, he saw his city teaching job as a temporary expedient until new positions opened up in the more desirable suburbs.

I reluctantly decided to apply to [city schools]. I had liked the suburban schools a great deal, but I needed a job even if it was going to be in a place that I was unfamiliar with. I was placed at the Wilson Intermediate School in the city, and I have been there for 4 years. At first, I thought that I had made the biggest mistake of my life. I knew that the city schools were tougher but I thought I would be able to handle the students with a few adjustments. This was not the case. The school threw me for a loop the first day. I walked into the school the first day and was told that even though I was hired for a social studies position, the only position that was available at the time was a corrective math position. I was not given any materials. They handed me my program and said, go teach math to students who were deficient in math and reading. The students were off the wall. It took me 15 minutes to get them in their seats and another 10 minutes to get them to be quiet, just in time to tell them about 3 out of the 10 rules for the class before the bell rang. I took a look at my schedule and realized because they had a scheduling problem, I had the class again three periods later. After the first day I thought I had made the biggest mistake of my life. After giving myself a pep talk and licking my wounds I went back the next day and was treated the same way.

Despite the challenges, Sam is coming to understand his students better than he did at the outset and is even reversing his earlier articulated preference for teaching in suburban schools:

> *It is much easier and more comfortable to teach in a suburban school but I would take the city school job any day and twice on Sunday because of the challenge. You have no idea what "real" teaching is like until you have heard a child who has all of these disadvantages say "I understand what you mean, Mister." You see the look on their face that says "I got it" and it means so much more than having a suburban student with many more advantages saying the same thing.*

Responding to the Issues

1. New teachers tend to want the familiar, to teach in communities and schools similar to the ones they know. How can education students and new teachers learn about a variety of schools so that they can make fully informed choices about where to teach?
2. Should teachers make some sort of ethical commitment to a set of values that define the teaching life, something like the Hippocratic Oath that doctors take? If there were such an oath, what should it say?
3. Are there certain traits that define a good urban teacher? Is it dependent on having grown up in the city? Why do so many people who grew up in the suburbs feel they would not be successful in teaching in urban areas? How can these attitudes be changed?

MOVING BEYOND MISCONCEPTIONS

The voices of the teachers profiled in this section are those of individuals who grew up in the suburbs. To their own surprise, they have come to see that teaching in the city offers unique opportunities as well as forms of professional satisfaction that they feel are not available in wealthier suburbs. Some now teach in the suburbs and enjoy what these environments have to offer. Others now teach in the cities and are satisfied with their work in these schools.

Harry is a 6-year veteran of teaching, 3 years spent in the city, and 3 years in the suburbs. These contrastive experiences have given him insights about teaching that many new teachers do not yet have. Harry's personal experiences of these two environments and capacity for reflection have allowed him to arrive at conclusions that have moved his thinking about city and suburban schools away from simplistic dichotomies. Obviously, his judgments are rooted only in his own experiences. Nevertheless, they offer a sense of the possibilities inherent in both school settings:

> I have been teaching for 6 years: 3 in the city and 3 in the suburbs. There are many differences, but the major difference is cultural diversity. Teaching world history in a city school was much more interesting for me because the students shared personal cultural practices with the class. It not only helped the students learn from their peers, but it taught me as well. On the other hand it is great teaching in the suburbs because of the extra funds the school has. I am able to have a slide projector, an overhead projector, television, VCR and computers in my classroom. All of these extra items enhance my teaching and I feel allow the students to become more knowledgeable.

> I find that teaching in the suburbs is a bit easier to an extent because of all the extra technological devices at hand, but also because the kids tend to be better at reading and writing—English tends to be their only language. Discipline is also much easier because there is great support from their parents. Of course sometimes parental involvement might be too excessive and, therefore, bothersome. But for the most part it's a good thing to have parent involvement.

> In the city it was hard to get in touch with parents, and when I did I usually found a language barrier. They did not know English that well and I had to depend on their child, my student, to be the translator.

> City kids also seem to be more tolerant of others, probably because they always deal with others. I find suburban kids are more isolated and are sometimes prejudiced or not as tolerant of groups different from them.

Louis, like many new teachers, began his teaching career in an urban school. He has taught a variety of grade levels, all in urban schools. He also plans to stay in city schools for the near future. In this passage, he points out the difficulties in making suppositions about types of schools without hard evidence. Nevertheless, Louis, like his suburban counterparts, has chosen to teach in an environment he knows, in this case, the city.

> I have taught for over 2 years. June will make 3 years. I have no idea of what it is like to teach in a suburban school. There is, of course, what is published in newspapers and magazines, and definitely what people "say."

> Theoretically, suburban schools are "supposed" to be better funded, with smaller classes, newer more up-to-date equipment and texts. It is my understanding that there are more parents who are more involved in the schools on a regular basis. "If" the above is true, then I would be more than

willing to give suburban schools an 8- to 10-year test period! [That would take him into his 70s.]

I've taught 1 full year as a substitute teacher, worked in three different schools, and in grades K to 12. The last 2 years I have been teaching in two middle school grades, 6 to 8. When I have the choice, I believe I'll choose high school.

I live in the city and am learning about the city's department of education. One piece of prior knowledge that applies ... is the tried and true old gem, "The grass is not always greener on the other side of the street." I will teach in the city schools because I live here ... I want for the kids I teach to get what I wish for my [own children].

Like other teachers, Barbara is well aware of the ambiguities surrounding city teaching. She talks here about her decision to leave city teaching for the suburbs. She readily acknowledges that this suburban school is changing and becoming more like the one she left in the city.

As a teacher of 5 years, I feel my talent and skill level is entering its prime. I still have a high level of passion for my craft and a desire to learn more. I developed my classroom persona, expectations, and methodology in an urban setting. I taught at a high school in a poor, mainly Hispanic neighborhood for 4 years. Developing my skills in a city school was a challenge, but one that every teacher should go through. I saw many teachers leave due to stress and mismanagement, and many who were not asked back because they were missing the structure that would build a good teacher. But all of the teachers that entered that door were pushed to their limits: creativity, discipline, patience, and every other way imaginable.

My current school [in the suburbs] is similar to my old school, with 3,000 or so students in a large building. It is a very suburban area, but really? The neighborhood has some resemblance to an urban neighborhood. What makes this building more attractive to me? If I had to boil it down to one thing, it would be the lack of a large bureaucracy. There is one high school in the district, and only two middle schools and four elementary schools. There is a carefully structured administration that is small enough to keep abreast of all events and policies. These administrators are able to set strict and precise measures across the board that work because they are ingrained from Day 1! Resources are devoted to putting these policies in place and carrying them out.

The students are very similar to those in my old city school, but the difference is they have been taught how to learn from an early age. Appropriate punishments are given because the code of conduct is spelled out and followed across the board. They have learned there are few loopholes in the system.

Barbara's story suggests the importance of schools that function in coherent ways, both for students and teachers. She feels, as do others, that these characteristics are more likely to be found in smaller scale environments. Small schools, with few administrators and teachers who wear many hats, have provided some of the features Barbara sought in her teaching life within city limits. Still, the issue of financial resources and their contribution to making schools function well is never far from the surface of satisfactory teaching environments for teachers, both new and experienced ones.

Janine's story picks up on themes present in Harry's vignette. Janine values diversity and echoes some of the reactions of family and friends featured earlier in the book about the decision to teach in an urban setting. However, hers is clearly a voice that defends the satisfactions of the urban teaching life:

> *Where else could I get this unique opportunity? When I go home to my family they think I am insane for teaching here in the city. But I have come to love it. The neighborhood of Jamaican and Haitian and Spanish people is great—I can feed myself for a week just shopping in the neighborhood—and I have developed a relationship with the parents and with the students. They trust me, and have come to accept me because they know now—and they didn't at first—that I am here to help them. That I am not a racist or a burnout, and that I want to teach here. I don't know if I will be here forever, but I can't think of teaching in another place where I would have the stories that I do. Sure there are problems. The school is not perfect. The administration definitely is not perfect. But all in all, I am very happy where I am.*

Finally, Chris's words raise once again the problem of pay differentials across school districts. These pay differentials are significant in the New York City area, with school districts in Long Island, New Jersey, and Westchester County, New York, offering significantly higher pay scales and better salaries than what is available to teachers in New York City. Chris's story suggests that even if an individual is happy teaching in an urban area, the lure of better paying jobs might put pressure on this decision once a young person marries or starts a family. Or, it might simply be the case that an individual wants to capitalize on the higher top pay rate afforded in the suburban districts than what is available in the city. Whatever the reason, these pay differentials, tied to issues of school funding and school districting introduced at the beginning of this chapter, have negative consequences for staffing urban public schools:

> *I am really happy where I am now, in a New York City public school … I don't know enough to equate my school with all the "city schools" or to compare city schools to "island schools," but I have no real complaints about the spe-*

*cific place I am in now. I do think that I am going to need a better paying posi-
tion than a city school teacher, which is a terrible shame, but you know I don't
want to make this decision until it comes time.*

Responding to the Issues

1. What policies could politicians and policymakers develop that
   might keep veteran teachers in urban schools?
2. What specific recommendations can you suggest that would make
   teaching in poor, urban schools more attractive to a broader group
   of new teachers?
3. How will you approach the option of urban teaching? What might
   make urban teaching attractive to you?
4. What have you learned from this chapter about the structural issues
   that shape schools in the 21st century?

REFERENCES

Apple, M. (2000). *Official knowledge: Democratic education in a conservative age* (2nd
ed.). New York: Routledge.
Banks, J. (2001). *An introduction to multicultural education*. Boston: Allyn & Bacon.
Costigan, A. (2003, February 18). *Finding a name for what they want: A study of New York
City's Teaching Fellows*. Presentation given at the Association of Teacher Educators
Distinguished Research in Teacher Education Award, Jacksonville, FL.
Gallucci, C. (2003). Communities of practice and the mediation of teachers' re-
sponses to standards-based reform. *Educational Policy Analysis Archives, 11*(35). Re-
trieved September 29, 2003, from http://epaa.asu.edu/epaa/v11n35
Hargreaves, A. (1993). *Changing teachers; changing times: Teachers' work and cultures in
the postmodern age*. New York: Teachers College Press.
Howard, G. (1999). *We can't teach what we don't know: White teachers and multiracial
classrooms*. New York: Teachers College Press.
Lagemann, E. C. (2000). *An elusive science: The troubling history of educational research*.
Chicago: University of Chicago Press.
Nieto, S. (1999). *The light in their eyes: Creating multicultural learning communities*. New
York: Teachers College Press.
Thornton, S. J. (1991). Social studies teachers as curricular instructional gatekeep-
ers. In J. Shaver (Ed.), *Handbook of research on social studies teaching and learning*
(pp. 237–248). New York: McGraw-Hill.

Going Further
and Checking It Out

The first question one veteran educational professor asks those interested in his college's teacher education program is, "Why do you want to be a teacher?" Almost always those who want to teach speak of it as a profound choice, one that they hope will be fulfilling to them throughout their lives. They talk about their desire to nurture the next generation, to make a difference in the world through their life work, and to engage daily with the great heritage of knowledge that this world has accumulated over the millennia.

Too often in this country today, a different view of teaching is promulgated; it plays on this sense of idealism but couples it with the notion that teaching involves a rather low-level set of skills that can be picked up in a crash course of only a few weeks. Or, at the very least, that this is all that is necessary to put teachers into schools in urban areas where the intellectual demands of teaching are viewed minimally. In this commonly held view, teaching is delivering a lesson, managing a classroom, and meeting curriculum mandates. The work is seen as more about mechanics than artistry. The great divide between what most middle-class Americans wish for their own children and what they will tolerate for other people's children is in no domain more vividly expressed than in the differences between urban and suburban education.

Part IV has only skimmed the surface of the multitude of complex, historically influenced factors that have contributed to shaping urban and suburban schools and the teaching lives of those who work in them. In considering those factors, these two chapters have suggested that individual choice is an appropriate response to those factors: choices concerning where to teach and choices in how to respond to the inevitable problems one faces wherever one teaches. We have asked readers to consider working to improve their schools, but acknowledge that such decisions will depend on many considerations. In the end, three principles should govern this process, ones that have served as the large themes running throughout this book.

First, teaching is a profoundly autobiographical experience, for new teachers as well as veterans. Teaching is a "lived experience" that exists within the context of vocational desires and personal aspirations for fulfillment and growing out of the context of family and friends. Making choices about teaching can only reflect the interplay of personal experience and values as well as professional aspirations.

Second, teaching should not be a solitary enterprise. In other words, new teachers should not see the work the way it so often is portrayed, as a solo performance, something one does in front of a student audience on a private stage. Teaching is, instead, a highly communal and collaborative type of work, an interaction among the individual, the students, other teachers, administrators, parents, and the community. Classrooms and schools are relational places where serious ethical obligations mark the kinds of interaction that should be tolerated and avoided. Teaching always takes place within the context of historical, social, and economic factors, which influence the kinds of schools in which teachers choose to teach and how they view those schools.

Finally, new teachers can become agents for educational reform if they recognize the importance of reflective inquiry in their practice and collaborate with others in improving the schools in which they work. Within the educational community of researchers and practitioners, acknowledgment grows of the importance of partnerships between schools and colleges and of communication and collaboration across stakeholders in the work of reforming schools nationwide. Finding groups of other teachers to share stories and problems with is essential to surviving and growing as a teacher.

We believe that no better way exists for simulating the challenges inherent in teaching practice than through sharing new teachers' compelling stories and opening up space in teacher preparation programs for honest dialogue. Giving voice to their words here will, we hope, encourage new teachers to begin conversations with others interested in contemporary issues of accountability, urban schooling, and the profession of teaching.

All citizens who value education as a right deeply rooted in the fabric of American democracy and as a means for improving that fabric need to work together across boundaries of race, gender, and class to produce more equitable and excellent forms of education in this country. However, without caring, competent, and committed teachers, who remain in the profession and grow in it, all other efforts will be in vain. "*As I enter my teaching prime, I can't picture my life without my career.*"

These words provide a companion statement to Tracy's poem presented at the beginning of this book. They are the words of an individual who has successfully negotiated the first few years of teaching. Now in her fifth year,

Tracy has made it beyond the watershed moment of those treacherous first years of teaching that conspire to drive so many new teachers from teaching. She is, by the standards of urban schooling, a veteran, and not only one who has persisted, but one who has claimed teaching as central to her identity and seems clearly satisfied with her choice.

Many of the young people featured in this book have embarked on lives motivated by concerns for social justice. They work long hours at salaries that are relatively modest in terms of their skill levels, features of their work rarely appreciated by many citizens. They work in schools that are generally poorly resourced and in climates that strain from the burdens that have been imposed on them, none more so than through the agency of new measures of school and teacher accountability.

What these stories demonstrate on so many levels is the deep thought and careful consideration so many new teachers bring to their profession. As their years in the profession unfold, and they move into the status of veteran teachers themselves, clearly schools will be better served if most of them remain in teaching. Making that more likely is the chief reason this book was written. If teachers retain the idealism that has brought them into this work, then their students, especially those in urban schools who have been so greatly shortchanged by this country's public schools, will stand a better chance of gaining a decent education.

Research shows that new teachers tend to leave the profession not because of low salaries but because of what might be called quality-of-life issues. They cite lack of autonomy in teaching (Claycomb, 2002), limited input into school decision making (Gordon, 2003), increased accountability and high-stakes testing (Costigan, 2002; Crocco, 2002), chaotic teaching environments (Johnson et al., 2001), and lack of support by administrators (Costigan, 2002), as well as the low status of teaching as a career among family and friends (Hartocollis, 2002).

As teacher educators, we acknowledge that schools of education often do not do an adequate job in inducting future teachers into the realities of teaching in an age of accountability. This book is an effort to provide a reality check for the work of teacher preparation in the brave new world of teaching. We have offered candid testimony about the messy, complex, difficult, and sometimes backbreaking work of learning to teach these days. The picture is challenging, but not entirely bleak. We are certain that bright, dedicated new teachers can find space for creating teaching practice in line with the focus of this book, drawing on reflection, inquiry, and collaboration in sustaining them in this tough work.

The following activities are based on the qualitative methodology used in this book. As opposed to quantitative research, which uses questionnaires, surveys, and statistics, qualitative research uses observation and interviews to arrive at a deeper understanding of individuals or groups situated in a particular location or human condition. This definition is an oversimplification, of course, but increasingly qualitative research is used in education to make sense of the human dimensions of the educational system. In an era of increased politicization of education, qualitative research can offer profound insights into teaching and learning. These insights are important in a standardized academic environment that seems to take little interest in the on-the-ground effects of large-scale policies on students, teachers, and schools.

1. Being sure to take no notes, literally "hang out" outside of a school before the school day begins. Listen and observe for 10 minutes, making sure to time yourself with a watch. As soon as possible after the 10 minutes are up, go to a place where you can write everything you remember. What was the experience like? What did you notice? What surprised you? What did you see that you never saw before? What cultures do you notice associated with the school? Repeat this observation in other parts of the school you are not familiar with (e.g., offices, lunchroom, hallways, athletic fields).

2. Next, go to a school in a different part of town, with a different population of students. Repeat the same steps. See what differences you can find.

3. Investigate issues of school financing in your community. Explore the history of the school budget, its development, and if it's voted on each year, its success in being passed over the last ten years. Look at the records of the local newspapers to discover what the "burning issues" have been as regards school finances in this community during that time.

4. Look into the history of segregation in your community or local neighborhood. Go back to the early part of the 20th century to discover what arrangements were made, if any, for African American students in neighborhood schools. What other ethnic groups were represented in schools throughout this century? Were there racial conflicts related to busing, desegregation, or another topic during this period? Do some research into this topic online, or in your local library, or by doing oral histories of neighborhood "elders." What insights does this investigation provide about the contemporary state of schooling in this area?

REFERENCES

Claycomb, C. (2002, Winter). High-quality urban school teachers: What they need to enter and to remain in hard-to-staff schools. *The State Education Standard*, *1*(1), 17–21.

Costigan, A. T. (2002). Teaching and the culture of high stakes testing: Listening to new teachers. *Action in Teacher Education: The Journal of the Association of Teacher Educators, 22*(5), 35–42.

Crocco, M. S. (2002, February). *Accountability and authenticity: Beginning teachers in the social studies*. Paper presented at the meeting of the American Association of Colleges of Teacher Education, New York.

Gordon, D. T. (Ed.). (2003). *A nation reformed? American education 20 years after A nation at risk*. Cambridge, MA: Harvard Education Press.

Hartocollis, A. (2002, April 17). As social status sags, teachers call it a career. *The New York Times*, p. B3.

Johnson, S. M., Birkeland, S., Kardos, S., Kauffman, D., Liu, E., & Peske, H. G. (2001, July–August). Retaining the next generation of teachers: The importance of school-based support. *Harvard Educational Letter Research Online*. Retrieved July 17, 2001, from www.edletter.org/current/support.shtml

Part V

CONFRONTING THE AGE
OF ACCOUNTABILITY

INTRODUCTION

The stories found in this book have been sobering renditions of the challenges facing new teachers today. Although the events captured in these accounts occurred in schools located in a major metropolitan area of the United States, they might have happened anywhere—in rural regions of the United States or outside the United States—for example, in Great Britain, where the pressures of educational accountability have also been keenly felt over the last two decades.

It would be easy to get discouraged from becoming or remaining a teacher in the face of such tales. As you will see here in the final chapter, however, such a response is not the aim of this book. In Chapter 12, Karen Zumwalt draws on her own life experiences and extensive understanding of teacher education, schools, and teachers to encourage you to take a different lesson from these stories: the need to confront the challenges of accountability with all the intellectual, theoretical, and practical capacity you have built over the course of your teacher preparation and remain committed to teaching despite or even because of these difficulties.

Zumwalt has fittingly entitled her contribution to this book, "Choosing to Make a Difference." Her approach mirrors the theme of "choice" introduced in Chapter 1, which was called "Choosing to Become a Teacher." She reminds readers that one of the most significant decisions we make in our lives is the choice of career. Few professions offer the opportunity to change lives to the degree found in teaching. Some might argue that such idealism went out with bell-bottom jeans and the 1960s, but the authors of this book have found lots of evidence among the young people we interviewed that this sentiment is still alive and well.

Some might say that talking about idealism and making a difference undercuts the professionalism of teaching and makes this career choice sound like joining a monastery. Characterizing teaching in this fashion hardly implies that the work of teaching requires only commitment rather than expertise or that its real human satisfactions justify poor compensation. Teaching does provide an avenue for engagement with young people in ways that truly can make a difference—by enhancing their sense of future possibilities and developing their capacity for seizing such possibilities. However, it also demands a range of different skills and knowledge and loads of hard, even exhausting work if it is to be done well.

Life, like teaching, is all about making decisions. Zumwalt candidly acknowledges the challenges of the current historical moment we have labeled the age of accountability. In the end, she insists that teachers can manage the new challenges of accountability as long as they recognize and respond creatively to the demands this era, like many others, presents. We share the hope that you, along with the talented and resilient young people we meet in our own teacher education classes, can and will make a difference.

Chapter 12

Choosing to Make a Difference

Karen K. Zumwalt

The journey you are embarking on, although having some similarities to those of your classmates, will undoubtedly be different because of the life experiences you bring with you, the choices you make along the way, the evolving circumstances of your personal and professional lives, and your commitment to a particular vision of good teaching. Your journey will also be shaped by how actively you choose to engage yourself as a teacher.

No matter how well developed during your teacher preparation program, the reflection, inquiry stance, and collaboration encouraged in this book will take effort to sustain. Without making such an effort, the daily demands and intensity of teaching can easily carry you along year after year. It is as easy to be lulled by teaching in a relatively ideal situation as it is to be discouraged by a tough situation. The choice is yours—you can let your job carry you along or you can take an active role in reflecting, inquiring and collaborating. It is you who can decide how much of a difference you will make as a teacher.

That said, although most of the reality challenges faced by beginning teachers in this book sound very similar to those I faced as a beginning teacher in the late 1960s and my students have faced over the last 30 years, the increased demands for accountability through student testing have provided a new context for all teachers. I have no trouble critiquing the misguided nature of some of this effort. However, as a teacher educator, I believe that arming my students with a critical perspective is important, but it is not an adequate response for teachers and their students who have to deal with the phenomena on a daily basis. In some cases, they might find themselves in a situation where they can work collaboratively to change the

247

way testing is enacted in their schools, but in the face of increasing state and federal mandates, more are likely to find themselves having to cope with tests over which they have little control. Throwing up one's hands, moving to a different school or grade level, or leaving teaching might be appropriate responses in some cases. However, to advance these as the only reactions short of changing state and federal testing requirements leaves me with the unsettled feeling that I would just be compounding the problem. Such a defeatist attitude would seemingly minimize the difference I can make as a teacher educator and my students can make as teachers.

Quite frankly, my thoughts about how to work with teachers in the current political climate are still evolving, but I share them with you in hope that they might help sustain you in the tough and important work ahead of you as teachers. The authors of this book argue that teaching is an autobiographical act. Hence, perhaps the best way to explain my perspective is to briefly share with you some aspects of the journey that have led me to my current thoughts about teaching.

My motivations for becoming a teacher were similar to those expressed by the beginning teachers in this book. After college, many of my political science classmates joined the Peace Corps or went to law school. Not sure what I wanted to do in the long run, I headed for Washington and a job in civil rights. That experience helped me decide that I could make more of a difference in addressing troubling inequities as an educator than as a lawyer. Teaching was also appealing to me because I would be working with young people who often were denied the benefits of a good education and for whom social studies might be empowering. From a less lofty perspective, I also saw teaching as an occupation that would be personally satisfying because it allowed even beginners a level of autonomy and creativity not available in many other jobs.

I was challenged, but not disappointed, by my student teaching in inner-city Boston and by my first job teaching in the largest junior high school in Ohio. Besides teaching eighth-grade American history and ninth-grade economics, my primary first-year teaching assignment was in a single-sex, Title I program teaching social studies, English, math, and science to seventh-grade girls. Although texts and general expectations were provided, the level of autonomy granted and creativity needed more than fulfilled my needs for personal satisfaction. Although standardized tests were given, the primary indicator of my success from my principal's perspective was the engagement of my students. My students came to school and were actively engaged in the classroom.

Marriage meant leaving Cleveland and looking for a similar situation teaching in Chicago. Unfortunately, the Chicago Public Schools, at the time, did not accept certification in social studies, but only in history. My social studies certifications in Massachusetts, New York, Ohio, and Illinois were not adequate. However, they were fine for getting a job in suburban Chicago. Now instead of teaching in the inner-city schools, which had been my plan, I was another White teacher teaching mostly White children in an affluent suburb. Although disappointed, I must admit that I quickly found these privileged seventh and eighth graders needy in different ways, presenting a new set of challenges. My naive view that teaching would be easy in this affluent setting was quickly dispelled.

Although I was free to enact the curriculum in ways that I saw fit, the actual curriculum expectations were more specifically drawn than in the urban schools in which I had taught. I also had my first taste of needing to "teach to the test." Because my seventh graders were expected to pass a schoolwide grammar test at the end of the year, I was supposed to teach them sentence diagramming. The other teachers warned me to start early because sentence diagramming was not easy for the students. I did not admit that, as a social studies teacher and a graduate of a progressive public school where grammar was taught primarily in foreign language class, I had never learned diagramming sentences myself. After trying to learn how to do it on my own, I quickly realized that I was not confident that I could answer my students' questions. Before panicking, I decided that perhaps my expectations for mastery of the intricacies of diagramming were too high. I asked to see a copy of the previous year's grammar test. Much to my surprise, students were expected to identify parts of speech and use them appropriately, but did not actually have to diagram any sentences. Because diagramming was just the means rather than the desired end, I decided to teach grammar in a way I thought would make more sense to my students (and to me). I also remembered my tenth-grade biology teacher explaining he was going to teach biology the way he thought it should be taught, and then prepare us for the New York State Regents Biology test in the last month or so. So I decided to spend my time on other goals in my social studies/English classes, and do a crash course directly teaching the parts of speech in the last months before the test. It worked; students in my classes achieved the highest scores on the end-of-the-year grammar tests. In retrospect, I am aware that they might not have learned other things that diagramming sentences was supposed to teach them. However, they achieved the grammar test goals, and I still like to believe I spent the saved time on other curricular goals that made more of a difference.

The autonomy, within reasonable parameters, I had in my teaching has been shared by most of the student teachers and teachers with whom I have worked as a professor of education for the past 30 years in Massachusetts and in the New York metropolitan area. Being able to be responsive to one's students and the current context as one works to achieve curricular goals is one of the reasons teaching can be so stimulating and rewarding. Teaching, as I have experienced it, directly and indirectly through my students, has been intellectually and emotionally challenging, calling on one's knowledge, life experiences, creativity, organizational skills, and personal sensitivities.

Perhaps this is why some of the stories I have read in this book and have heard recently from my own students at Teachers College, Columbia University have been so troubling. When teaching is reduced to the technical task of strictly following a script and measured solely by test scores, it not only changes the nature of the job, but also restricts the learning of many students. It has the potential of chasing good teachers as well as students away from schools. That is troubling.

It is unclear whether the current trends will accelerate or moderate, but it is likely that the reality of teaching in an age of accountability will continue to be with us. The public does have a right to feel confident that its schools are preparing youth to meet the challenges of the future. Although we might believe that achievement test scores are not the whole picture and could actually distort the picture, they do give some indication of what students know and can do. In some form—hopefully improved—they are a reality that needs to be faced by teachers, students, parents, administrators, and teacher educators.

I remain hopeful for many reasons. The first reason is that every day I meet prospective teachers, teachers, and administrators who enter and remain in teaching to make a difference. They are not giving up because the costs to our children and our future are too great. Their commitment and resilience in the face of difficult situations is encouraging. Second, I am encouraged that in most teaching situations, active teachers can find space for themselves and their students to break through in all but the most prescriptive environments. Generally they are rewarded for doing so by their students—and often by parents and administrators whose conceptions of good teaching go beyond test scores.

You have met some of these teachers in this book and, hopefully, in your own experience as students, student teachers, and teachers. Remember Theo, who started his course for his students who had failed the World History Regents, with the hieroglyphics activity that got them actively engaged. It is not surprising to hear that despite teaching in a school that had been placed under administrative review because of poor performance, that he enjoyed his first year of teaching. Unlike Steve who later borrowed the activity, Theo used the activity and the subsequent flow of activities in a way to engage the students in the content as well as the activity. Barbara adopted the district's approach to writing and conformed to the curriculum pacing calendar. However, she also thought up activities, such as having students come up with their own origin tales, that both she and the students enjoyed. You learned in more detail how Andy worked in the concepts and skills to be tested through the books his students chose to read, portfolios, field trips, service projects, and "ethnographic" reports about their communities. Despite not using the scripted program that he had been given, his students outperformed all the other eighth-grade classes in the school. Instead of just walking through the Regents sequences, George got respect from his department chair for teaching social studies through central concepts and trying to make it relevant to his students. And although Sophie was increasingly discouraged by the scripted curriculum and the things she could no longer fit in, she does manage to continue her "culture of excellence" literacy projects. Chapter 9, describing the classroom as a global village, has a multitude of examples in which teachers actively introduced content that went beyond what might be expected in an attempt to relate to students and to expand their understanding of the perspective of others. In some cases, like Joanne's approach to writing, administrators recognized it as something to replicate, whereas in other cases, like Marla's lunch group, administrators squashed a good idea because of unintended consequences. However, in all these cases, whether applauded or not, the teachers were taking an active role in making decisions about the curriculum their students were experiencing.

As the authors comment, "finding room for creative decision making … is essential to sustaining interest in a profession that intelligent people find attractive largely due to its intellectual and knowledge demands." Except for the most extreme situations, space does exist in most teaching situations for more curricular decision making than might seem possible on the surface. However, it does take a concerted effort to continue to see curriculum as something to be created rather than something to be implemented, particularly in the present political context when policymakers are trying to "fix" the schools by mandating curriculum.

The situation in New York City is illustrative of the political context in which many teachers, especially but not exclusively, in urban areas, find themselves. If the No Child Left Behind federal regulations are implemented without modification, it is a context most of our nation's teachers in urban, suburban, and rural schools might need to negotiate in the future. These days in New York City, the "curriculum" is often talked about as the punishment given to schools that are not successful enough, according to test scores, to get a waiver from the city. After politically necessary adjustments to the test scores were made, 208 schools were exempted from the mandated city curriculum in the first year. Despite the fact that the mandated reading and mathematics curriculum were not based on highly structured, skills-based approaches, schools scrambled to be declared exempt from the "progressive approaches" that many of them have embraced for years and continue to practice.

To obtain a waiver was a badge of honor, but there were other reasons for wanting to be exempt. School communities knew that a mandated curriculum often leads to rules and checklists regardless of the nature of the curriculum. At one point, news media reported that all classrooms needed "rocking chairs" for teachers to read and discuss books with students. Although school officials quickly denied that they were requiring certain furnishings, it is not surprising that principles of designing classrooms that are conducive to reading and deep discussion got translated at some level down to specific furnishings and seating arrangements. Obviously, this represents a lack of understanding of the conception of teaching and learning implicit in the mandated reading and mathematics approaches. These administrators were probably used to implementing curriculum in the form of particular texts or programs and then checking to see that all teachers were using them in the prescribed ways. They, and often the teachers they supervise, view curriculum as something to be implemented rather than adapted or enacted by empowered teachers.

This traditional conception of curriculum is deeply embedded in many school systems, and is one that the news media and general public apparently embrace as well. It is also the conception of curriculum that underlies policies that view teaching as a technical act that can be accomplished with minimal preparation, controlled by increasingly specific prescriptions, and measured by standardized achievement tests.

To see beyond this currently popular use of curriculum will help you make a difference—to make the most of each situation for your students and for you as a teacher. Intuitively, most people understand that curriculum is a far more dynamic concept than what is described in a written document.

Think back to before you started a new school year—be it in elementary, middle, or high school. Even though you knew there was a curriculum for sixth grade, first-year algebra, or 11th-grade American history, you probably hoped you would be lucky enough to get a particular teacher or be spared another one. You knew that your assigned teacher and your classmates would make a big difference in how you experienced sixth grade, algebra, or American history. You realized that different teachers would interpret the curriculum differently and add their own special dimensions; their reputations foreshadowed what the curriculum might be. More recently, these factors, along with meeting time, probably influenced which sections or semester you chose to take particular courses in college or graduate school.

Most of you have had some experience in understanding that the curriculum of a particular class is greatly influenced by the interaction of the teacher, students, and content as their lives evolve over the school year. This is what is called the *enacted curriculum*. It is at the classroom level that curriculum comes alive—this is where curriculum is given meaning and where you as the teacher play a critical, interactive role.

As a teacher, you start with the *formal or explicit curriculum*, which can be articulated in your school in any number of ways. You might be given curriculum frameworks or guidelines, content standards, a pacing calendar, a required list of topics or skills to be developed, textbooks, programs, or required assessments. Using the formal curriculum, knowledge of your particular learners and your own professional expertise and judgment, it is your job as teacher to create the *planned curriculum*. No matter how detailed or prescriptive the formal curriculum you have been given, you need to plan how you are going to carry it out with your particular students. At this planning stage of teaching, your curriculum intentions are developed for each class period, for each unit of content or activity, for each marking period, for each semester, and for each year.

Typically, new teachers slowly increase their ability to plan for longer periods of time. The longer you can think ahead in your planning while maintaining a degree of flexibility, the more likely you will achieve the goals of the formal curriculum and your planned curriculum. Adaptation and modification, however, are likely to continue on a daily basis, not just because experience makes you a better planner, but because the curriculum that is enacted invariably differs from the planned curriculum, thus affecting future plans.

Even if three of your teaching assignments involve one "prep," you are likely to find that the enacted curriculum in your first-period English class, the class right before lunch, and the class scheduled for the last period of the day is different. Maybe it is the time of day; maybe the different mix of ability levels, student personalities, or life experiences; maybe what is happening in other classes students are taking; and maybe what you have learned from doing the lesson or unit once or twice before. In any case, the interactive stage of teaching invariably modifies the planned curriculum so that the enacted curriculum is different in each class.

The enacted curriculum also has another dimension. Curriculum is not just what a particular class experiences, but it also has individualistic meanings. Think back to the teacher you had hoped for because your older sister was always talking about her or your friends thought she was the coolest social studies teacher in the school. Just because you got the teacher you wanted, your experience did not necessarily match your expectations. Your experience might have been disappointing, not just because of unrealistic expectations or because the teacher was having an off year or because of new testing demands, but because each student experiences the evolving curriculum differently. This is what is called the *experienced curriculum*. As a teacher, you try to anticipate and understand the experienced curriculum, but it is unrealistic to believe that you will know how each student experiences the curriculum as it is enacted in your classroom and as they reflect on it afterward. This is one of the endemic uncertainties of teaching—knowing how much of a difference you are really making with a particular class, and with particular individuals in that class, especially because that difference might not manifest itself until long after the students have left you.

Besides the long-term nature of your potential impact and the large number of students most of you will teach on a daily basis, another reason it is hard to determine what the experienced curriculum is for students in your classes is that another type of curriculum is also operating. The *hidden or implicit curriculum* is "what students learn that is not necessarily part of the planned or even the enacted curriculum, although it might be part of both either intentionally or unintentionally. In the first case, the hidden curriculum is planned by the teacher but not made explicitly known to the students. A teacher, for instance, might decide to assign students to particular group projects to expose students to new topics or to others with different perspectives or to keep groups mixed by ability or gender. In some cases, curriculum might be "hidden" from both student and teacher. For instance, the practice of rewarding students with no homework nights if all homework is turned in on time could send an unintended negative message about homework. Through individual and collaborative reflection, some aspects of the hidden curriculum can be uncovered and become another source for your curricular planning, inquiry, and action. Doing this deep thinking about curriculum is another way for you to make a difference as a teacher.

Earlier in this chapter, references were made to some of the ways teachers in this book took an active role in making decisions about the planned curriculum in their classrooms. Looking at curriculum more broadly, as what students learn in school, we can see a multitude of ways curriculum is enacted, intentionally or unintentionally, affecting the curriculum students experienced.

Some teachers, like Joseph, set out with a broad view of their role as a teacher that goes beyond the formal curriculum. Joseph hoped to "change the way young people think in many aspects so as to help them mold themselves into what they feel is their path ... Being a teacher and person, to me, is measured by the mark you leave on those around you—be that academic or social." Others were not so conscious about how they were going beyond the formal curriculum. Although Susan needed to set limits on her after-school availability, think about the message of caring she sent to the immigrant children who gathered in her room after school hours to work on their homework. Some quickly realized that they themselves were part of the curriculum and worked to take advantage of it. Clarissa knew that her presence as a Black teacher said something to her students who "didn't know Black students went to college" and were surprised that she did not have children of her own.

How you manage your classes also becomes part of the curriculum—that is, part of what students learn by being in your class. Patrick learned to take hold of a powerful influence on the curriculum, the impact of a potentially disruptive pupil, by creatively engaging him in a new role as the class janitor. More typical is Jonathan learning the hard way the importance of deliberately thinking through classroom management and organization so he could enact curriculum that focused on content rather than behavior problems. For Susan, setting limits and having clear class rules was a given. However, having a co-teacher who set up "walls around her" convinced Susan that she did not have to shut off her personality. "So I showed a lot of my personality and told a lot of stories, a lot of personal stories, and funny things." Not only did she become part of the curriculum, but she impacted the curriculum by establishing a comfortable classroom climate where "students can speak their mind without fear of being criticized." As Sarah commented, management is about "creating a safe space where learning can take place." Learning does take place in all classrooms, but the kind of learning that takes place in "out-of-control" classrooms often has little to do with the formal curriculum. In fact, the experienced curriculum might actually be miseducative. At the other extreme, one might question whether authoritarian, teacher-dominated and student-passive classrooms "prepare students to participate in a democracy." The ways teachers organize and manage their classrooms and interact with students are an integral part of the curriculum, whether intentional or not.

The way teachers handle seemingly minor interactions is part of the hidden curriculum even if it does not become part of the enacted curriculum. What would Mizzi and her classmates have learned if Sharon had decided to forbid her from drawing swastikas on her arm? Whereas Sharon's telephone calls and research did not eliminate Mizzi's isolation, her minilesson on the meaning and misunderstanding surrounding symbols might have introduced or reinforced for some students the multiple perspectives needed in a diverse society. Students' lived experiences are there to enrich the enacted curriculum if teachers are sensitive to the cues picked up in discussions and informal interactions. Remember Marybeth's surprise when teaching about the triangle trade to learn that two thirds of the students in one of her classes had worked in sugar cane fields. Don used his students' understanding of the isolation of different cultures in urban neighborhoods to help his students understand the Puritans' desire to maintain a culturally pure Puritan way of life.

Sometimes, teachers develop curricular goals to address issues that arise in their particular school communities. Nancy worked in an affluent school where "nose jobs" and tanning salons were part of the culture. She decided that one of her goals was to get her female students to think about alternative ways of looking at themselves. By including women's history in her planned curriculum, and actively engaging students as the curriculum was enacted, she worked hard to get the girls to see themselves as active participants in the classroom. In a different approach, Katrina brought gender into her curriculum through the hidden curriculum by decorating her room with pictures, posters, and quotes from women in history. Although the intent of the room decorations was not hidden to her nor perhaps some of her students, she did not make them part of the enacted curriculum until the day Scott commented about the "women all over the room." Even when not explicitly part of the planned curriculum, when teachers have strong beliefs about what they want to accomplish, the conversations they have with students as they interact with them in class, between classes, and before and after school, become part of the experienced curriculum as it did for the girls Clarissa talked to about being strong females.

Your students also learn lessons in school that are not as directly under your control—how the school is organized, the use of tracking or heterogeneous grouping, how people with special needs are treated, the gender and race of teachers and administrators, how the school handles discipline problems, what subjects really count, what activities are valued, and what can be interrupted. They learn about knowledge—are courses taught as discretely separate disciplines or in interdisciplinary ways? They learn a lot from watching how teachers work together as teams or as lone rangers, and about how community and school cultures are created, maintained, or threatened. They learn a lot from their peers—an influential factor in the hidden curriculum, how curriculum is enacted in the classroom, and how it is experienced. As Neva found out, in the affluent community where she worked, parents can also be so intrusive that they affect the enacted curriculum by interfering with teacher decisions. They were also part of the hidden curriculum—what were these students learning about power and authority? What were they learning about personal problem solving when their parents jump in to rescue them?

Thinking of curriculum in all its manifestations—the formal or explicit curriculum, the planned curriculum, the enacted curriculum, the hidden or implicit curriculum, and the experienced curriculum—provides a much fuller and powerful conception of curriculum. Hopefully, it will allow you to think beyond the commonly used, one-dimensional meaning of the term. It provides an analytic tool to deepen your reflection and inquiry about curriculum and can enrich collaborative inquiry and action. It also enables you to look beyond the formal curriculum that might seem too restrictive or inappropriate or boring as you plan and enact curriculum with your students. The space for your voice and your students' voice to be manifested in the curriculum will vary in different settings, but the very nature of curriculum, as defined broadly, ensures that there is a place for that voice. In fact, as teacher you cannot help but be part of the curriculum—the learnings that your students take with them. However, by being aware of the many dimensions of curriculum, you gain an opportunity to shape what your students are learning—an opportunity to make more of a difference.

Think back to the teachers that have made a difference in your life. What was it about each one that affected you in such a way? What was it about them that might even have affected your decision to become a teacher? When I have asked prospective teachers, beginning teachers, and experienced teachers to describe the best K–12 teacher they ever had, their responses are very similar to the responses I received when I asked a group of school superintendents from a very test-conscious county to describe the best teacher in their district. High student test scores are not mentioned. Invariably, however, the "best" teachers are described as having high standards and expectations for students, engaging the students in memorable curriculum activities, and, most frequently, personally connecting to individual students in some meaningful way—making students feel special, confident, able, valued, connected, motivated, or empowered. These are teachers who made a difference in the lives of their students. Now, regardless of the circumstances you find yourself in, it is your turn to make a difference in the lives of your students. The choice is yours.

Author Index

Subject Index

DATE DUE

FE 10 '06			

#47-0108 Peel Off Pressure Sensitive